MAKE YOUR OWN
DOLLS' HOUSE
FURNITURE

MAKE YOUR OWN DOLLS' HOUSE FURNITURE

MAURICE HARPER

GUILD OF MASTER CRAFTSMAN PUBLICATIONS LTD

First published 1995 by
Guild of Master Craftsman Publications Ltd,
166 High Street, Lewes,
East Sussex BN7 1XU.

ISBN 0 946819 59 9

The publishers would like to thank ERCOL and Aga–Rayburn for their kind
permission to reproduce plans based on their original designs. The modern
dining chair in Chapter 13 and the dining table in Chapter 14 are based on
classic designs by ERCOL Furniture. The Aga cooker in Chapter 30 is based on
Aga Cooker Design by Aga–Rayburn.

The photo on page 13 is reproduced courtesy of ARCO Ltd.
Photography by Peter Walton
Line illustrations by Tim Benke, Top Draw (Tableaux)

Designed by Ian Hunt Design

Colour Reproduction by AD.VER Srl - Gorle (BG) - Italy

Printed and bound by
Tipografia Umbra Srl - Città di Castello (PG) - Italy

CONTENTS

ACKNOWLEDGEMENTS

To Ann, my wife, who has always supported
me in whatever undertaking I have
pursued with a greater degree of patience
than I can boast.

To Kirsty, my daughter, whose birth started
me off with an interest in dolls' houses and
furniture. An interest that has almost become
obsessive.

To Marion Fancey, editor of *Dolls' House and
Miniature Scene*, who gave me the opportunity
to publish some of my models.

To Michael, my son, for printing the black-
and-white photographs.

To Ian, my son, for helping with some of the
necessary reproduction of the drawings.

MEASUREMENTS
AND REFERENCES

CAUTIONARY NOTE

The dimensions given in all of the cutting lists, with the exception of the Aga Cooker, are generally greater than required by a small amount to allow for waste in cutting, shaping and fitting parts together. Timber thicknesses are variable but consistent with those available from reputable suppliers.

Imperial conversions may vary fractionally, but those given err on the right side and will not lead to undersized parts.

Always use one system of measurement only. Do not mix metric and imperial measurements.

As the projects are so small, it is recommended that a drawing is made of the work in imperial sizes to ensure that the measurements have not lost anything in the translation. (*See also* the Metric Conversion Table on page 166.)

SCALE OF PLANS

All plans are actual size. Pictorial views and some details, as noted, are not to scale. Measurements can be taken directly from drawings, but for shaped pieces, tracing is recommended.

SUPPLIERS

To locate stockists and suppliers of the materials referred to in this book, please consult your local telephone directory or the many excellent magazines available.

RECOMMENDED READING

In the course of writing this book, the author found the following publications helpful:

Plant, Oliver, *Woodturning*, The Crowood Press, Ramsbury, 1993
The International Book of Wood, AH Artists House, London, 1976

INTRODUCTION

The object of this book is to help anyone with an interest in 1/12 scale models to make their own. The emphasis is on dolls' house furniture, with a few models of miscellaneous character included, to add interest to 1/12 scale generally.

If you have never attempted this kind of work before, but on browsing through this book your interest has been aroused, then this is the book for you. Some of the models do look a bit daunting at first glance, but don't despair because if I can do it then so can you, however amateur you may be. It is whether you have the interest to begin with that matters.

I began by simply measuring furniture, drawing it to 1/12 scale and looking for sources of timber which would meet my needs without having to buy elaborate machinery to produce the thicknesses that I required.

You don't have to be a cabinet maker to achieve good results, but if you are, you may be able to improve upon the jointing methods indicated. For the beginner I have set out a cutting list, and a step by step guide for the construction of each piece. When using the cutting list, it would be advisable to make the individual parts slightly oversize so that you can 'fit' them together by rubbing the edges with a fine abrasive paper.

Your workshop need only be the living room until you need to use a lathe or do any dusty work. I constructed my own workshop at the rear of the garage. Its measurements are 2.73 x 1.5m (8ft x 5ft) and although I would like more space it is adequate for my present needs.

I strongly suggest that if you haven't attempted anything like this before you only buy the basics. When you have a little more confidence in your work, then is the time to stock up on timbers, brassware and finishing materials. So carry on and enjoy a very rewarding hobby whether creating pieces for home use of for sale.

Workshop with scroll saw on swivelling frame

Workshop showing Hobbymat variant lathe and tool racks

TOOLS

As far as equipment is concerned, many of the models require only the very basic tools such as modeller's knives, straightedge and cutting board: others will need extra tools to make life easier. I have split these tools into two groups, A and B. Group A indicates the less expensive items but ones which I have found to be invaluable. Group B are the more expensive items that I have managed to acquire over a period of time after much hard saving. The photographs on the following pages show my own particular preferences.

GROUP A

1 Knives
2 Fret saw
3 Cutting board
4 Rule/steel straightedge
5 Bead saw
6 Mitre block
7 Try square
8 Clamps
9 Set of drills
10 Awl
11 Needle files

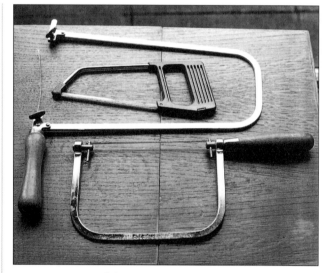

Fig 1.2 It is useful to have a variety of saws for working on jobs with different shapes and angles

Fig 1.3 A cutting board and straightedge are basic modelling tools

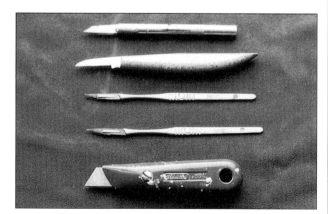

Fig 1.1 A good set of knives is essential

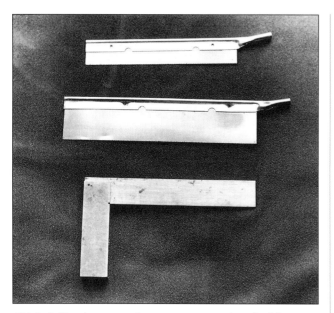

Fig 1.4 *Bead saws and try squares are invaluable*

Fig 1.5 *Mitre blocks can be bought in miniature*

Fig 1.6 *A collection of miniclamps*

Fig 1.7 *Long-armed Chinese clamps, and small clamps*

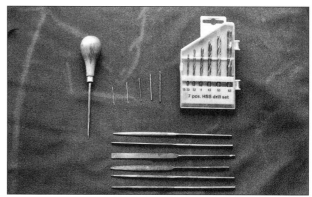

Fig 1.8 *Awl, drills and needle files: part of the basic tool kit*

GROUP B

1 Tweezers
2 Flat-nosed pliers
3 Set of miniature chisels
4 Minicraft bench saw
5 Minicraft drill and stand
6 Minicraft lathe attachment
7 Lathe for woodturning
8 Set of turning tools
9 Pin vice
10 Grinding machine
11 Vernier gauge
12 Scissors
13 Clippers
14 Minicraft sanding machine

Of these group B tools, the most useful one, if you can afford it, is the Minicraft bench saw with its transformer, followed by the Minicraft drill and parts. (*See* Figs 1.11, 1.12 and 2.6.)

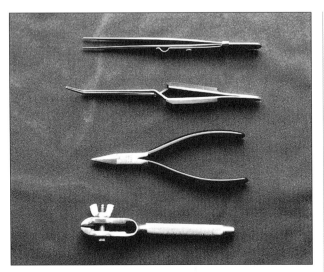

Fig 1.9 *Tweezers, flat-nose pliers and pin vices become necessary with more difficult work*

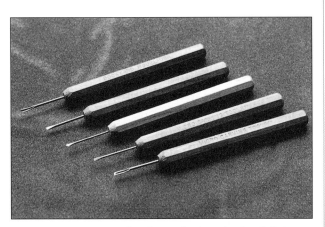

Fig 1.10 *Miniature chisels can be bought for dolls' house work*

Fig 1.11 *Minicraft drill with transformer*

Fig 1.12 *Minicraft drill with lathe attachment*

Fig 1.13 *Multi-purpose grinding machine*

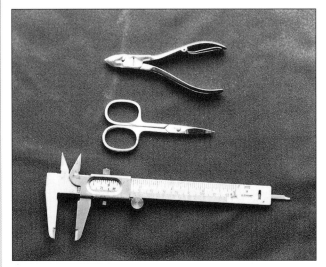

Fig 1.14 *Vernier gauge, scissors and clippers: useful additions to the tool box*

TECHNIQUES

TRANSFERRING INFORMATION

Plans can be traced from the drawing onto the timber surface using carbon paper. Place the drawing on a sheet of carbon paper that is face down, place both onto the timber surface, and then trace the outline of the drawing.

Half plans can be copied onto the timber surface as full plans. To do this, place the half plan on a sheet of carbon paper face down, place this on a sheet of paper that is folded so that the folded edge lines up with the centreline of the drawing, and place under all of this, a piece of carbon paper face up. Now trace the outline.

When you open up the paper it should reveal the complete plan, always dependent upon the careful lining up of the fold with the centreline. All you need to do then, is transfer this plan view, via carbon paper face down, onto the plan view. (*See* Fig 2.1.)

A = Original drawing
B = Carbon paper FACE DOWN
C = Folded paper with folded edge lined up with the centreline on the drawing.
D = Carbon paper FACE UP
E = C opened out
F = Carbon paper FACE DOWN
G = Timber surface

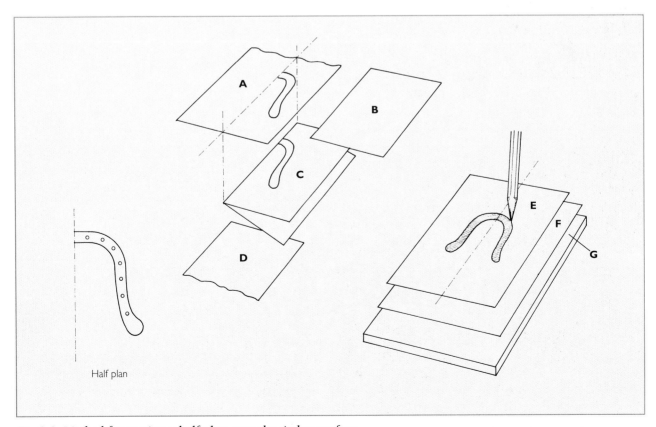

Half plan

Fig 2.1 Method for tracing a half plan onto the timber surface

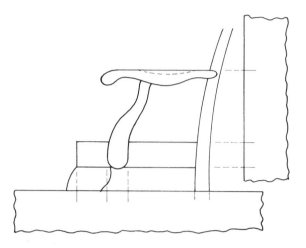

Fig 2.2 *Transferring information by means of a paper template*

Another method I use to transfer information from the sketch is by means of paper templates, as shown in Fig 2.2. Place the sheet of paper, or card, next to the sketch and mark onto it all the relevant points. Now place this paper or card next to the timber and transfer the points from the template to the timber surface.

CUTTING

In order to enable the beginner to gain some knowledge of the way in which timber should be cut and of its jointing in small scale work, the following sketches have been provided and should be of some assistance. For more detailed information please refer to books on carpentry generally and try to adapt what you read to what you intend to make.

To get the best results you must always cut with the grain. Cutting against the grain will only make the

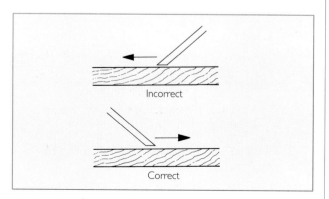

Fig 2.3 **For best results, always cut with the grain**

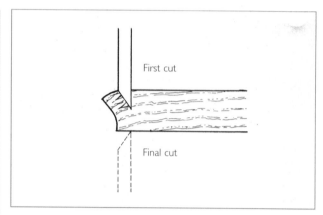

Fig 2.4 *Cut only half way from either side, to avoid splitting the timber*

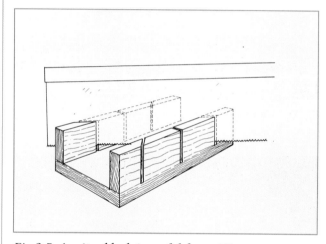

Fig 2.5 *A mitre block is useful for a 45° cut*

chisel, or knife, dig deeper. (*See* Fig 2.3.) When cutting across the grain with a chisel, it is advisable to cut only halfway or a little more, and then turn the piece around and do the same from the opposite side. This is so that the timber won't split along the bottom edge. (*See* Fig 2.4.)

If a 45° cut is required for mitreing purposes, a mitre block is very useful and can be bought in a miniature size if necessary. (*See* Fig 2.5.)

For small pieces that are required to have parallel edges and square corners such as thin sheet material for drawer construction, the Minicraft bench saw is a must. (*See* Fig 2.6.) Trying to cut at right angles with a try square and knife can be very frustrating, especially when it comes to putting the parts together and finding that they don't quite fit. By all means experiment, after all you may be better at it than me. (*See* Fig 2.7.)

Fig 2.6 Minicraft bench saw and sanding machine: expensive but extremely useful

Fig 2.7 Using a try square and knife to cut at right angles

Fig 2.8 Square blocks enable a perfect right angle to be cut

To ensure that you get perfect right angles to adjacent faces during drawer construction, you will require a square block. I use a metal one made up for me by a friend and it has proved to be indispensable. (*See* Fig 2.8.) Metal was used to prevent the glue, which seeps out of the joints, from sticking to its surface.

When carving is carried out, especially with cabriole legs, it is essential that you follow the directions given earlier with regard to the grain direction and, slope. To repeat this message, the arrows shown on the following sketch give the direction of cut with the knife blade. (*See* Fig 2.9.)

JOINTING

Where possible, well-formed joints are to be sought in order to add strength to the model. Having said that, there will often arise a situation where jointing is either difficult to do, or not worth the effort because the parts are too thin.

The following sketches illustrate various joints that I have found useful. I would not necessarily recommend dovetail, or mortice and tenon joints, unless you are a perfectionist, because you will then

Fig 2.9 A cut must always be made with the grain slope

be required to cover the joint with a thin veneer, adding to the workload. As you become more proficient, however, there is no reason why you should not resort to such sophisticated techniques but they are beyond the scope of this book. (*See* Fig 2.10.)

For greater stability I sometimes 'peg' the joints. This is done by simply drilling into the faces of the two parts to be joined, using a suitable sized drill bit. Then, from a cocktail stick or dowel, cut out a length to fit into each hole and enable the parts to meet. The pegs can then be glued in place.

HINGEING

There are an amazing number of different kinds of brass hinges especially made for miniaturists. These can be obtained by mail order, unless you are lucky enough to be living near a supplier. The brass hinges I have found useful are shown in Fig 2.11. They are, unfortunately, very fiddly to apply and can be time-consuming but when they have been fitted properly, they add to the overall effect of the model. To fit either kind you will need to chase out some timber from the adjoining faces which are to receive the hinges. What I end up doing is to superglue the hinges in position and then stick the small nails in. It may sound a bit cock-eyed but it works. When you do come to chase out the timber, be very careful not to cut out too shallow or too deep. The reason is obvious if you look at Fig 12.2.

For hingeing very thin members such as window frames and bureau door frames, I tend to favour the pivot method as shown in Fig 2.13. Also, if there is

enough timber to work with, I sometimes form a spigot on the end of the vertical member which is to fit into a pre-drilled hole in the adjacent edge. (*See* Fig 2.14.) This does have a tendency to squeak, however, and a variant of this can be seen in Fig 2.15.

Linen hinges can be used but prove useful under certain conditions only. This is because they tend to cause the joint to flap about somewhat. The best situation for them is shown in Fig 2.16.

LATHE WORK

It is beyond the scope of this book to go into any kind of detail on lathe work techniques and I would strongly advise you to go to a craft fair where a practitioner is showing off his skills, take lessons, or try to pick it up from books.

FINISHING

To do the finishing properly you should spend as much time on it as you do to make the model and the best time to do it is during the initial preparation: each piece should be finished off completely before the parts are assembled, with all traces of glue being removed before polishing and varnishing to avoid ugly streaks. At least, that is the theory. I have yet to do this for every model I make, but you may wish to do better.

The correct way to prepare a timber surface for receiving a finish is to first use a scraper to remove any roughness (*see* Fig 3.2), then to rub it down with a fine abrasive paper, and finally to rub it with a grade 0000 wire wool, working along the grain. This procedure is not always possible unless the model has a nice flat surface to work with, such as a table top, but you can only do your best to achieve the smoothest surface that you can.

When using a wax finish, after first sealing the wood with a coat of sealer, you should impregnate the wire wool with the wax and then rub it well into the timber, working along the grain. Repeat this procedure after about a week for each coat applied and then buff the surface with a lint-free duster to make it shine. It will not be as glossy as a varnish but for certain pieces, such as the office bureau, it is more in keeping with the style of furniture it is modelled on.

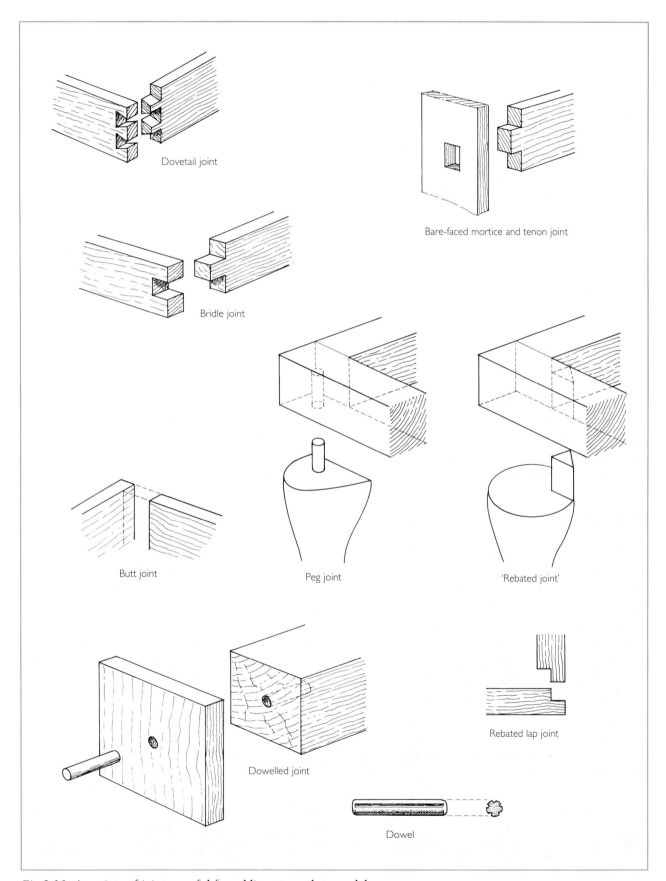

Fig 2.10 A variety of joints, useful for adding strength to models

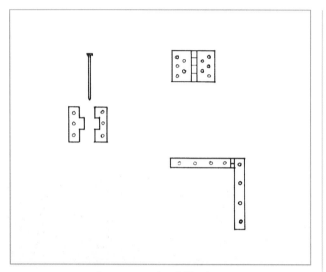

Fig 2.11 Brass hinges can be difficult to apply, but add to the overall effect

When varnishing, care must be taken to remove all traces of glue showing through at the joints as this will lead to ugly stains. Eight hours should be allowed between applications and each coat should be rubbed down with wire wool before the next coat is added.

If you need to stain your timber, then make sure that the timber surface is free from dust and grease. Apply the stain with a brush or rag, working quickly along the grain, and leave to dry for 24 hours. The wood sealer is then applied to prepare the surface for the final polish and to prevent the stain from bleeding through.

If you wish to use a beeswax polish, this would be applied using the fine wire wool. Work along the grain and leave for about three hours before polishing with a soft cloth.

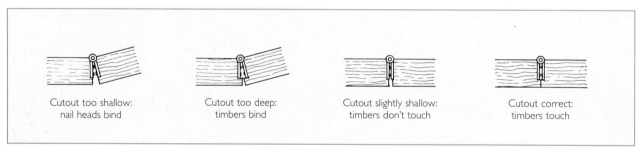

Fig 2.12 Correct depth of cutout is vital if a hinge is to fit

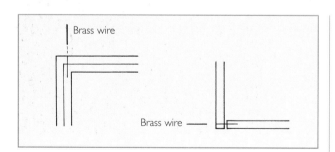

Fig 2.13 Pivot hingeing works well for thin members

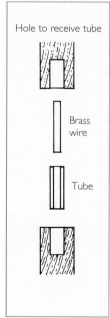

Fig 2.15 A 'quieter' variant of spigot

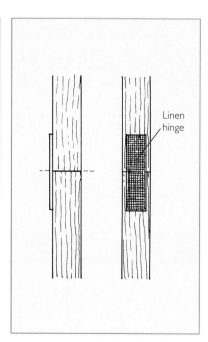

Fig 2.16 Linen hinges can be used where it is difficult to apply brass hinges

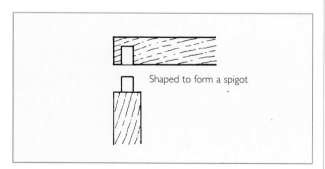

Fig 2.14 Where timber width allows, spigots add strength to pivot hinges

MATERIALS

Fig 3.1 As much time should be given to the finish of a job as to its preparation

FINISHING

Materials for this consist of:

1 A dust-free rag
2 Cotton wool
3 Wire wool grade 0000
4 Abrasive paper, grade 320 grit
5 Shellac wood sealer
6 Beeswax
7 Stains of various colours
8 Teak oil
9 Danish oil
10 Paint brushes
11 Methylated spirit
12 Scraper
13 Varnishes

A rag and cotton wool are important for ensuring that the timber surface is clean and free of dust and grit. Wire wool, abrasive paper and scrapers are used to remove any blemishes from the surface of the wood, making it smooth and thus producing a good finish.

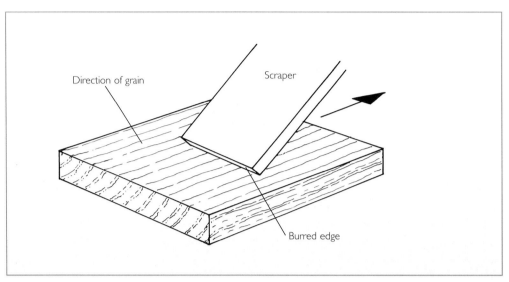

*Fig 3.2 **The burr on a scraper reduces the height of the grain and so, gives a smooth finish***

The scraper consists of a flat piece of metal with a sharp edge. It is drawn across the surface of the timber in order to reduce the height of the grain and form a perfectly smooth finish. (*See* Fig 3.2.)

You may like to use a certain stain to give a piece a more authentic appearance. If you do so, the use of a sealer before applying varnish will prevent the stain from leaking out. Use methylated spirit to clean the brushes and to remove any unwanted sealer.

Stains and varnishes can be purchased from DIY shops and specialist timber merchants. They are available in various colours. I use 'mahogany', 'mid oak' and 'dark oak' as well as clear varnish, and simply follow the maker's instructions regarding application. A lint-free material is usually specified to apply the stain or varnish, but I find a cheap brush is suitable, and these can be bought from an artists' suppliers. The only problem with using a brush is that you have to be careful not to let the varnish run or you will end up with unsightly blobs.

If you would like to polish your work, you can use beeswax which can be bought from furniture stores, or furniture polish from a supermarket.

Teak oil brings out the natural beauty of the timber but may need regular brushing to feed it. Danish oil contains tung oil which penetrates deep into the timber and gives a hard, durable seal. It can be used as a primer before varnishing is carried out, but if you do use it in this way, remember to leave about eight hours for it to dry.

TIMBER

The timbers which I have found to be easy to carve and turn are:

1 mahogany
2 boxwood
3 walnut
4 yew
5 beech
6 yellow pine
7 lime

There are others, but those listed are readily available as offcuts from hardwood suppliers at a reasonable price.

As far as timber sheets are concerned, I have found that, in the kind of thicknesses you will require, they are mostly imported from America. They can be a bit expensive but unless you can discover a source of supply here in England, then you are obliged to pay a bit extra for them. There are several suppliers who deal in mail order. If you have a thicknesser/planer, or if you have a friend who has a thicknesser/planer in his workshop then you may be able to make up some sheets.

I once enquired about the cost of rosewood in the appropriate thicknesses and was staggered by the price, which turned out to be four times the cost of imported timber. If you can afford it, however, it produces a lovely finish.

SAFETY

The question of health and safety in the workshop is an important one. Accidents happen easily and quickly, and the work itself poses potential health risks. Care, concentration and a set of basic safety procedures are needed.

Be aware that all tools have sharp cutting edges. When using electric tools, always switch the power off before setting them up and whenever they are not in use, and always read and follow the manufacturer's instructions. With all tools, keep fingers away from sharp or moving blades.

It is important to wear appropriate clothing. Open shoes offer no protection against falling knives or spilt liquids, and loose clothes can become entangled in equipment. Keep sleeves rolled up and, for the same reason, keep long hair tied back.

When sanding or turning, a great deal of dust will become apparent as it settles around your work. This is especially true of hardwoods such as mahogany. I

have found, when washing my hands after working with mahogany, that the dust mixing with the water looks like fine mud. Imagine what this can do to lungs if breathed in! You should always wear a dust mask to protect against this. All dusts pose a health risk, and the dust of some woods, being toxic, can cause bronchial problems. Dust masks have a life of about eight hours and should be replaced after this time.

When using electric tools, such as the lathe and minicraft bench saw, chips of timber will fly off from time to time and unless protected, your eyes will be vulnerable. It is in your own interest to cover your eyes with safety glasses. (*See* Fig 4.1.)

Keep your workshop floor clear of dust and offcuts, and your workspace free from odd bits of timber, containers and tools. This will help to avoid slipping or tripping: falling onto a sharp tool, or with one in your hand, is not advisable.

Another reason for keeping the workshop clean is to reduce the risk of fire. Wood shavings and volatile liquids are a part of every workshop, so the risk of fire must be acknowledged, and steps taken to reduce it. Sweep the floor and remove rags that have been used for finishing at the end of each day.

Many of the liquids and adhesives used in finishing give off pungent fumes and when using them you should maintain adequate ventilation. Bottles should be clearly labelled and kept out of reach of children. Always wash your hands and affected areas of skin immediately if they are contaminated by any of the liquids used, and to avoid contamination, wear disposable gloves when handling them.

Finally, it is a good idea to have a first aid cabinet in your workshop, where it can be easily seen and reached. Cuts and abrasions should be kept clean and covered and splinters are an occupational hazard, so bandages, scissors, antiseptic and tweezers should all be included.

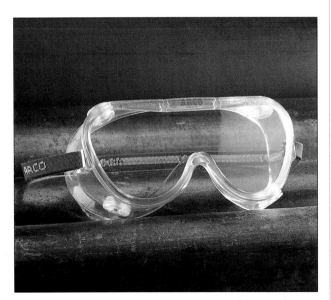

Fig 4.1 Safety glasses protect your eyes from timber chips and grit

Photo reproduced courtesy of ARCO Ltd

CHAIRS

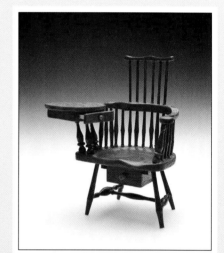

HEPPLEWHITE CARVER

If you intend to produce a dining room layout that could be found in a stately home, then this model should fit the bill. The finished result can be seen in the photograph, which also shows a dining chair made from the same set of instructions but with the arms omitted. Because there is a great deal of hand carving to be done, I have chosen to use mahogany throughout.

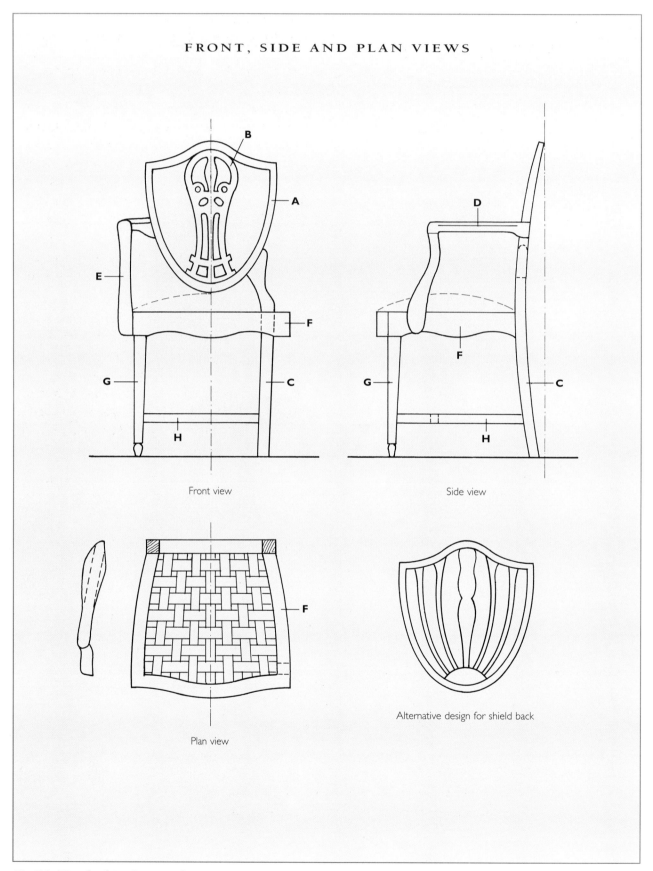

FRONT, SIDE AND PLAN VIEWS

Front view

Side view

Plan view

Alternative design for shield back

Fig 5.1 Hepplewhite Carver: Plan

CUTTING LIST

All mahogany.

A Back rest (1) 40 × 40 × 10mm (1½ × 1½ × ⅜in)

B Splat (1) 35 × 15 × 5mm (1½ × ⅝ × ³⁄₁₆in)

C Rear legs (2) from 2: 55 × 10 × 10mm (2¼ × ⅜ × ⅜in)

D Arms (2) from 2: 30 × 7 × 5mm (1¼ × ⁵⁄₁₆ × ³⁄₁₆in)

E Arm supports (2) from 2: 30 × 10 × 5mm
(1¼ × ½ ×³⁄₁₆in)

F Seat surround (2) from 2: 50 × 45 × 7mm (2 × 1¾ × ⁵⁄₁₆in)

G Front legs (2) from 2: 35 × 5 × 5mm (1½ × ¼ × ¼in)

H Stiles (3) from 3: 35 × 3 × 3mm (1½ × ⅛ × ⅛in)

The sizes given allow for some waste to facilitate the shaping. If multiple chairs are required then I would suggest that the parts be cut from a single sheet of timber of appropriate thickness. For example, should you need, say, six chairs and two carvers, the back rests can be cut from a piece of timber measuring 350 × 40 × 10mm (14 × 1½ × ½in).

PREPARATION AND CONSTRUCTION

BACKREST A Place a sheet of carbon paper face down under the drawing and trace the outline onto the timber surface. Using a fine drill, bore a hole on the inside curve near a corner through which to insert the blade of your fret saw, then cut around the curve and remove the inner shaped piece of timber. (*See* Fig 5.2.) Before the outer curve is cut around, it will be necessary to rub down the timber on the face and back to the shape shown on the side view in the drawing. This should be done using a coarse abrasive paper. Once you are happy with it, you can then cut around the outer curve and put aside until required.

SPLAT B Following the same procedure, cut out the splat. This will require a steady hand and eye, especially if the splat is to fit snugly into the back rest. An alternative design for the shield back is given should you prefer a simpler approach, but even with this, great care is required in making sure that the internal bits that make up the shield back are able to fit properly.

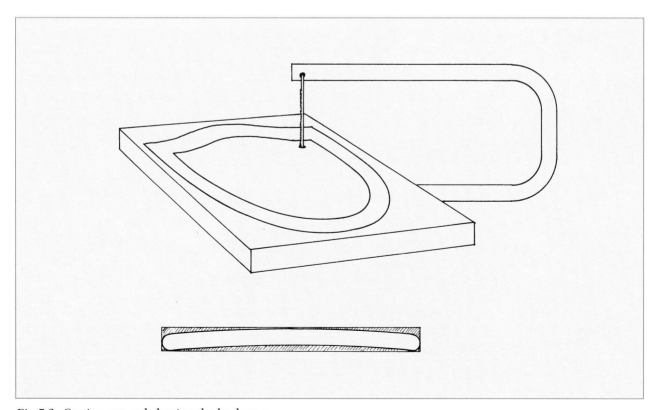

Fig 5.2 Cutting out and shaping the back rest

ARMS D AND ARM SUPPORTS E The next tricky operation occurs when the arms and their supports are cut out and shaped. This is where a sharp modeller's knife becomes necessary, along with some patience, in order to get the arms and their supports to meet as shown in Fig 5.3.

REAR LEGS C These are cut out and shaped in a similar manner, making sure that they marry up to the shield of the back rest. Note how these legs are curved in two directions. (*See* Fig 5.4.)

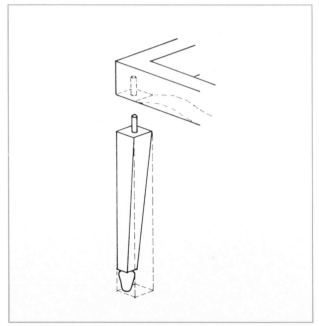

Fig 5.5 The front legs, tapered on the inside only, are attached to the frame with a spigot

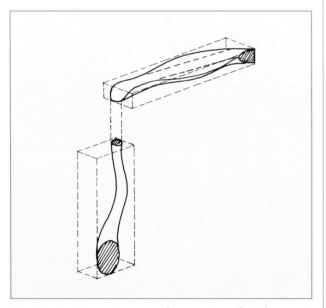

Fig 5.3 Cutting out arms and supports so that they meet

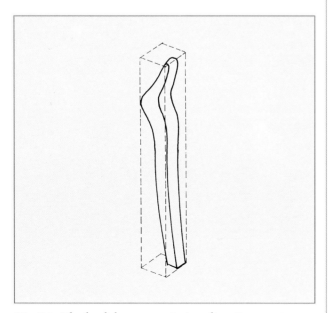

Fig 5.4 The back legs curve in two directions

SEAT SURROUND F The seat surround is made up in two parts, as can be seen from the plan view in Fig 5.1, with a three-sided front piece and a straight back piece. I suggest that you cut out the shape from one piece of timber in the same way as the back rest was done and when you are satisfied with the result, then simply cut away the corners where the seat frame meets the back legs. The shaping of the underside edge of the front and sides of the seat frame can be achieved by eye and a steady hand. Leave a square portion of timber at each of the front two corners underneath the frame, so that you can drill them to receive the front leg spigots as shown in Fig 5.5.

FRONT LEGS G Note that the front legs are tapered along their insides, leaving the front and side faces perpendicular to the seat frame.

ASSEMBLY When it comes to assembling the carver, it will be necessary to do a dry run first to make sure that all the parts meet as they should. A certain amount of rubbing down will probably be required before applying the glue. Start with the seat frame and the back legs, ensuring that the top of the seat frame is at the correct height by laying the parts on the drawing whilst the glue is still wet.

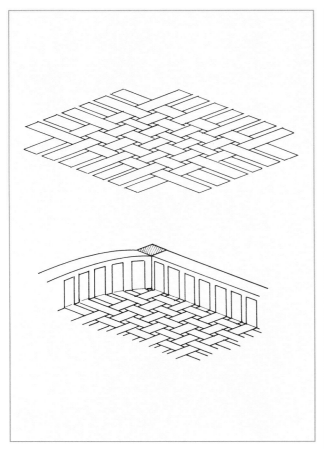

Fig 5.6 Seat webbing should be interlaced before being glued to the frame

SEAT WEBBING Once the legs are set in their correct positions the next task will be to fix the webbing to the seat frame. To do this you should first cut out some strips of stiff fabric and interlace them as shown, away from the seat frame and before attempting to glue the ends to the frame. (*See* Fig 5.6.)

ASSEMBLY

The splat should now be glued into the back rest, when they are found to fit snugly together, and this assembly can then be fitted and glued into the back legs. The arms and their supports follow, but whilst the glue is still wet, I would recommend that you offer them up to the seat frame and back rest to check that they do in fact meet where they should. Once they are set, the front legs can be glued into the seat frame. The stiles, which brace the legs, can be cut to the lengths shown in Fig 5.1 and then fitted and glued in position.

SEAT COVER When all this has been achieved, the final thing left to make is the seat cover. Cut out the shapes shown in Fig 5.7 from some soft leather, or fabric. I use very thin leather or Leatherette with a linen backing, which can be obtained from most drapery shops. The fabric needs to be fairly stiff, and where patterns are involved, these need to be in keeping with the scale of the model. The stuffing for the seat can be cotton wool or kapok. This needs to be carefully measured out so that the final shape of the seat does not ride up too high. When you are reasonably satisfied with it, you can glue the leather or fabric to the sides of the seat frame using Copydex. All that is left to do then is to apply a finish to the timber.

FINISHING

All exposed timber parts should be rubbed down with a fine abrasive paper followed by a fine steel wool. The finish to be applied is left to your own preference. Not being an expert in this field, I recommend that you refer to books on the subject. On this model I used mahogany varnish, but care is needed to ensure that no glue is showing at the joints, otherwise the varnish won't take and ugly streaks become apparent. To make the chairs, simply leave off the arms and their supports.

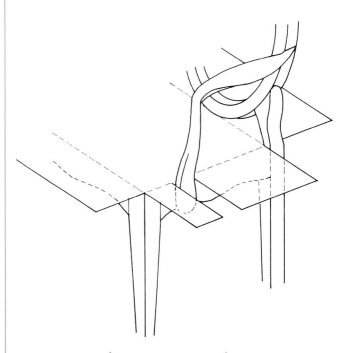

Fig 5.7 Pattern for seat cover material

CHIPPENDALE CHAIR

Here is an example of the versatility to be found in the design of Chippendale-style chairs. The one shown is a dining chair which, with arms added, becomes a carver, and by extending the width it can be turned into a two-seater as shown in the photograph. It is a particularly testing piece to make, requiring a high degree of patience and a steady hand when it comes to carving out the splat, but don't let that put you off because the results are quite beautiful and well worth all the effort. I have used mahogany throughout because of the amount of carving called for and also because this type of period furniture can only be found in a darkish wood.

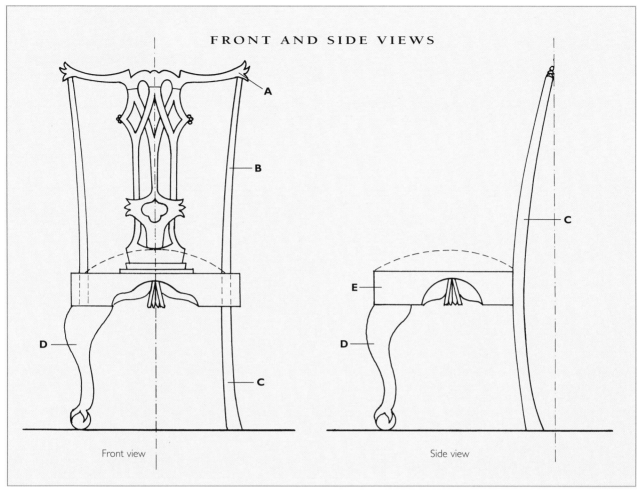

FRONT AND SIDE VIEWS

Front view

Side view

Fig 6.1 Chippendale Chair: Plan

CUTTING LIST

All mahogany.

A Headrest (1) 50 × 10 × 2mm (2 × ½ × ³/₃₂in)

B Splat (1) 50 × 25 × 4mm (2 × 1 × ³/₁₆in)

C Rear legs (2) from 2: 95 × 10 × 10mm
(3¾ × ½ × ½in)

D Front legs (see Fig 6.6) (2) from 2:40 × 15 × 15mm
(1½ × ⅝ × ⅝in)

E Outer seat frame (1) 165 × 10 × 5mm
(6½ × ⅜ × ³/₁₆in)

F Inner seat frame (1) 145 × 4 × 1.5mm
(5¾ × ³/₁₆ × ¹/₁₆in)

G Gussets (1), thin ply or lime, 15 × 15mm (⅝ × ⅝in)

These sizes are slightly larger than required to enable carving to be executed with the minimum of waste. If you have a stock of different thicknesses it will be to your advantage to judge your individual needs directly from the drawing.

Where multiple chairs are wanted, the necessary adjustments can be made to accommodate the parts from a single sheet of timber. Most of the sheets on sale measure 450 × 75mm (18 × 3in), in thicknesses ranging from 0.75 to 6mm (¹/₃₂ × ¼in).

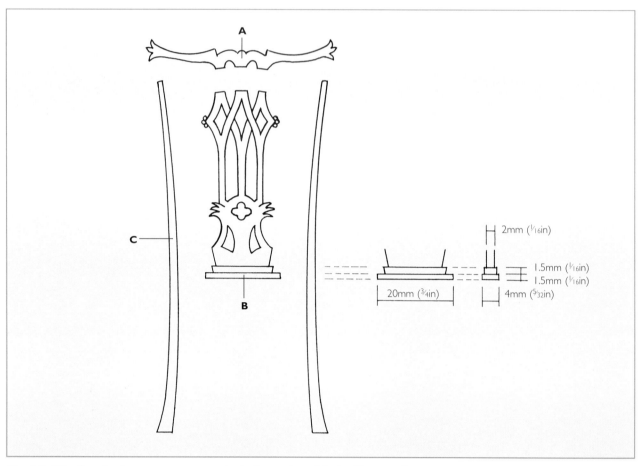

Fig 6.2 The four back rest components, including splat with double step-down

PREPARATION
AND CONSTRUCTION

The back rest is made up of four parts: the headrest, the splat and two rear legs. (*See* Fig 6.2.) As the splat is the most time-consuming element it would be best to start there, followed by the headrest and the rear legs.

SPLAT B   Trace the splat details onto the timber surface, with the aid of carbon paper placed face down under the drawing. Drill a number of holes through which to thread the blade of your jig saw and cut out the internal bits first, following the basic shapes.

Before the outer shape is executed, it would be advisable to rub down the front and rear faces of the splat in order to develop a curved surface which is to follow the curve of the chair legs (*see* the side view in Fig 6.1).

Cut out the outer pieces of timber around the splat using a sharp modelling knife and then begin to carve the individual elements of the splat. Use great care to avoid splitting the timber. From the photograph you will notice how the three vertical elements appear to intertwine near the top. You will perhaps also see how all parts of the splat are cylindrical in cross section. This can be achieved with the use of fine abrasive paper or an emery board.

Make sure that the base of the splat has sufficient timber to be able to step down in two stages. (*See* Fig 6.2.)

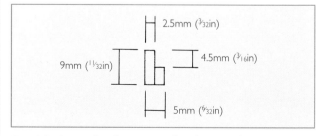

Fig 6.3 A simple alternative for the seat framework: glue two timber pieces together

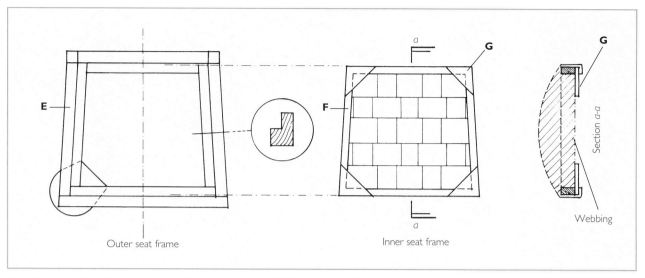

Fig 6.4 Seat details showing webbing to support filling material

HEADREST A This is not as difficult to carve as it would first appear. Trace the details onto the timber and carefully carve away the design. As with the splat, the headrest is fundamentally cylindrical in cross section, this can be achieved by using fine abrasive paper.

REAR LEGS C Because of their slenderness and awkward shape, I found the rear legs to be the most tedious to carve. From the front and side views in Fig 6.1 you will see how these legs curve in two directions and, once again, are basically cylindrical in cross section. I suggest that you trace the front view of the legs onto the timber surface, leaving enough thickness of timber to accommodate the pronounced curve of the legs in the other direction. During the carving, it would be as well if you keep on checking that the legs

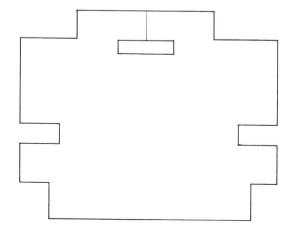

Fig 6.5 Pattern for seat cover material (not to scale)

are conforming to the drawing and that they meet the headrest where shown.

OUTER SEAT FRAME E Begin by taking the length of timber for the outer seat frame. Using a modelling knife and a straightedge, cut out a slice of timber along the centre of each of two adjacent edges to form an L-shaped cross section. If you feel nervous about doing this, simply make up the framework by gluing two pieces of timber together as shown in Fig 6.3. Next, cut the timber into the appropriate lengths as shown on the plan. Glue the back rail of the frame to the rear legs, making sure they are at the correct height by laying rail and legs on the plan whilst the glue is still tacky. When the glue has set you can then glue the rest of the framework to the rear legs, once again laying the assembly onto the side view to ensure that all is in accordance with the drawing. The carving along the front and sides of the frame is not as difficult to achieve. The way I did it was to first draw the shapes onto the timber face and then carefully cut away the superfluous bits.

INNER SEAT FRAME F AND GUSSETS G This is made up of simple strips of timber glued together as shown in Fig 6.4, with corner gussets glued to the underside to add stiffness to the frame. Note that the frame is smaller in size than the inside of the outer seat frame because of the need to accommodate the seat cover material.

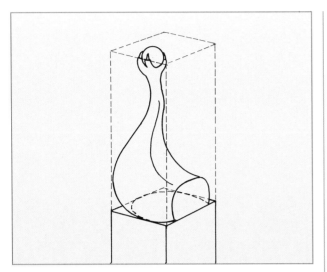

Fig 6.6 Carving the front legs from one long piece of timber will avoid difficulties

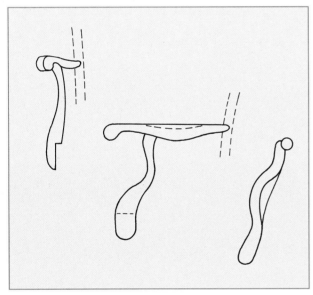

Fig 6.7 The addition of arms and supports will produce a carver

WEBBING The webbing is made up as described in the previous model. (*See* Seat webbing in Chapter 5, and Fig 6.4.) The seat cover can be in soft leather, or a regency-striped fabric in keeping with the period. The seat cover pattern is shown in Fig 6.5.

FRONT LEGS D The sizes for these as given in the cutting list will make it awkward to handle. It would be simpler to cut them from a long piece of timber as shown in Fig 6.6. The claw and ball feet can only be carved by eye (and a sharp blade, of course).

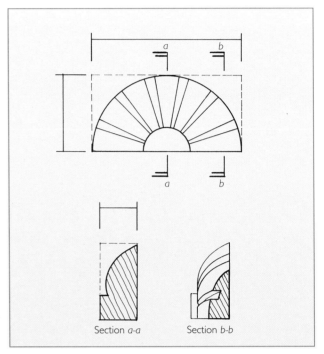

Fig 6.8 Shape and carve the shell from an offcut of timber

CARVER Although not drawn here, a Chippendale carver can be achieved by adding arms and supports as shown in Fig 6.7.

TWO-SEATER If you would like to make a two-seater as seen in the photograph, all you have to do is make two splats, the two outer rear legs, and the front legs as for the chair. The two inner rear legs only extend downward to the top of the seat frame. The headrest is made up in one piece after tracing the profile onto the timber surface using the drawing as a guide. The centre front leg is exactly as for the chair, and the shell, which is cut out and carved separately (*see* Fig 6.8), is glued to the frame as shown. The overall length of the seat. frame is 90mm ($3^{17}/_{32}$ in), and the inner frame has an overall length of 82mm ($3^{7}/_{32}$ in), otherwise everything else is as for the chair construction.

FINISHING

After carefully rubbing down all exposed surfaces with a fine abrasive paper and fine wire wool, the finish can be applied. I used mahogany varnish to give a glossy appearance to the timber, but you may decide on a different system.

CHIPPENDALE CARVER

Of all the chairs I have made, this one is my favourite. Many of the features to be found on Chippendale furniture of the late eighteenth century are incorporated in its design. Examples of these include: (a) bow-shaped headrest; (b) carved and pierced splat; (c) stuff-over seat; (d) ball and claw feet; (e) acanthus leaf carving at the front leg knees.

Dining chairs can also be produced from this drawing by simply omitting the arms. Mahogany is used throughout to facilitate carving and to produce a colour in keeping with the period. As with all models of this kind, a great deal of care is needed when carving the splat and headrest, especially in view of the fact that they are made in one piece.

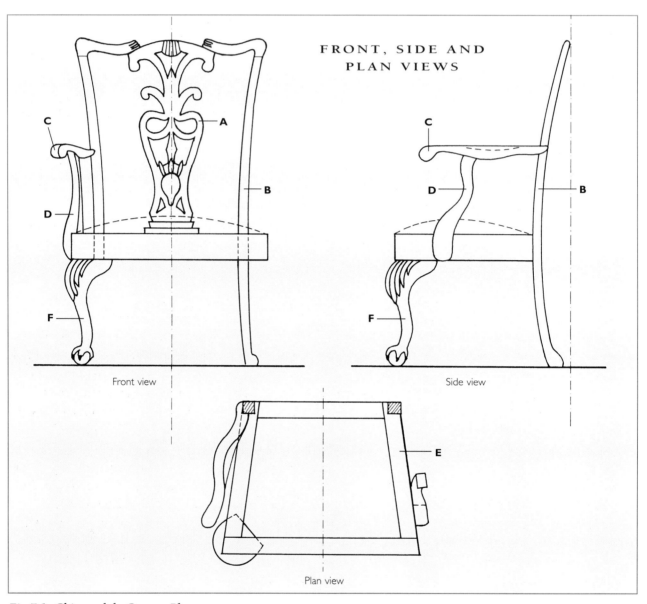

Fig 7.1 Chippendale Carver: Plan

CUTTING LIST

All mahogany.

A Headrest and splat combined (1), sheet, 52 × 50 × 4mm (2⅛ × 2 × ³⁄₁₆in)

B Rear legs (2) from 2: 85 × 10 × 10mm (3⅜ × ⅜ × ⅜in)

C Arms (2) from 2: 40 × 10 × 5mm (1½ × ⅜ × ¼in)

D Arm supports (2) from 2: 30 × 10 × 5mm (1¼ × ⅜ × ³⁄₁₆in)

E Seat frame (1) from 165 × 7 × 5mm (6½ × ⁵⁄₁₆ × ³⁄₁₆in)

F Front legs (2) from 2: 30 × 15 × 15mm (1¼ × ⅝ × ⅝in)

To allow for the carving and fitting together of parts, these sizes are slightly larger than required and much of the material can be cut from sheets of the appropriate thickness in order to reduce waste. For example, the arms, arm supports and seat frame can be cut from a 5mm (³⁄₁₆in) thick sheet of timber.

PREPARATION AND CONSTRUCTION

HEADREST AND SPLAT A Rub down the sheet from which they are to be cut in order to follow the curvature as seen on the side view. Trace their configuration onto the surface of the timber, using carbon paper face down and under the drawing. (*See* Tracing in Chapter 2.) The greatest possible care is now needed in cutting out the shape because, should the grain run from top to bottom, the headrest can quite easily snap off. Likewise, if the grain runs from side to side, the splat uprights are liable to break.

When the drawing has been transferred to the timber surface, begin by drilling a series of holes within the splat and, using a fret saw, cut out the inside bits first. Follow this by removing the timber from outside the splat and from the underside of the headrest. Now, before removing the timber from the headrest, complete your work, carving out the splat with its detail. This is to retain stiffness in the headrest and so avoid a calamity. When this has been done you can remove the timber above the headrest and complete the carving thereof.

REAR LEGS B Now trace the rear legs from the front view onto the appropriate timber surface, making sure that there is sufficient thickness of material to accommodate the curvature seen on the side view. As you carve, place the legs on the drawing at intervals, to check that the shapes are in agreement with the drawing.

ARMS C AND ARM SUPPORTS D Trace onto the timber surface, and,using the modelling knife, carve away the superfluous material, making sure that the end of the support meets the arm rest as shown on the drawing. Notice how the upper surface of the arm rest is scooped out where the elbows are to be placed. Again, checks should be made periodically by placing the work on the drawing to make sure that the shapes conform to those shown.

SEAT FRAME E This is made up from timber having a simple rectangular cross section. The jointing can be plain butt joints. Cut away the corners where the rear legs are to be fitted and begin to assemble.

ASSEMBLY

1 Glue rear legs to headrest. *Lay parts on the front view whilst the glue is still wet, to get their relative positions correct.*
2 Glue seat frame to rear legs. *Check the height of the seat from the drawing before the glue sets.*
3 Glue arm rests and supports to seat frame and rear legs. *This will prove rather tedious work and it would be as well if you were to either hand hold them in position until the glue has set, or support them in some way by making a jig from some scrap material. If this is not done then you may find that the arms are not symmetrical about the centreline of the chair when seen from above.*

FRONT LEGS F Cut from a length of timber as shown in Fig 6.6, carving the claw and ball feet by eye. You may like also to try your hand at carving acanthus leaves at the knees as shown. (*See* Fig 6.8 for a similar task.) I used a set of miniature chisels and carving tools but if you don't have these, you can quite easily carve the leaves using a normal modelling knife.

WEBBING On this model I included webbing in the seat as described for the Hepplewhite Carver (*see* Seat webbing in Chapter 5) but, as a matter of fact, it would be more authentic to just glue a plain sheet of canvas to the underside of the frame. This supports the filling which can be either cotton wool, kapok or foam rubber.

SEAT COVER This can be soft leather or fabric, whichever you prefer. Cut out to the pattern shown in Fig 6.5 and use Copydex to attach the cover to the framework. Trim off any excess with a sharp knife.

FINISHING

As with the previous models, I used a mahogany varnish after rubbing all parts down with abrasive paper and wire wool. Ensure that the joints are free from glue, otherwise, when the varnish is applied, you will see some rather ugly stains. Should extra coats of varnish be needed, allow up to eight hours between applications and rub down with wire wool before the next coat is added.

8

ROCKING CHAIR

I came across the large scale version of this chair when touring Wales and was so taken with its beauty of line and its stability that I bought it on the spot. The model shown here is as near to the original article as is possible to get at this scale. When completed, this is an outstanding model which could grace any modern dolls' house. As will be seen, there is a certain amount of turning to be done for the arm rest supports, legs and stiles. Methods that can be used are explained in the text. In order to complete the overall impression and authenticity, I decided to make it in beech, which is available in thin sheets.

FRONT, SIDE AND PLAN VIEWS

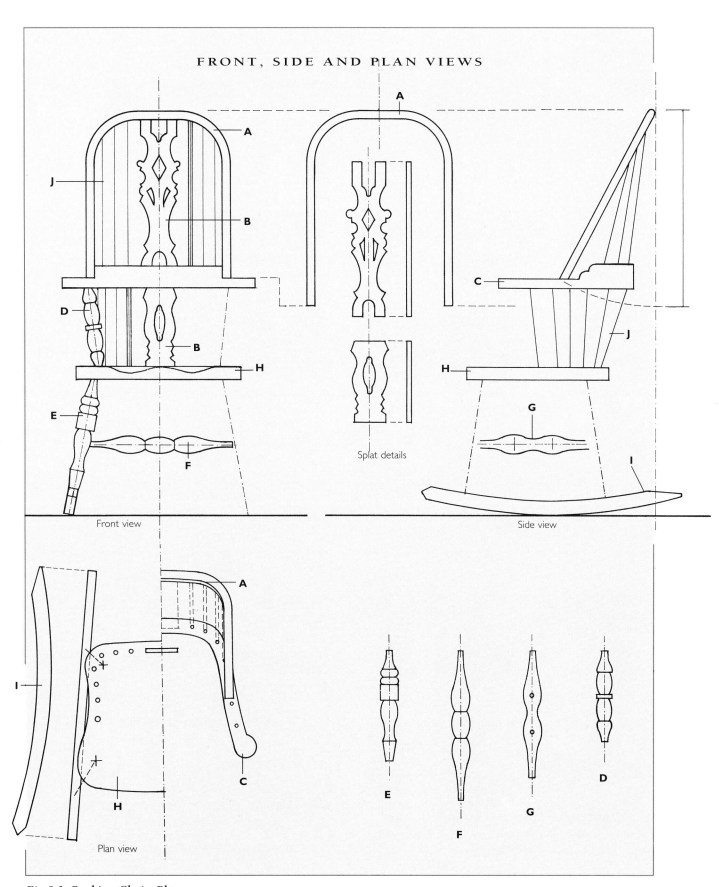

Front view

Splat details

Side view

Plan view

Fig 8.1 Rocking Chair: Plan

CUTTING LIST

Beech.

A Back rest frame (1) 55 × 40 × 2mm (2¼ × 1½ × ³/₃₂in)

B Splats (2) 80 × 15 × 0.75mm (3⅛ × ⅝ × ¹/₃₂in)

C Arm rests (2) 40 × 60 × 7mm (1⅝ × 2⅜ × ³/₁₆in)

D Arm rest supports (2), dowel or beech strips, 10mm diameter (⅜in)

E Legs (4), dowel or beech strips, 10mm diameter (⅜in)

F and **G** Stiles (4), dowel or beech strips, 10mm diameter (⅜in)

H Seat (1) 40 × 50 × 3mm (1½ × 2 × ⅛in)

I Rockers (2) 75 × 10 × 2mm (3 × ⅜ × ⅛in)

J Frame supports (20), dowel, 1mm diameter (¹/₃₂in)

PREPARATION AND CONSTRUCTION

ARM REST C Begin with the arm rest since the proportions of the chair depend upon the carving out of this member producing the correct contours. The grain should travel from back to front to avoid splitting the arms.

There is no easy way to deal with the shaping of this piece but I have found that, after transferring the basic outline from the plan view onto the timber surface, using carbon paper face down and under the drawing, the best way to start is to cut around the inside curve with a fret saw and then smooth down the profile formed using abrasive paper wrapped around a piece of dowel. You can then cut away the outer curve using a modelling knife and finish off with abrasive paper.

Now that you have the basic shape sorted out, the next thing to do is cut a groove about 45°, in the position shown in Fig 8.2, and carefully cut away the excess material over the arm rest areas. This can be done using either a knife or a saw, whichever you feel most comfortable with. The wiggly bit joining the top surface of the arm rest to that of the back part can be nicked out with a knife, or filed down.

Now comes another tricky operation. This is to drill a series of holes along the top edge of the back piece and the underside of the arm rests. I did this by marking out the positions of the holes first, then, using an awl or hole punch, I punctured each mark ready to receive the drill bit. The slope of the drill bit required to enter the timber was done by eye, but if you feel unable to do this you can make a system of card cutouts to act as formers to assist in acquiring the correct slope. The drill bit in question should be 1mm (¹/₃₂ in) diameter for the dowel and 2mm (³/₃₂ in) diameter for the arm supports. With regard to the card formers, Fig 8.3 will give a clear idea of what I mean.

Don't drill too far into the timber or full penetration will occur which won't look good on the finished chair.

BACK REST FRAME A Trace the outline of the back rest frame from the projected view shown, with the timber grain running from top to bottom. Cut away the inside first, using a fret saw and then carefully cut away the outside material with a fret saw or knife.

Rub down the finished article and offer it up to the drawing to check that it conforms to the shape shown. Remember to cut a chamfer at each end so that it will sit comfortably on the arm rest in the position shown on the side view.

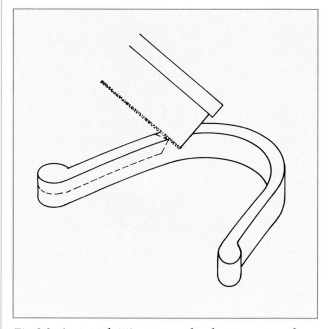

Fig 8.2 An initial 45° cut is used to begin carving the arm rests

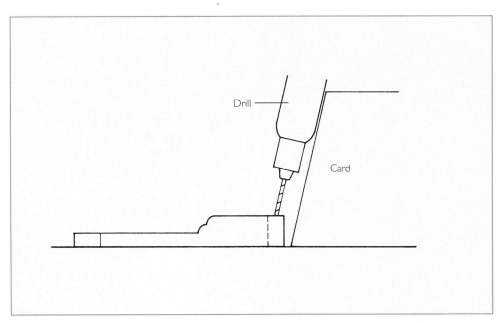

Fig 8.3 A card cutout will help with drilling at an angle

SPLATS B Make the splats next by transferring the shapes shown on the drawing to a sheet of timber, using carbon paper, and drill a series of holes to receive the fret saw blade. Cut out the inside bits first and then carefully cut around the outside with a modelling knife.

SEAT H Make the seat to the profile shown on the plan view and drill a series of holes as explained before, but this time you can penetrate the seat. The tricky bit is in getting the correct angle for penetration so that the arm supports and the legs correspond with the drawing.

Now hollow out the top surface to accommodate the buttocks. This can be done by wrapping some abrasive paper around a cylindrical object and rubbing down until you are satisfied with the result. (*See* Fig 8.4.)

ROCKERS I Cut out the rockers to the shape given alongside the plan view, marking it onto the timber first if you wish.

LEGS AND STILES E, F AND G AND ARM REST SUPPORTS D This assumes that you are in possession of either a Minicraft lathe or a drill. Place the dowel or beech strip of the appropriate thickness in the lathe, with enough length to allow for ease of operation with the chisel. Using a gouge, rough down

the timber surface with the lathe running, until you have reached the greatest diameter required on the piece to be shaped. A chisel is supplied with the Minicraft equipment but it is a useful addition to buy a 6mm ($\frac{1}{4}$ in) gouge as well. It is not easy to use a drilling machine for this operation unless you can purchase the equipment needed to convert it into a lathe.

When the timber has been roughed down, and with the equipment still running, mark out the portions to be cut away using a Biro, or pencil. If it scares you to do this then by all means turn the work by hand whilst you mark its surface. (*See* Fig 8.5.) Now proceed to cut away the timber until the required shape materializes.

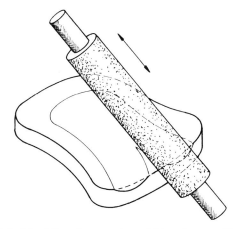

Fig 8.4 Moulding the seat by rubbing down with abrasive paper wrapped around a cylinder

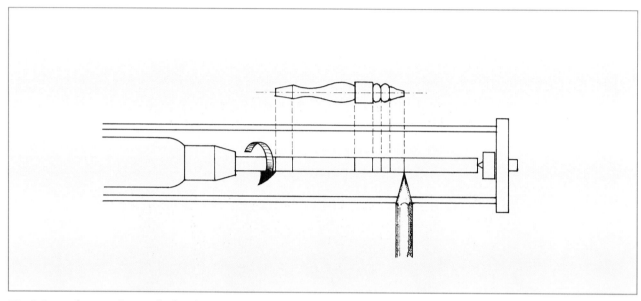

Fig 8.5 Timber can be marked either turning by hand, or in the lathe

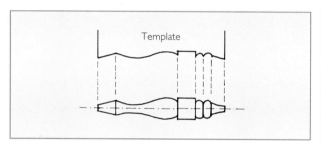

Fig 8.6 A template will save time and effort when making a repeated piece

When making pieces that are repeated, a template would be useful. A typical example is seen in Fig 8.6. This can be made from stiff card or sheet metal. To ensure that you have the same diameter on the pieces a vernier gauge is handy, but as long as you are happy without it, fair enough. After all, there is no need for absolute accuracy – what you are aiming for is to end up with a model that is pleasing to the eye.

ARM REST SUPPORTS D AND FRAME SUPPORTS J These are trimmed to fit as the chair is assembled.

ASSEMBLY

1 Glue back rest frame and upper splat to arm rest as shown.
2 Trim upper supports J to meet the back rest frame and penetrate arm rest. Glue in position.
3 Glue arm rest supports D and lower splat to seat and arm rest.
4 Glue lower supports J to seat and arm rest. *Note the dowel can be fed in from the underside of the seat and trimmed off when the glue has set.*
5 Glue cross stile to side stiles.
6 Glue stiles to legs and legs to seat.
7 Glue rockers to legs. At each stage of the gluing operation, check against the drawing to see how you are progressing.

FINISHING

Carefully rub down all parts with a fine abrasive paper and wire wool, rounding off the edges of the back rest frame. To enhance the timber and make it look like the real thing I used a clear varnish.

GEORGE I CHAIR

The best George I chairs were mostly made in mahogany and carried embellishments to the knees, feet and rail in the form of a shell motif. The feet were generally of the claw and ball variety, but others can be found with a paw or pad design. With the addition of arms, the chair becomes a carver. This model can be made in either mahogany or walnut which are both easy timbers to carve and take a good finish.

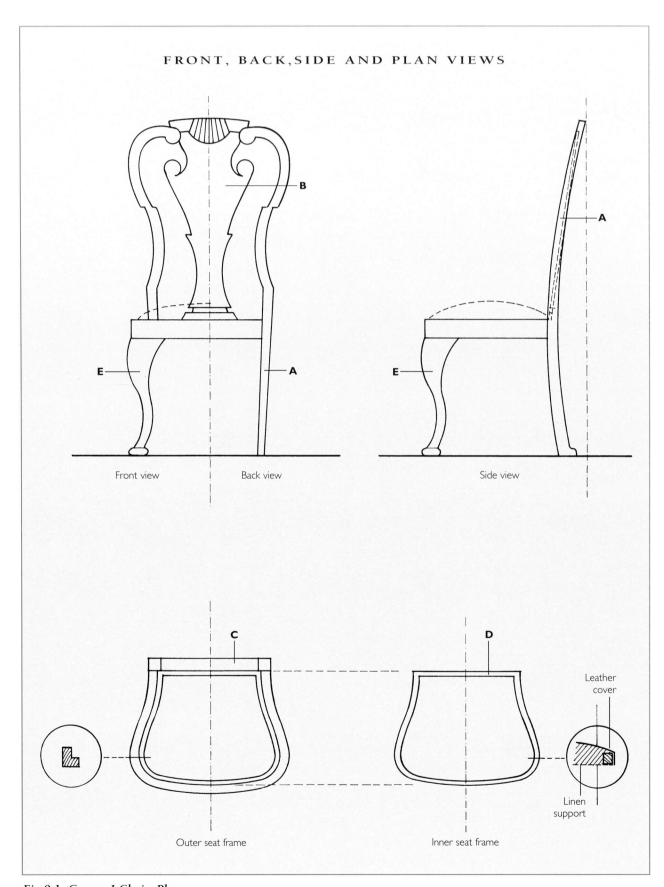

FRONT, BACK, SIDE AND PLAN VIEWS

Front view   Back view

Side view

Leather cover

Linen support

Outer seat frame

Inner seat frame

Fig 9.1 George I Chair: Plan

CUTTING LIST

Mahogany or walnut.

A Back rest frame and rear legs (1) 100 × 50 × 10mm
(4 × 2 × ⅜in)

B Splat (1) 50 × 30 × 0.75mm (2 × 1¼ × ⅟₃₂in)

C Outer seat frame (1) 50 × 40 × 5mm (2 × 1½ × ³⁄₁₆in)

D Inner seat frame (1) 40 × 30 × 2.5mm (1½ × 1¼ × ⅛in)

E Front legs (see Fig 6.6) (2) 35 × 12 × 12mm
(1½ × ½ × ½in)

The sizes given allow for a certain amount of wastage.

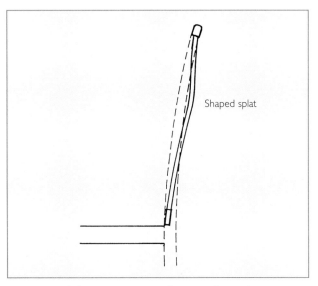

Shaped splat

Fig 9.3 Whilst more commonly curved, a splat may sometimes be flat

PREPARATION AND CONSTRUCTION

BACK REST FRAME A Begin by tracing the back rest frame onto the timber surface, using carbon paper face down and under the drawing. Notice that the rear legs form part of the back rest. Next, cut around the inside curves using a fret saw.

Before cutting around the outer curve, the timber should be rubbed down with a coarse abrasive paper in order to form the curvature shown on the side view. You will need to re-draw the shape of the frame at this point.

Now cut around the outer profile using a knife. The headrest forms part of the back rest even though it may appear to be independent. This effect is created when the shell motif and the back rest scrolls are carved.

You will find that the resultant frame is extremely fragile, so put it somewhere safe until it is required.

SPLAT B The splat is cut from a plain sheet of timber. On this model it is shown as a flat surface though on much of this type of furniture the splat is curved, as can be seen in Fig 9.3. To form a curve you will need to soak it for some time in hot water and clamp it in the required shape until it dries. You may be able to achieve the shape by holding the timber over steam. As the timber will attempt to recover its shape, it would be better to exaggerate the curve when carrying out the process.

At the foot of the splat you will see a small, stepped piece which can be made from a scrap piece of timber and glued onto the splat or seat frame.

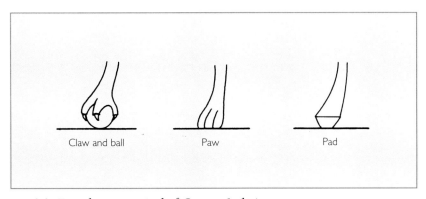

Claw and ball   Paw   Pad

Fig 9.2 Foot designs typical of George 1 chairs

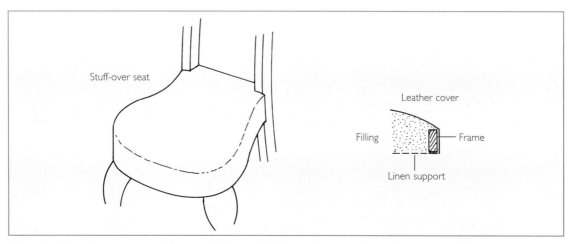

Fig 9.4   A stuff-over seat, with material over the frame, is an easier alternative to the drop-in seat

OUTER SEAT FRAME C   Trace its shape from Fig 9.1 onto the timber surface, using carbon paper face down and under the drawing, then drill a hole to receive the fret saw blade and cut out the middle portion. The inside top-edge then has to be cut away to form a shelf upon which the inner frame is to rest. I managed to do this by eye, using a knife and making sure that the cut was not too deep in either direction. I then finished the shelf off by means of my miniature chisel.

Cut out each corner of the seat frame at its junction with the back rest frame to accommodate the legs.

INNER SEAT FRAME D   The inner seat frame will need some patient handling, but if you cut out the inside portion first then it won't be so bad, just awkward to handle. The outer profile can be cut with a knife and 'fitted' to the inside shape of the main seat frame, remembering to make sure that there is a small gap between frames to accommodate the seat cover thickness. If the inner frame does break during its creation, don't panic, just glue it back together. Should you feel that this drop-in type seat is too difficult to do, make the drop-in frame from a solid sheet of timber, or use a stuff-over seat as seen in Fig 9.4.

SEAT COVER   Leather or fabric can be used for the cover material in each case. A canvas sheet can be glued to the underside of either frame to act as a support for the filling which can be cotton wool, kapok or foam rubber. Alternatively, a webbed undersurface can be applied to inner frame D (*see* Seat webbing in Chapter 5; *see also* Fig 6.4).

FRONT LEGS E   To avoid difficulties, these are made by carving the shape from one long piece of timber (*see* Fig 6.6). For a design typical of George I chairs, carve a simple pad, paw or claw for the feet.

CARVER   To make the chair into a carver, all that is required is to cut out the arms and their supports as described for the Chippendale Carver. (*See* Fig 6.7.)

ASSEMBLY

1   Glue back rest to seat making sure the seat is at the height shown on the drawing.
2   Glue splat to seat frame and headrest. It will need to be shaped so that it nestles neatly into the headrest.
3   Glue front legs to seat frame.
4   Glue seat covers to seat frame, using Copydex.

FINISHING

After rubbing down all exposed timber with a fine abrasive paper and wire wool, you can apply a varnish of the same colour as the timber used.

When applying varnish, it is necessary to make sure that no glue is showing, otherwise ugly streaks will show. Some model makers advocate that all of the individual pieces should be varnished before gluing but there is no need for this if you are very careful. Try both methods if you wish and stick to the one that suits you.

WINDSOR WRITING CHAIR

This is just one example of the wide variety of Windsor chairs that can be found. It incorporates a writing area with a drawer and a storage area beneath the seat. Because of the nature of such chairs, I once again chose mahogany to make life easier when carving and turning. However, it would look good in any kind of timber that is easy to carve. To authenticate a lighter timber, you may wish to stain it afterwards.

FRONT, SIDE AND PLAN VIEWS

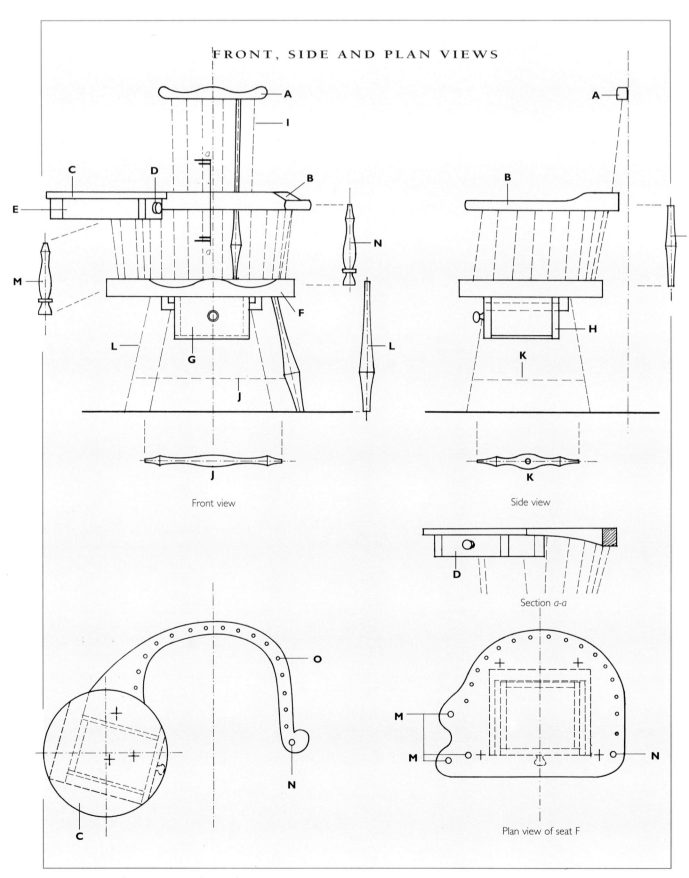

Front view

Side view

Section *a-a*

Plan view of seat F

Fig 10.1 Windsor Writing Chair: Plan

CUTTING LIST

Mahogany or any timber easy to carve.

A Headrest (1) 30 × 5 × 3mm (1¼ × ³⁄₁₆ × ⅛in)

B Arm rest (1) 40 × 60 × 2mm (1⅝ × 2⅜ × ³⁄₃₂in)

C Writing area (1) 40 × 40 × 2mm (1⅝ × 1⅝ × ³⁄₃₂in)

D Upper drawer

side panel (1) 25 × 5 × 1.5mm (1 × ¼ × ¹⁄₁₆in)

top and base panels (2) from 2: 25 × 25 × 1.5mm
(1 × 1 × ¹⁄₁₆in)

side block (1) 25 × 10 × 5mm (1 × ⅜ × ³⁄₁₆in)

end block (1) 25 × 5 × 3mm (1 × ¼ × ⅛in)

front (1) 25 × 5 × 1.5mm (1 × ¼ × ¹⁄₁₆in)

drawer pull (1), dowel or cocktail stick, 3mm diameter
(⅛in)

F Seat (1) 40 × 60 × 5mm (1⅝ × 2⅜ × ³⁄₁₆in)

G Drawer under seat

side panels (2) 18 × 10 × 1.5mm (¾ × ⅜ × ¹⁄₁₆in)

side pieces (2) 20 × 1 × 1mm (¹³⁄₁₆ × ¹⁄₃₂ × ¹⁄₃₂in)

base (1) 22 × 20 × 0.75mm (1 × ¹³⁄₁₆ × ¹⁄₃₂in)

side rails (2) 20 × 3 × 3mm (¹³⁄₁₆ × ⅛ × ⅛in)

end panel (1) 12 × 10 × 1.5mm (½ × ⅜ × ¹⁄₁₆in)

end piece (1) 28 × 3 × 3mm (1⅛ × ⅛ × ⅛in)

front (1) 22 × 11 × 2mm (1 × ½ × ³⁄₃₂in)

drawer pull (1), dowel or cocktail stick, 3mm diameter
(⅛in)

H Drawer frame (1) 75 × 3 × 3mm (3 × ⅛ × ⅛in)

I Head rest supports (6), dowel or cocktail sticks, 1mm
diameter (¹⁄₃₂in)

J to **O** Stiles, legs and arm rest supports (27), dowel, 5mm
(³⁄₁₆in)

Some waste is inevitable with the sizes given, which allow
for the parts to be 'fitted' together.

PREPARATION
AND CONSTRUCTION

ARM REST B Begin by tracing the outline of the
plan view of the arm rest onto the timber surface with
the grain travelling from back to front. (*See* Fig 10.1.)

Using a fret saw, cut away the inside portion first
and rub down the edge to the profile shown. Then cut
away the timber from the outside of the curve with a
knife or fret saw, and very carefully rub down the
edge. Should the timber break during this operation,
either glue it together again or repeat the exercise.

Now cut out the surplus timber above the arm rest
as shown on the side view and cut out that under the
arm rest as shown on section *a-a*. Put aside until required.

SEAT F Trace the seat from Fig 10.1 onto the timber
face and cut it out with a fret saw. Form the
indentations shown on the top surface (*see* Fig 8.4)
and mark the position of the holes to take the
supports, with an awl or hole punch.

WRITING AREA C Draw a circle onto the timber
surface with a pair of compasses, then cut it out with a
fret saw and rub down the edge to the diameter shown
on the plan view. Notice how the arm rest fits into the
edge of the circle and is of the same thickness where it
meets the edge of the writing area.

HEADREST A AND HEADREST SUPPORTS I
At this point you can cut out the headrest to the
profile shown, rub down and put aside until later. Cut
the headrest supports to size directly from the front
view in Fig 10.1.

**FRONT PANEL D AND FRAME OF UPPER
DRAWER E** The timber for the construction of the
drawer under the writing area needs to be carefully
cut out, otherwise, when assembled, the front or rear
of the drawer will stick out beyond the edge of the
writing area. An exploded view of the drawer
construction is shown in Fig 10.2 to indicate the
relative position of the drawer to its container.

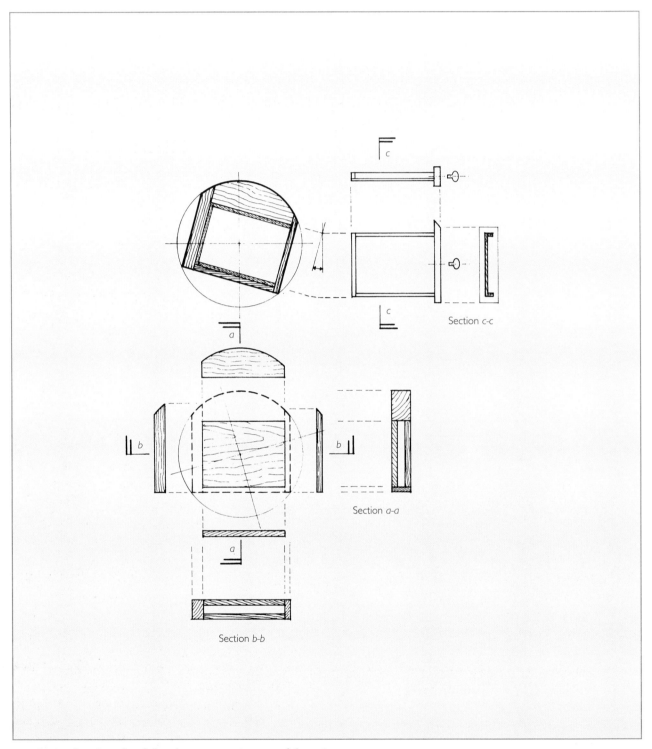

Fig 10.2 The close fit of this drawer requires careful cutting out

Make up the framework to house the drawer as shown. Glue the parts together and to the underside surface of the writing area and when set, construct the drawer itself to fit snugly into the space provided. Make sure that the front panel of the drawer is flush with the underside of the writing area and also the bottom edge of the drawer container.

A simple turned knob can be made and glued into a pre-drilled hole as shown, using a 1mm ($^1/_{32}$ in) diameter drill.

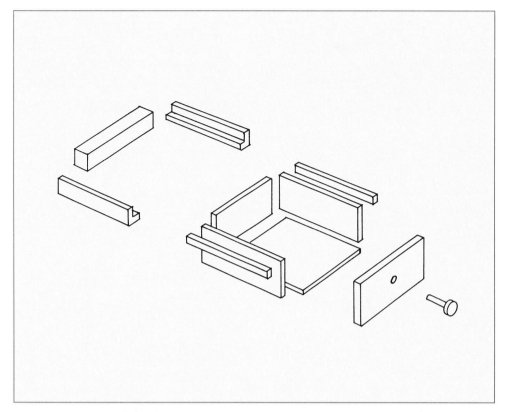

Fig 10.3 Framework for drawer under seat

**DRAWER G AND DRAWER FRAME UNDER
SEAT H** First make up a framework as shown in the
exploded view in Fig 10.3. The groove to receive the
drawer runners can be chased out with a knife, or
made up from two pieces of timber. (*See* Fig 6.3.) The
rear rail of this frame is a simple rectangular piece of
timber. Once the frame is made you can begin to
assemble the drawer, this time gluing some small
strips of timber along the top edges to act as runners.
Make sure that they fit comfortably into the frame
guides to prevent them binding when in use. Now
glue the framework to the underside of the seat,
taking care not to overlap any of the four crosses
where the legs are to fix.

Turn and fit a simple timber knob as indicated
in the exploded view (*see* Fig 10.3) and glue into the
pre-drilled hole. The drill to use for this will be 1mm
($^{1}/_{32}$ in) diameter.

**STILES, LEGS AND ARM REST SUPPORTS J,
K, L, M, N AND O** The stiles J and K, the legs L
and the supports M, N and O, should now be turned
on the lathe. The quantities for each can be
ascertained from the sketches on the plan. To transfer
details from the sketches to the dowel, use a strip of
plain paper and mark the prominent points from the
sketch onto it. Now put the dowel in the lathe and
transfer these marks from the paper to the dowel as
shown in Fig 10.4.

When turning it will be convenient, where possible,
to turn two or more pieces from a single piece of
dowel. (*See* Fig 10.5.) Before you remove the turned
piece from the lathe, it would be worthwhile to apply
the finish with the lathe in operation.

The next operation takes a lot of nerve and must be
done very carefully. That is, to drill the arm rest and
seat to receive their supports. To get the correct
inclination for the drill bit, you can use a system of
card cutouts as formers as described in the Rocking
Chair (*see* Fig 8.3).

Look at the plan views and you will see three
crosses on the writing area and four on the seat. These
indicate where the supports and legs are located. On
the plan view of the seat you will also see four small
circles marked M and N. These indicate where the arm
rest supports are located.

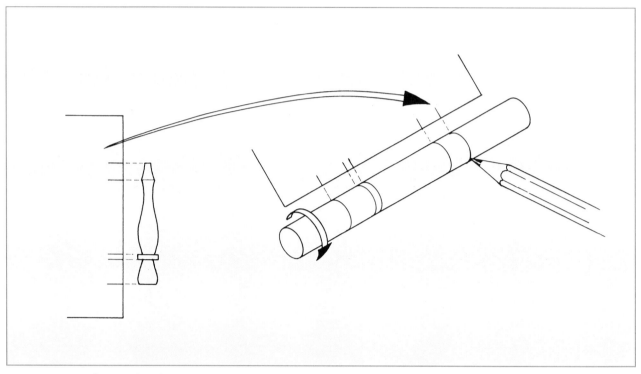

Fig 10.4 Transferring details to the timber, using a paper marker

ASSEMBLY

1 Glue stile J to stiles K.
2 Glue legs L to stiles K and to seat.
3 Glue supports O into locating holes in B and F.
4 Glue supports M and N in positions shown, before supports O set hard.
5 Glue headrest supports to arm rest B.
6 Glue headrest to supports. Hold in place until set.

FINISHING

Remove any surplus glue with a knife and rub down the timber with a fine abrasive paper and wire wool then apply an appropriate varnish to give it that glossy appearance. If more applications are to be administered, allow up to eight hours between each coat and rub down the surfaces with wire wool before applying the next coat of varnish.

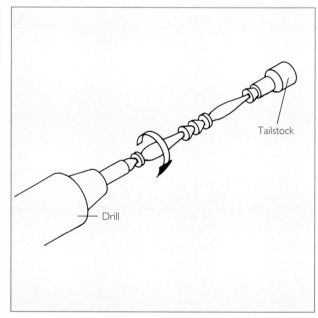

Fig 10.5 Multiple pieces can be turned from a single piece of dowel

CHILD'S HIGHCHAIR

These were known as 'Mechanical Highchairs' when first developed. The one shown here is of the late Victorian period. The making of the individual pieces is not too difficult but can be a bit fiddly because of the fineness of detail. The hardest part is when it comes to assembling the chair. So much will depend upon the accuracy of drilling and preparation of the pieces if it is to look presentable. Don't despair or be put off by these comments, just take your time over it and remember, if I can do it, so can you. The timber used for this model was mixture of lime and beech. The original chairs were generally made of birch or beech and were later painted or stained a dark colour. I have chosen lime where carving is to be done and beech for the legs and other supports.

SIDE, UNDERSIDE AND FRONT VIEWS

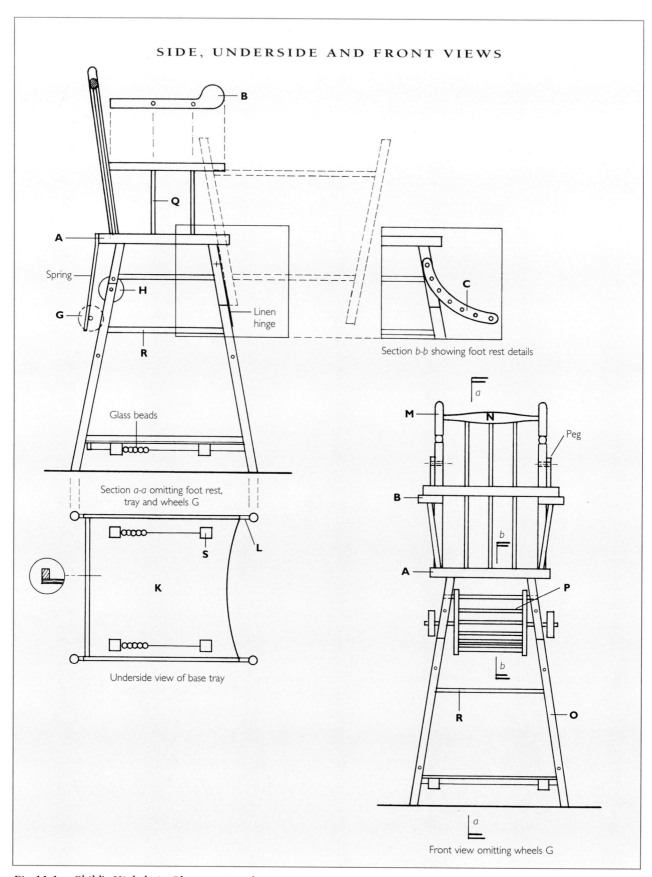

Section *b-b* showing foot rest details

Section *a-a* omitting foot rest, tray and wheels G

Underside view of base tray

Front view omitting wheels G

Fig 11.1a Child's Highchair: Plan - *continued over*

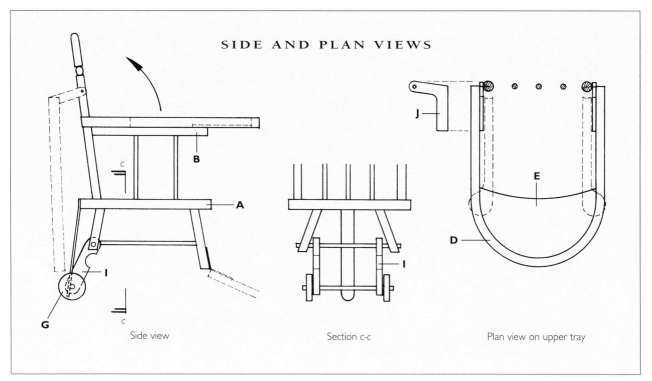

SIDE AND PLAN VIEWS

Side view

Section *c-c*

Plan view on upper tray

Fig 11.1b Child's Highchair: Plan - continued

CUTTING LIST

Lime; beech.

A Seat (1) 40 × 35 × 2mm (1½ × 1½ × ³⁄₃₂in)

B Arm rests (2) 35 × 10 × 2mm (1½ × ⅜ × ³⁄₃₂in)

C Quadrants (section *b-b*) (2), thin ply

D Tray edge (1) 50 × 40 × 2.5mm (2 × 1⅝ × ⅛in)

E Tray (1), thin ply, 35 × 20mm (1½ × 1in)

F Spring (section *a-a*) (1), thin ply or brass strip

G and **H** Wheels (4), dowel, 7mm diameter (⁹⁄₃₂in)

I Wheel-carriage supports (2) 40 × 10 × 1.5mm (1⅝ × ⅜ × ¹⁄₁₆in)

J Side arms (2), thin ply, 15 × 20mm (⅝ × 1in)

K Lower tray (1), thin ply, 45 × 40mm (1¾ × 1⅝in)

L Edging (3), thin strip, 130 × 1× 1mm (5 × ¹⁄₃₂ × ¹⁄₃₂in)

M Back rest supports (5), dowel or cocktail sticks, 2mm diameter (³⁄₃₂in)

N Headrail (1), dowel or cocktail sticks, 2mm diameter (³⁄₃₂in)

O Legs (4), dowel or cocktail sticks, 2mm diameter (³⁄₃₂in)

P Footrests (7), dowel or cocktail sticks, 1mm diameter (¹⁄₃₂in)

Q Arm rest supports (4), dowel or cocktail sticks, 2mm diameter (³⁄₃₂in)

R Stiles (6), dowel or cocktail sticks, 2mm diameter (³⁄₃₂in)

S (4), scrap timber

The rest of the framework can be made from dowel or cocktail sticks and the lengths taken directly from the plan. I used 2mm (³⁄₃₂in) diameter beech dowel, which is easier to operate on when it comes to drilling holes for the legs, headrail and principal back supports: elsewhere I used 1mm (¹⁄₃₂in) diameter dowel.

The small strips attached to the edges of the lower tray, shown on the underside views, can be made from odd scraps of timber.

PREPARATION AND CONSTRUCTION

SEAT A Start with the seat because so much depends upon the angle with which the timber is penetrated by the drill bit. To make sure of the correct angle you will need to make some stiff card templates as described for the rocking chair earlier. (*See* Fig 8.3.) The seat is a simple rectangular piece of timber rounded off at the corners. Trace its shape from the drawing onto the timber, using carbon paper, and cut out with a knife.

Mark out the position of the holes required by reference to the front view and section *a-a* in Fig 11.1a. Use an awl to give the drill bit an initial purchase and employ the techniques mentioned for drilling at an angle (*see* Fig 8.3) so that you can fairly accurately determine the slopes of the legs and other supports which are to be attached to the seat. For this exercise you will require 2mm ($^3/_{32}$ in) and 1mm ($^1/_{32}$ in) diameter drill bits.

Now, before you carry on, wipe the perspiration from your brow and take an aspirin, because the next operations need a steady hand.

BACK REST SUPPORTS M Prepare the two principal back rest supports by turning the shape shown and, using a 1mm ($^1/_{32}$ in) diameter drill bit, make a hole in each to receive the headrail. Do not penetrate right through the support. Now lay the two supports side by side and mark off, as close as possible, the positions of the peg holes shown on the front view.

The other three supports can be fitted at the assembly stage.

HEADRAIL N Turn the headrail to the shape shown in Fig 11.1a remembering to allow a little bit of extra length for the rail ends to penetrate the principal back rest supports. Drill the headrail to receive the back supports using a 1mm ($^1/_{32}$ in) diameter drill bit. Make sure that the holes are in agreement with those in the seat by marking their positions on the rail whilst it is next to the seat.

ARM REST B Trace these onto the timber surface and, using a fret saw and knife, create the projected shape shown on section *a-a*, Fig 11.1a. With a 1mm

($^1/_{32}$ in) drill bit, make the necessary holes to receive the four arm rest supports, which will be fitted at the assembly stage. The angle of the drill bit needs to be at the slope shown on the front view and symmetrical about the centreline of the chair.

TRAY EDGE D Trace this onto the timber surface and carefully cut out the profile along the inside curve with a fret saw. The outer curve can then be cut with a knife. You will find this a very fragile piece to handle so take care.

TRAY E Now trace the tray itself onto some thin ply and shape it with a knife to fit the profile of the tray surrounds as shown on the plan view on the upper tray.

SIDE ARMS J Cut out the two side arms shown on the plan view on the upper tray from some thin ply and, using a 1mm ($^1/_{32}$ in) diameter drill bit, make a hole to receive the peg shown on the front view. These pegs are made from scrap pieces of timber, preferably hardwood. You will need to check them to see that they enter the back supports easily.

LEGS O Prepare these next by making them very slightly longer than the elevations show in case you need to trim them down later. Notice how the legs next to the chair seat are of different lengths. The dotted outline of the opened up frame explains the reason for the difference.

A tricky operation is now to be done. This is the drilling of the holes in the legs to receive both the stiles R and wheels H. It will be seen that all four legs splay out which makes the drilling operation nail-biting to say the least. I suggest you make up a balsa

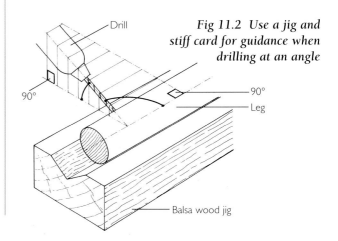

Fig 11.2 Use a jig and stiff card for guidance when drilling at an angle

wood jig and stiff cards cut to the appropriate angles to guide the drill into the legs. (*See* Fig 11.2.) A 1mm ($\frac{1}{32}$ in) diameter drill should be used for this.

QUADRANTS C The two quadrants forming the supports for the footrests P can be made from thin ply and drilled as shown on section *b-b*, in Fig 11.1a. The shape of these quadrants can be traced onto the ply surface and cut out with a knife.

FOOTRESTS P These can be made from cocktail sticks or 1mm ($\frac{1}{32}$ in) diameter dowelling. They can then be cut to length and glued to the quadrants making sure that the overall width of the footrest does not exceed the width between the upper legs (*see* front view, Fig 11.1a).

You will by now have realised how tight for room everything is becoming and this is why you must keep as close to the drawn details as you can.

When you have cut to length, from Figs 11.1a and 1b, all of the stiles for the legs, make a dry run by assembling the parts below the seat as far as you can at this stage. If you find the legs do not follow the slopes shown or are not aligned with each other, you must make the necessary adjustments before proceeding.

WHEEL-CARRIAGE SUPPORTS I Trace these onto the timber surface and cut out to the profile shown on the side view. The cut away slot is vital if everything is to come together when the frame is rotated into the open and closed positions and should engage with the axle of the wheels marked H.

SPRING SECTION F To ensure that the wheels marked G do not rotate too freely, a spring is made and attached to the rear seat frame. I made mine out of thin ply because of its springy nature and glued it to the seat as shown on section *c-c* in Fig 11.1b.

To drill the 1mm ($\frac{1}{32}$ in) diameter holes, in the wheel-carriage supports, through which the axles are to pass, place the two supports on top of each other and drill through them both so that the holes are in exactly the right place on each support.

Note that the wheel-carriage supports are glued to the upper axle but free to move on the lower axle. This is because the upper axle must be free to rotate in the leg holes and the lower wheels G must be glued to

their axles to enable the axle to rotate in the supports without the wheels falling off.

WHEELS G AND H These can be turned in a lathe or sawn from dowel. Drill the wheels to receive their axles.

LOWER TRAY K AND EDGING L This is cut to the shape shown on the underside view of the base tray and framed with thin strips of scrap timber to the height shown on the sectional detail on the underside view.

The underside edges of this tray will be glued to the two parallel stiles as shown. It is, therefore, important that you determine whether or not they will meet up when you do the dry run mentioned earlier. The working surface of the lower tray contains four small blocks of timber, S, which are to be pre-drilled to receive the fine wire onto which the small glass beads are threaded. I bought some coloured beads for this purpose from a dress shop.

ASSEMBLY

1 Glue headrail to side supports.
2 Glue back supports to headrail.
3 Glue headrail supports and back supports to seat.
4 Glue arm rest supports to seat. *Check height from drawing.*
5 Glue arm rests to supports.
6 Glue front upper legs complete with free moving footrest assembly to seat. *Check angle of legs.*
7 Glue upper rear legs to seat whilst glue is still wet, and fix the stiles and wheel-carriage axle to the upper legs. *Check angle of legs.*
8 Glue stiles to front and back face of lower legs. *Check angle of legs against upper legs.*
9 Glue stiles to sides of lower legs.
10 Glue tray to underside of bottom stiles.
11 Glue linen hinges to front legs. *See section a-a.*
12 Glue side arms J to upper tray. *When set, spring tray into position on the headrail supports.*

FINISHING

No finishing is required unless you wish to paint or stain the chair. If you wish to stain it, follow the procedure given under Finishing in Chapter 2.

CHAISE LONGUE

There are as many variations in the design of this style of furniture as
there are days in a year. The one shown here is of the Regency period. The model
is best made from hardwood with a close grain. Beech or mahogany, or even lime,
is suitable to help with the shaping of the head and footrests. Whatever you
decide will obviously depend upon your stocks of timber, but in any case
it will be covered with a dark varnish later.

FRONT AND BACK VIEWS

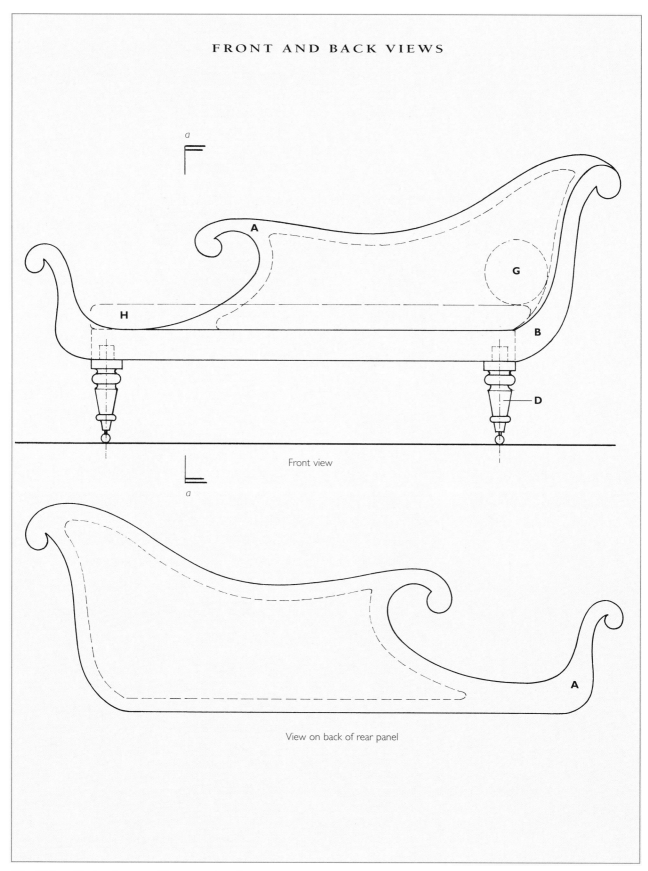

Front view

View on back of rear panel

Fig 12.1a Chaise Longue: Plan - *continued over*

CUTTING LIST

Hardwood with a close grain.

A   Rear panel (1) 170 × 60 × 3mm (6¾ × 2⅜ × ⅛in)

B   Front edge strip (1) 170 × 60 × 3mm (6¾ × 2⅜ × ⅛in)

C   Base panel (1) 115 × 40 × 8mm (4⅝ × 1⅝ × ⁵⁄₁₆in)

D   Legs (4), dowel, 10mm diameter (⅜in)

E   Headrest (1), balsa, 70 × 50 × 15mm (2¾ × 2 × ⅝in)

F   Footrest (1), balsa, 40 × 50 × 15mm (1⅝ × 2 × ⅝in)

G   Seat cushion (1), balsa cylinder, 40mm (1⅝in) × 15mm diameter (⅝in)

G   Seat (1), polystyrene, 120 × 40 × 7mm (4¾ × 1⅝ × ⁹⁄₃₂in)

The sizes given are slightly greater than required, to allow for rubbing down.

CROSS SECTION

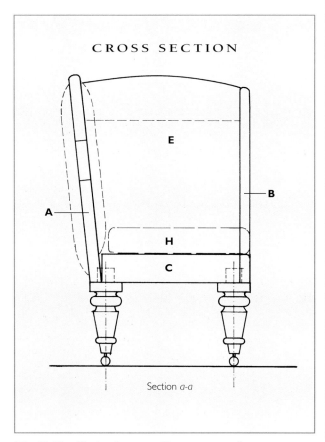

Section *a-a*

Fig 12.1b Chaise Longue: Plan - continued

PREPARATION AND CONSTRUCTION

REAR PANEL A   Start with the rear panel by tracing it from Fig 12.1a onto the timber surface, using carbon paper, and cut out the shape using a fret saw. Round off the edges with abrasive paper. A half-round needle file may be required to finish off the returns of the curved ends of this piece. Notice how the rear panel slopes back from the seat on section *a-a*, Fig 12.1b. To achieve this, insert a thin wedge-shaped piece of timber along the lower inside edge (*see* Fig 12.4) and glue in position.

FRONT EDGE STRIP B   Trace the front edge strip onto the timber, and follow the same procedure, but glue the strip into position without the wedge. Check that finished shapes of this and the rear panel coincide. At this stage it would be as well if you apply the finish, especially before upholstering takes place. If you have used a light timber you should apply stain, sealer and varnish as described under Finishing in Chapter 2.

BASE PANEL C   This is a simple rectangular block, the extent of which is shown by a dotted line on the front view.

Mark off the position of the four holes that are to receive the legs and drill with a 4mm (⁵⁄₃₂ in) diameter drill bit, or a size to suit the spigots on the end of each leg. Cover the under surface with fabric, to simulate hessian.

UPHOLSTERY   For the front and back of the rear panel, follow the details given in Figs 12.2 and 12.3. Don't use too much stuffing in the way of cotton wool or kapok or the result will look too fat.

For the front face of the rear panel (*see* Fig 12.2), a thin, polystyrene strip is required with holes pierced through it where shown. These are needed for the buttoning effect. To achieve this effect, simply sew fabric or soft leather through these holes, onto some stiff card and then shape the fabric around the card as indicated in Fig 12.3. Using Copydex, glue the fabric to the back face of the card.

The back face of the rear panel is shown without the buttoning effect. If you require this, just follow the procedure as for the front panel.

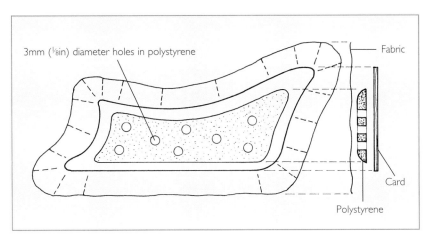

Fig 12.2 *Pattern for upholstery on front face of panel*

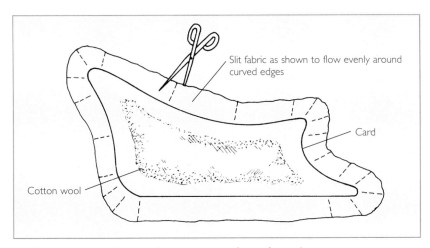

Fig 12.3 *Pattern for upholstery on rear face of panel*

SEAT H   This is made up of a polystyrene block with fabric wrapped around it and glued to its underside. Once again, if you wish to 'button' this area follow the instructions above.

SEAT CUSHION G   This is made up from balsa wood in a cylindrical form, covered with fabric and glued together with Copydex. Alternatively, you could make up the cylinder with a roll of fabric though with fabric there is a tendency for the Copydex to seep through and leave a messy stain, so be careful. You may like to glue small buttons to each end to cover up the joins of the cover fabric.

HEADREST E   This portion of the model is best made up from a balsa wood block and carved by hand to follow the profile shown in Fig 12.4. Notice how the headrest is curved.

FOOTREST F   Construct this in a similar way, making the piece up from a balsa wood block, and then carving by hand to the desired profile. Cover both pieces, for front and back faces, with fabric and glue this to the timber where it is not likely to be seen. To avoid stains spoiling the effect, make sure that the glue doesn't show through the fabric.

LEGS D   Turn the four legs to the profile shown. Transfer the prominent parts from Fig 12.1a or 1b to the dowel, using a strip of plain paper as a marker. (*See* Stiles in Chapter 10.) Where possible, make two or more from the same piece of dowel as suggested in Fig 10.5. Apply the finish whilst the piece is still in the lathe.

To add to the effect, attach a small castor to each leg. These can be obtained from miniaturist suppliers.

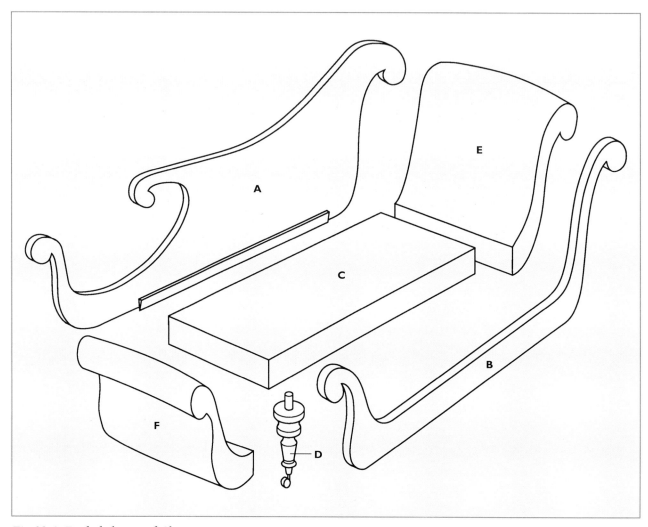

Fig 12.4 Exploded view of Chaise Longue

ASSEMBLY

1 Glue rear panel to base.
2 Glue front edge strip to base. *Check the alignment with the rear panel profile before the glue sets, and adjust if necessary.*
3 Glue head and footrests to frame. *Clamp the frame to the rests until the glue has set.*
4 Glue rear panel upholstery to front and rear faces. *Make sure that the glue doesn't show through the fabric.*
5 Glue legs to base by puncturing through the 'hessian' which is glued to the underside of the seat.

FINISHING

If you wish to embellish the chaise with some carving along the exposed edges, do it before you stain the timber.

To darken the timber, use a suitably coloured stain and when it is dry, apply a wood sealant to prevent the stain leaching out. Once this has been done you can apply a varnish. Remember to get rid of any unsightly glue stains before you varnish and should more coats be required, then allow up to eight hours between applications and rub down with wire wool as each coat dries.

MODERN DINING CHAIR

This is a replica of a dining chair which I bought some 30 years ago but which is still fashionable. It is made in a two-tone timber to give it more appeal; the original was made in beech. The darker timber is mahogany for ease of carving, and the rest is in lime for contrast.

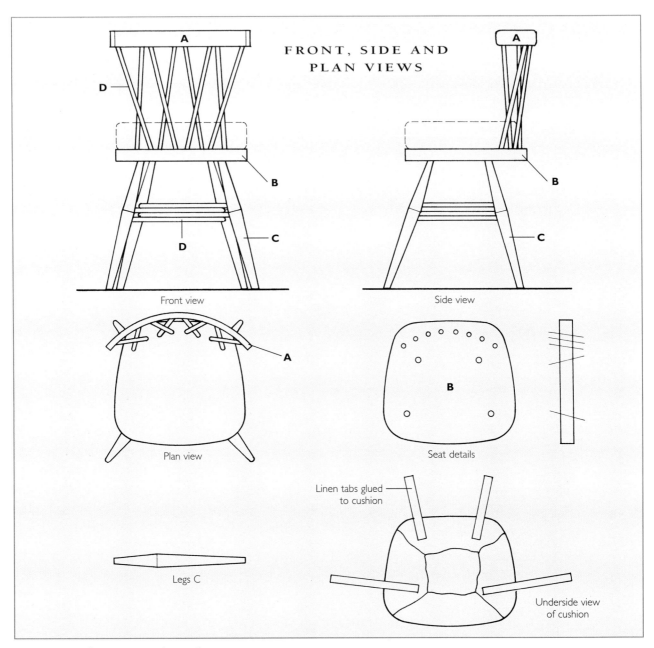

FRONT, SIDE AND PLAN VIEWS

Front view

Side view

Plan view

Seat details

Legs C

Linen tabs glued to cushion

Underside view of cushion

Fig 13.1 Modern Dining Chair: Plan

CUTTING LIST

Mahogany; lime.

A Back rail (1), mahogany, 40 × 10 × 4mm ($1^5/8 × ^3/8 × ^3/16$in)

B Seat (1), lime, 35 × 40 × 3mm ($1^1/2 × 1^5/8 × ^1/8$in)

C Legs (4), dowel, 5mm diameter ($^3/16$in)

D Stiles and back rail supports (12), dowel or cocktail sticks rubbed down, 1mm diameter ($^1/32$in)

With these sizes, allowance has been made for rubbing down and turning.

PREPARATION AND CONSTRUCTION

SEAT B Trace the outline from Fig 13.1 onto the timber surface, together with the position of the eight holes that are required to accommodate the back rail supports. Cut out the shape with a knife or saw and rub down with abrasive paper. Note that the top surface of the seat is perfectly flat since the chair is to have a cushion. The position of the holes for the legs can be obtained from the front and side views.

A card template can be made to cater for the angle of the drill bit when drilling through the seat. (*See* Fig 13.2.) The eight holes to receive the back rail are to be 1mm ($^1/_{32}$ in) in diameter and those to receive the legs 2mm ($^3/_{32}$ in) in diameter.

BACK RAIL A Trace the shape from the plan view onto the timber surface and carefully cut away the inside timber first, by using a series of saw cuts and a chisel as indicated in Fig 13.3. Cut the rough pieces that are left on the surface with a knife and rub down with abrasive paper wrapped around a suitably curved object to obtain a smooth finish. Now cut away the timber outside the curve with a knife and rub down until you are satisfied that the thickness and curvature conform to the drawing.

LEGS C Turn these from the dowel as described for the stiles of the Windsor Writing Chair, in Chapter 10. (*See* Figs 10.4 and 10.5.)

STILES AND BACK RAIL SUPPORTS D These can be cut out from dowel or cocktail sticks, when the legs have been glued in position. Since the rail

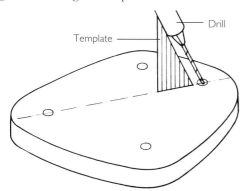

Fig 13.2 Using a stiff card template to ensure drilling is done at the correct angle

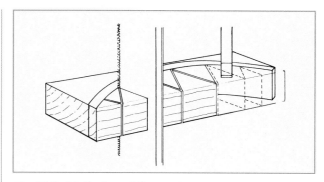

Fig 13.3 Method used for cutting out arcs

supports cross over each other, they will need to be pre-bent so that they meet at rail and seat in a single curved line. This can be done by steaming the supports, or soaking them in hot water, bending them to a slightly exaggerated curve and drying them off in this position. Any small adjustments can be made when gluing takes place.

CUSHION Cut out the basic shape from the plan view in 6-7mm ($^1/_4 - ^9/_{32}$in) polystyrene, using a sharp knife. Round off the top edges with the knife.

Cover the polystyrene in fabric, allowing enough to overlap as shown in the under view of the cushion and glue to the polystyrene with Copydex. Now attach four strips of linen which will eventually be glued to the underside of the seat.

ASSEMBLY

1 Glue legs to seat. *Check against the drawing to see that the correct slopes are maintained before the glue sets. Symmetry is all important.*
2 Glue stiles to legs. *The length of the stiles can only be found by trial and error.*
3 Glue back rail supports to seat. *Again, look for symmetry in both directions.*
4 Glue back rail to supports. *The rail will have to be held in position until the glue sets.*

FINISHING

Before applying the finish, remove any glue lines. If you have made this model out of beech, then all you will need is a clear varnish. In the case of the two-toned timber, use the appropriate coloured varnish.

TABLES

DINING TABLE

This is a modern style of table which would go well with the modern dining chair of the previous project. At first glance it would appear that the table is circular, but if you measure it you will find it to be slightly oval in shape. The original was made in beech but, except for the dowel used for the parts D, I have used mahogany throughout.

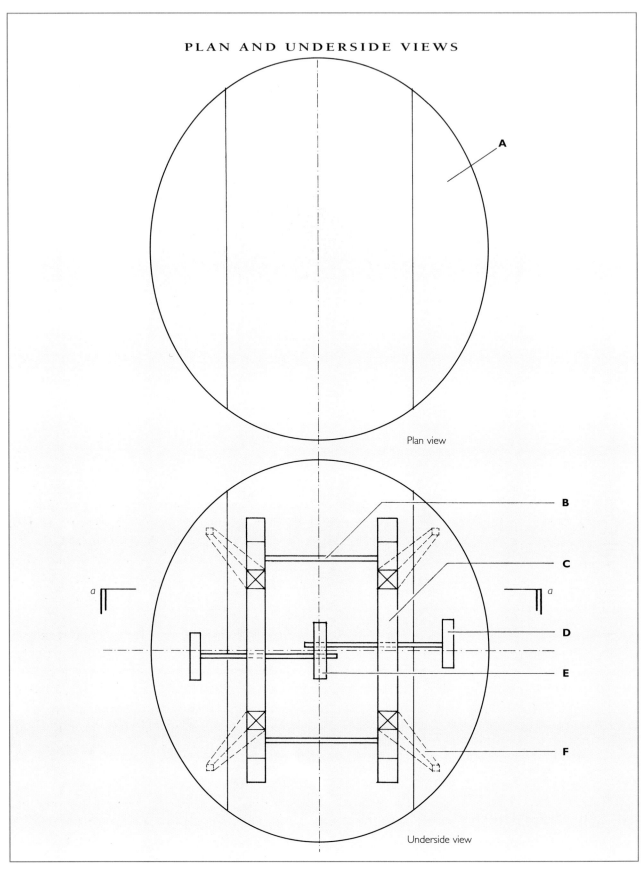

PLAN AND UNDERSIDE VIEWS

Plan view

Underside view

Fig 14.1a Dining Table: Plan - *continued over*

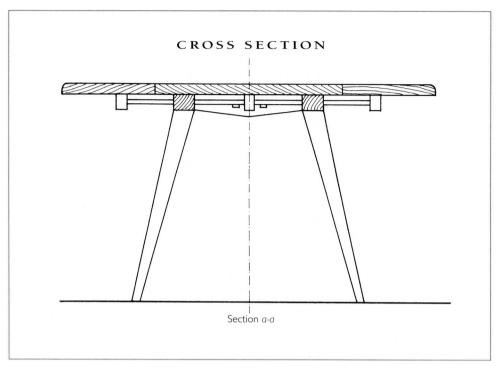

CROSS SECTION

Section *a-a*

Fig 14.1b Dining Table: Plan - *continued*

CUTTING LIST

Mahogany.

A Table top (1) 110 × 100 × 3mm (4⅜ × 4 × ⅛in) or from 2: 100 × 50 × 3mm (4 × 2 × ⅛in)

B (2) 65 × 6 × 1.5mm (2⅝ × ¼ × ¹⁄₁₆in)

C (2) 150 × 5 × 4mm (6 × ³⁄₁₆ × ³⁄₁₆in)

D (2), plus dowel, 20 × 4× 3mm (1 × ³⁄₁₆ × ⅛in) + 1mm diameter (¹⁄₃₂in)

E (1) (see assembly notes)15 × 4 × 3mm (⅝ × ³⁄₁₆ × ⅛in)

F Legs (4) 240 × 5 × 5mm (9½ × ¼ × ¼in)

The sizes stated allow for some wastage.

PREPARATION AND CONSTRUCTION

TABLE TOP A This is made up in three parts. Begin by tracing the centre portion plus one leaf onto the timber surface. Make sure that when you trace the second leaf onto the timber surface, you go around the same profile as that used for the first so that you achieve symmetry when seen from above.Now cut out the shapes with a fret saw or bead saw, and knife. Rub down the edges and round off the upper edge as shown, with abrasive paper.

It would be as well at this stage, if you prepare the upper surface of the table to receive the finish. Do this by rubbing down with a scraper, then with a fine abrasive paper, and finally with wire wool to obtain a smooth surface. You can apply the first coat of whatever finish you want at this point since if a varnish is used, it needs to rest between coats for a few hours.

PARTS B Trace both parts B from Fig 14.2 onto the timber and cut out the shapes with a bead saw and knife. Try not to cut too much off the length because you will need to 'fit' them later to conform to the drawing.

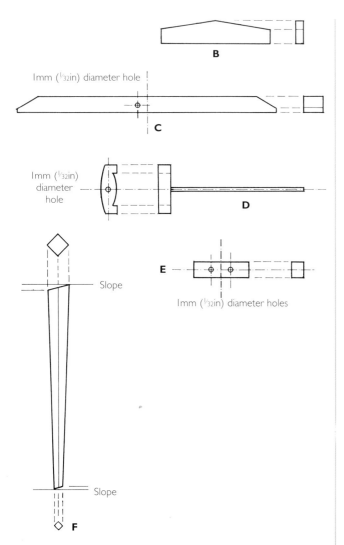

Fig 14.2 Details of parts

PARTS C Trace, or measure, both parts C from the details on Fig 14.2 and chamfer the top of each end as shown. Drill a 1mm ($^1/_{32}$ in) diameter hole in each part, in the position indicated, as accurately as you can because it is through these holes that the two parts D have to move.

PARTS D This is a bit fiddly to do and a lot will depend upon the accuracy with which you arrive at the final shape. Trace the outline of both parts from Fig 14.2 onto the timber surface on the 4mm ($^3/_{16}$ in) face and, before cutting out the profile indicated, drill the 1mm ($^1/_{32}$ in) diameter hole in the centre. This hole must line up with that in part C, so it would be advisable to clamp parts C and D together with the bottom edges flush and, using the hole in part C as a

guide, drill through it and into part D. I did say it was fiddly, so be very careful: the smooth action of parts D is vital on the finished model. Now rub down the 1mm ($^1/_{32}$ in) diameter dowel until it fits snugly into the hole, then glue this to the block comprising the head piece of part D.

PART E It would be a good idea for you to take a strip of timber to the cross section given in Fig 14.2 and, before you cut it to the length shown, drill the two holes in the position indicated. The best way to mark off the position of these holes is to do it by using a strip of paper and marking off the hole seen on part C, relative to the centreline, and then by transferring this to the timber face of part E. Do this on the 4mm ($^3/_{16}$ in) face. Then, using an awl, make the necessary indentations to give the 1mm ($^1/_{32}$ in) diameter drill bits its location. Now, before going any further, check that the dowels of both parts D pass easily through these holes and that parts C are properly aligned.

LEGS F The legs can be measured from the detail and tapered from 4mm ($^5/_{32}$ in) at the tops to 2mm ($^1/_{16}$ in) at the feet. I tapered mine with a sanding block made from a scrap of timber wrapped around with abrasive paper. If you are a perfectionist then you may like to make yourself a jig as shown in Fig 14.3.

The head and foot of each leg must be chamfered as indicated in the sketch detail. This must be done with care to ensure that symmetry is obtained when the legs are finally glued in place. See section *a-a*, Fig 14.1b.

ASSEMBLY

1 Glue B to parts C. *Make sure that they line up, passing the dowel of parts D through the holes in part C and holes in part E whilst the glue is still wet. Allow to set.*

2 Glue parts B, C and E to underside surface of the table whilst parts D and parts E are still in parts C following the operation above.

3 When the glue has set, make sure that the dowels move freely through the holes in parts C and E and then put a blob of glue on the ends of each dowel (but not in contact with the table surface) so that when set, the glue will form a stop to prevent the dowel from pulling right out.

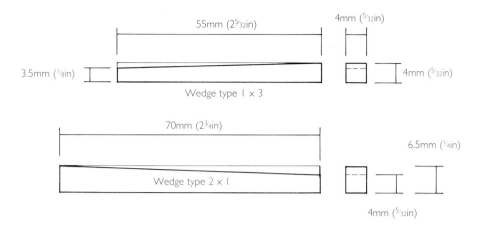

55mm (2⁵⁄₃₂in)

Wedge type 1 × 3

3.5mm (¹⁄₈in)

4mm (⁵⁄₃₂in)

4mm (⁵⁄₃₂in)

70mm (2³⁄₄in)

Wedge type 2 × 1

6.5mm (¹⁄₄in)

4mm (⁵⁄₃₂in)

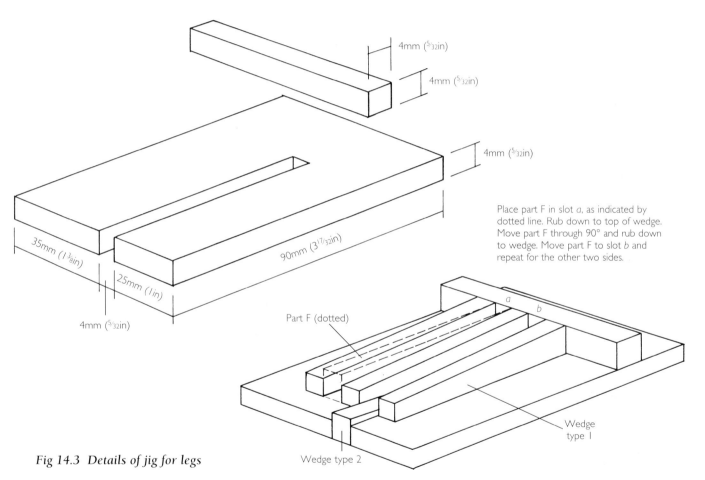

4mm (⁵⁄₃₂in)

4mm (⁵⁄₃₂in)

4mm (⁵⁄₃₂in)

35mm (1³⁄₈in)

90mm (3¹⁷⁄₃₂in)

25mm (1in)

4mm (⁵⁄₃₂in)

Place part F in slot *a*, as indicated by dotted line. Rub down to top of wedge. Move part F through 90° and rub down to wedge. Move part F to slot *b* and repeat for the other two sides.

Part F (dotted)

Wedge type 1

Wedge type 2

Fig 14.3 Details of jig for legs

4 Glue legs to part C. *I just glued the surface together, but for greater stability it would be better to 'peg' the ends to parts C as described under Jointing in Chapter 2. (See also Leg supports F in Chapter 15 and Fig 15.3.)*

5 Glue thin strips of linen to the underside face of the table top and leaves, to act as hinges. This is more satisfactory than messing about with brass hinges.

FINISHING

The table top should by now have received one coat of wax, or varnish. If so, rub it down with a fine abrasive paper and wire wool and give it a second coat. If you haven't rubbed down each individual part by now then do so and apply the finish you have decided upon. Where varnish is used, remove any glue lines before its application.

EXTENDABLE DINING TABLE

This model would be suitable for a large room area in a dolls' house which can accommodate an extended table. It can, of course, be used in a normal sized room in the closed position. The timber used for its construction can be any of the hardwoods such as beech, walnut or mahogany. I used mahogany because I have plenty in stock, but I think I would use either beech or walnut if I was to repeat the exercise. Due to its overall length, I have only drawn the one half of the table, in the closed position.

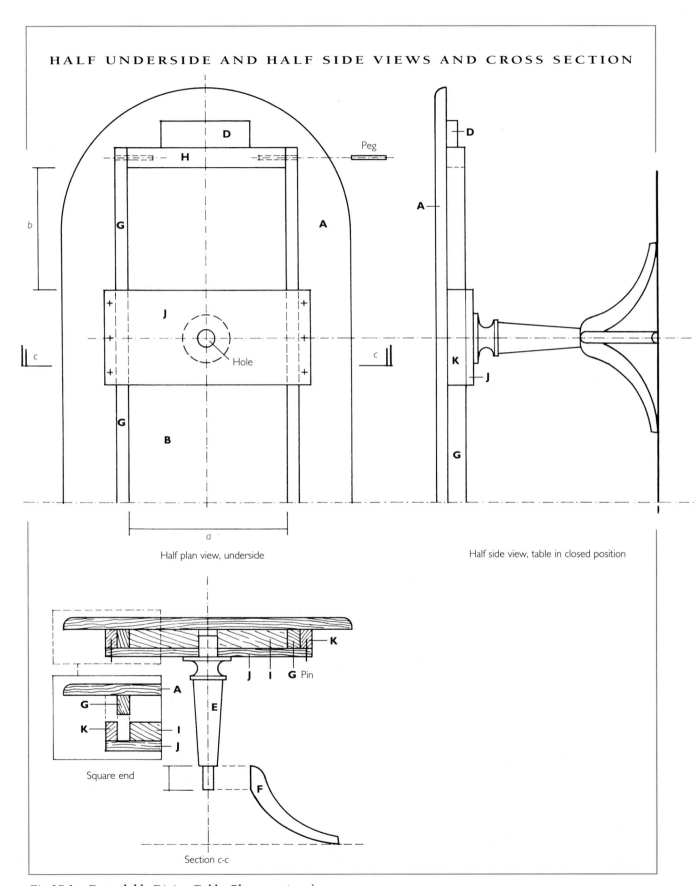

HALF UNDERSIDE AND HALF SIDE VIEWS AND CROSS SECTION

Half plan view, underside

Half side view, table in closed position

Square end

Section *c-c*

Fig 15.1a Extendable Dining Table: Plan - *continued over*

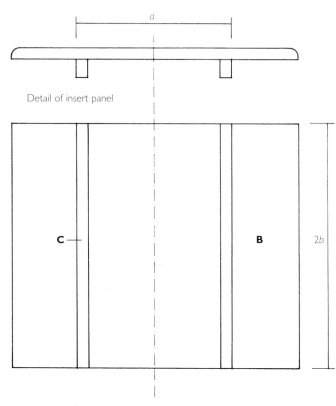

Detail of insert panel

Fig 15.1b Extendable Dining Table: Plan - continued

CUTTING LIST

Any hardwood.

A Table top (1) from 240 × 75 × 3mm ($9^5/_8$ × 3 × $^1/_8$in)

B Insert panel (1) 70 × 75 × 3mm ($2^3/_4$ × 3 × $^1/_8$in)

C Guides (2) from 140 × 4 × 3mm ($5^5/_8$ × $^3/_{16}$ × $^1/_8$in)

D End stops (2) 50 × 7 × 3mm (2 × $^9/_{32}$ × $^1/_8$in)

E Legs (2), dowel, 15mm diameter ($^5/_8$in)

F Leg supports (8) 280 × 10 × 3mm (11 × $^3/_8$ × $^1/_8$in)

G Slides (2) from 2: 190 × 5 × 3mm ($7^1/_2$ × $^3/_{16}$ × $^1/_8$in)

H (2) from 2: 45 × 5 × 5mm ($1^3/_4$ × $^1/_4$ × $^1/_4$in)

I (2) from 2: 45 × 25 × 5mm ($1^3/_4$ × 1 × $^1/_4$in)

J (2) from 2: 55 × 25 × 2mm ($2^1/_4$ × 1 × $^3/_{32}$in)

K (4) from 4: 25 × 5 × 3mm (1 × $^1/_4$ × $^1/_8$in)

Sizes given allow for wastage in the main. You will notice that the width of the table top is the same as the timber strip that can be bought from a model shop.

PREPARATION AND CONSTRUCTION

TABLE TOP A Trace the shape of the outline from Fig 15.1a onto the timber surface using carbon paper, or draw the end curve with a pair of compasses. Cut around the profile with a fret saw and then round off the edge with abrasive paper. Use a fine abrasive paper on the top surface and then rub down with wire wool until there is an acceptable finish to receive either wax or varnish. (*See* Finishing in Chapter 2.) The best kind of surface can be obtained with the use of a scraper before the abrasive paper is used.

PARTS I, J AND K Make up the block comprising these parts from the details given on the half plan view and section *c-c*, Fig 15.1a. Glue and pin parts J to parts K. Prepare block I and glue to part J, making sure that the gaps at each end are equal. These are where the slides will be travelling through.

Drill at the centre as indicated, using a 5mm ($^3/_{16}$in) diameter drill bit. Now rub down the outer surfaces, which will be on display, ready to receive the finish.

LEGS E Turn the legs from the dowel, using the technique described for the Rocking Chair, first roughing down the dowel to the greatest diameter required, and then marking out the portions to be cut away with a Biro or pencil. (*See* Legs and stiles in Chapter 8.) The lower end of the leg should be square in cross section, ready to receive the four legs supports. This can be done when turning is completed, with the use of a bead saw. Apply the finish whilst in the lathe.

LEG SUPPORTS F These are to be shaped from the timber strip, as shown in Fig 15.2, using a knife. They can be rubbed down with abrasive paper and wire wool, ready to take the finish.

To ensure that the leg supports are stable, you may like to peg them as shown in Fig 15.3. If so, then drill through the leg and insert a timber peg. Glue it in position and when fixed, drill through the adjacent face and insert the other peg. The hole in each leg support should not be allowed to penetrate fully, so take care. This is only offered as a suggestion because I found that by gluing the leg supports to the ends of the legs directly there was no problem.

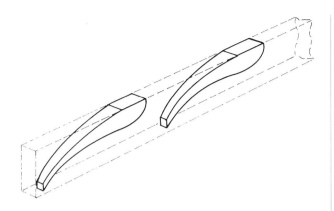

Fig 15.2 *Leg supports are shaped from a timber strip*

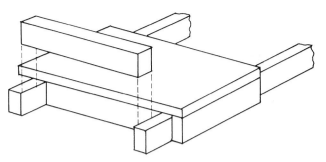

Fig 15.4 *Method for marking out sliding mechanism parts*

SLIDES G AND PART H The following instructions are an improvement upon the way I first made the sliding mechanism and are very much more positive in operation.

Prepare the timber as shown and check that the slides move easily through the blocks which are to receive the legs. Mark out part H with the slides just penetrating the block, as shown in Fig 15.4, to ensure that the parts will not bind when the table is opened out.

Glue the slides to part H and when the glue has set, drill the ends as indicated on the half plan view to receive 1mm ($^1/_{32}$ in) diameter pegs made from cocktail sticks rubbed down, or 1mm ($^1/_{32}$ in) diameter dowel. Now glue them in position. The slides and part H should now form an independent framework, ready for assembly.

INSERT PANEL B Prepare the length as shown on the plan view of the panel and prepare the top face as for the table top, ready to take the finish.

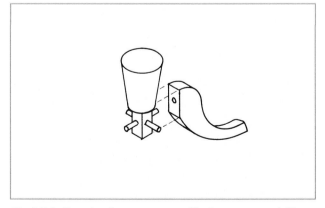

Fig 15.3 *Pegging leg supports will give extra stability*

GUIDES C Glue the two guides to the underside of the insert panel as shown and check that the dimension, *a*, (*see* Fig 15.1b) complies with the gap between the slides before the glue has set.

ASSEMBLY

1 With the table face down and opened out, put the insert panel in place and lay the slide framework on the table. *Make sure that the distances from the framework to the ends (or from the centreline) are equal. Check using a strip of paper as shown in Fig 15.5.*

2 Now clamp the slide frame onto the table top, using a card or timber strip to protect the table surface, and fix the position of the block comprising parts I, J and K as indicated in Fig 15.6. Mark the position of the slide frame onto the table surface and remove the clamps. When satisfied, glue the block to the table.

3 Transfer the clamps to the block as shown in Fig 15.7 and move the slide frame in and out to prevent any overspill of glue from adhering to it and thereby restricting its movement.

4 Repeat the operation for the other block.

5 Remove the insert panel and close up the table. Now move the slide frame until there is an equal distance at each end relative to the table top, then position and glue the end stops D to the table. *Before the glue has set, move the slide frame away by opening up the table, to prevent the glue from end stop D adhering to the slide frame end H.*

6 Glue the legs to the blocks attached to the table and when set, glue the leg supports to each leg. *Make sure that all four feet on each leg touch the ground.*

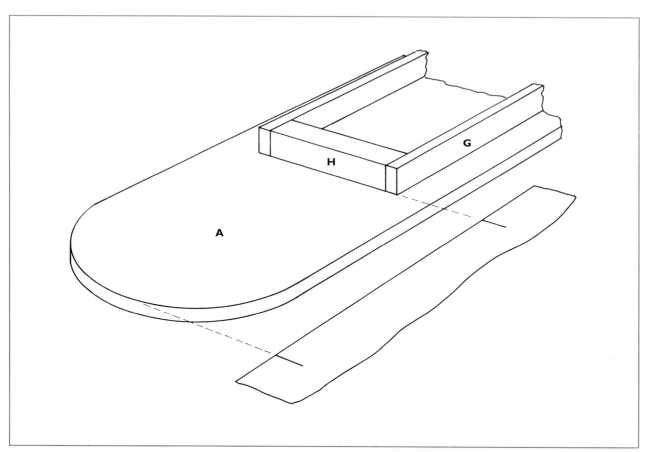

Fig 15.5 Using marked paper to check distances

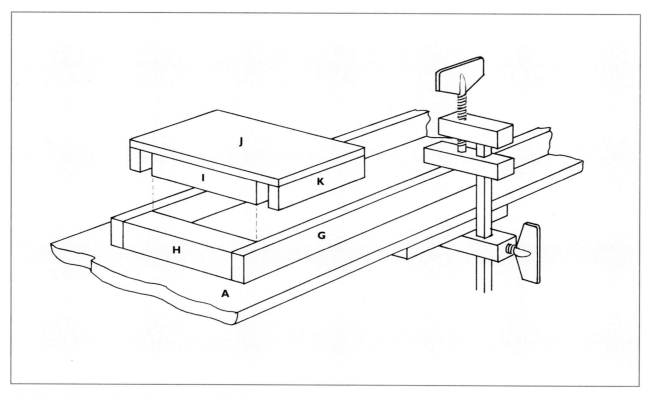

Fig 15.6 Clamp slide to fix position of block

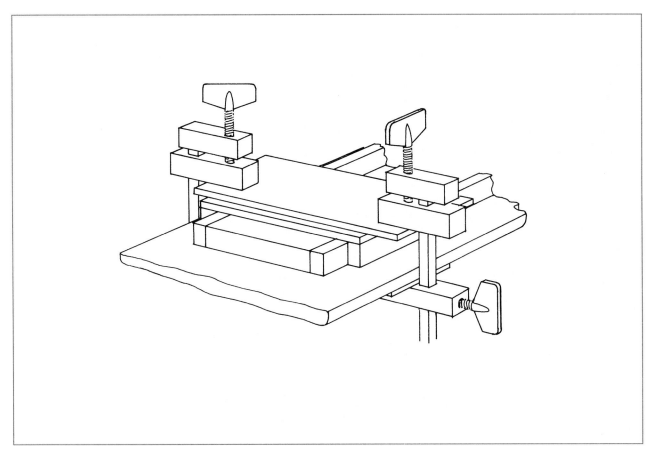

Fig 15.7 Clamp block to allow free movement of slide

FINISHING

Most of the finishing for this piece will have been done en route. If a wax finish is required, remember to first seal the wood with a coat of sealer, and to leave it off the faces that are to be glued together. If you prefer to varnish the model after assembly, ensure that any glue that has seeped out from the joints is first removed, otherwise it will show.

To get a nice, polished surface to the table, follow the instructions given during the construction procedure and after the first coat of varnish has been applied, let it rest overnight before rubbing down with wire wool and applying the second coat. Wax can be applied by impregnating some wire wool with beeswax and rubbing it into the surface by following the direction of the grain. This can be repeated after the wax has had time to harden.

GATE-LEG TABLE

Reference to folding tables can be found in sixteenth century manuscripts. The term 'gate-leg' came into being some 300 years later. They can vary in size considerably, the larger ones having eight legs with four folding gates. The model shown here is a typical Edwardian-style table. For ease of producing the barley-sugar twist legs, I used mahogany throughout. It is also a convenient timber to use, since the finished article should be of a dark appearance if it is to be authentic.

PLAN VIEW AND CROSS SECTION

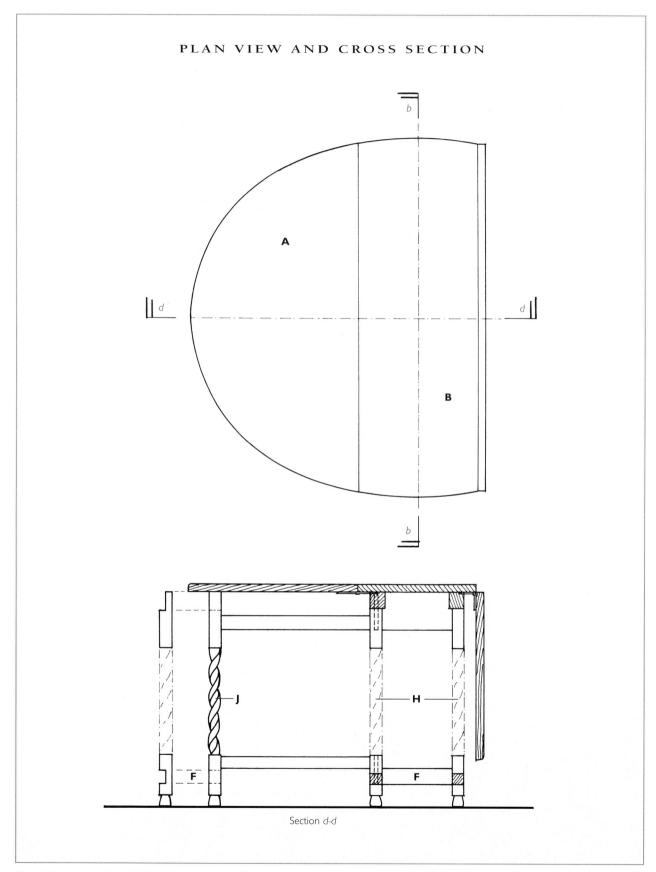

Section *d-d*

Fig 16.1a Gate-leg Table: Plan - *continued over*

CROSS SECTIONS

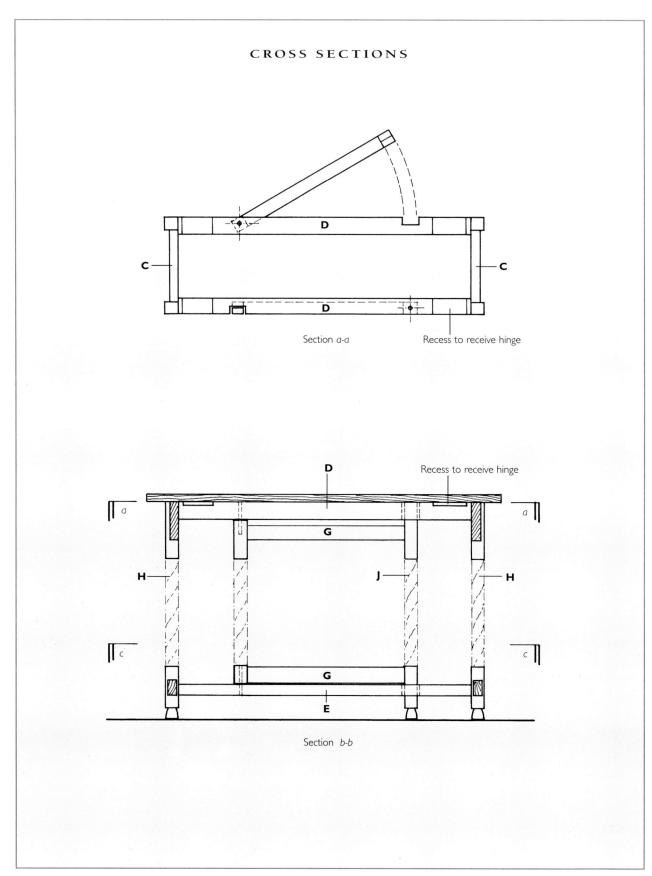

Section *a-a*

Recess to receive hinge

Recess to receive hinge

Section *b-b*

Fig 16.1b Gate-leg Table: Plan - *continued over*

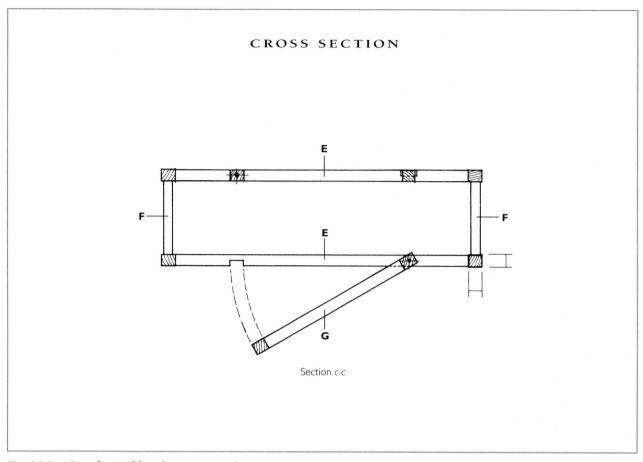

CROSS SECTION

Section *c-c*

Fig 16.1c **Gate-leg Table: Plan** - *continued*

CUTTING LIST

All mahogany.

A Drop leaves (2) 100 × 100 × 2mm (4 × 4 × ³⁄₃₂in)

B Central part (1) 100 × 35 × 2mm (4 × 1⅜ × ³⁄₃₂in)

C End rails (2) 40 × 10 × 3mm (1⅝ × ⅜ × ⅛in)

D Side rails (2) 160 × 5 × 4mm (6⅜ × ¼ × ³⁄₁₆in)

E Side stiles (2) 160 × 3 × 3mm (6⅜ × ⅛ × ⅛in)

F End stiles (2) 40 × 4 × 2mm (1⅝ × ³⁄₁₆ × ³⁄₃₂in)

G Inner stiles (4) 180 × 3 × 3mm (7⅛ × ⅛ × ⅛in)

H Legs (4) 320 × 3 × 3mm (12⅝ × ⅛ × ⅛in)

I Legs (2) 190 × 3 × 3mm (7½ × ⅛ × ⅛in)

J Legs (2) 120 × 3 × 3mm (4¾ × ⅛ × ⅛in)

These sizes allow for wastage during cutting and fitting.

PREPARATION AND CONSTRUCTION

DROP LEAVES A AND CENTRAL PART B
Trace the shape of the table top from Fig 16.1a onto the timber surface, using carbon paper. The drop leaves are done independently of the central portion. Cut around the profile with a fret saw and round off the edge with abrasive paper. Rub down the top surface first with a scraper, followed by a fine abrasive paper and then with wire wool to achieve an acceptable finish. (*See* Finishing in Chapter 2.)

END FRAMES C, AND F These are simple rectangular frames and can be made up fairly easily as long as you follow Fig 16.1b with regard to the heights of the rails. (*See* section *b-b*.)

LEGS H AND J The barley-sugar twist effect on the legs is achieved with a round needle file or rasp as shown in Fig 16.2. As you file at the angle required,

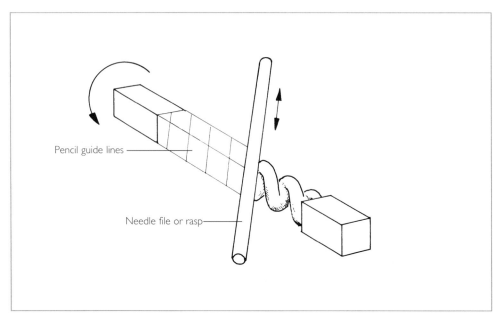

Fig 16.2 Turn the timber as you file to achieve barley-sugar twists

you must slowly turn the leg at an even pace to obtain a regular spacing for the barley-sugar twists. The feet can be carved to the profile shown with a knife. The two legs J are for the inner frame and are shaped differently at their ends. (*See* Fig 16.3.)

TOP RAILS D These are the long ones seen in section *a-a*, Fig 16.1b. Cut them to the length indicated and then chase out the slot with a bead saw and small chisel. Also, cut out the shallow recesses which are to accommodate the hinges. Check that the slots produced line up with their counterparts and are at right angles.

Now drill a 1mm ($\frac{1}{32}$ in) diameter hole through the top face to receive a pin which is to be made from brass wire. Note that the hole is not central in the width of the frame member.

BOTTOM RAILS E Repeat the procedure as for the top rails but this time the pin holes will be central on the top surface as shown on section *c-c*, Fig 16.1c.

PARTS G AND I These are made up as indicated on section *b-b* and *d-d*. The slots are cut out with a bead saw and chisel and the barley-sugar twist completed as described above. The false legs I which adjoin the side rails are to be drilled along their axes at top and bottom to receive the pins shown on section *b-b*.

ASSEMBLY

1 Make up the end frames and glue the components together (*see* Fig 16.3), making sure that they are at right angles to each other. *Lay the one end frame on top of the other to ensure that they are exactly aligned.*

2 Make up the gates and glue their components together as shown on section *b-b*, Fig 16.1b. *Again, lay one gate on top of the other to ensure that they are aligned.*

3 Glue the top and bottom side rails to each end frame in turn, ensuring that they are at right angles to each other and flush along the top edge. *Before the glue has time to set, check the relative position of these rails to the end frames by laying the gate on the frame containing these rails. It is important that the false leg, which is to be pinned, touches both rails as in section b-b and that the slots in top and bottom rails and legs coincide.*

4 Repeat for the opposite side to that shown in section *b-b*.

5 When the basic frame comprising two end frames and four rails is complete, insert the pins to secure the gate and check that everything works as it should.

6 Fix the hinges to the underside surface of the table top, making sure that they are positioned such that they marry up with the recesses in the top rails.

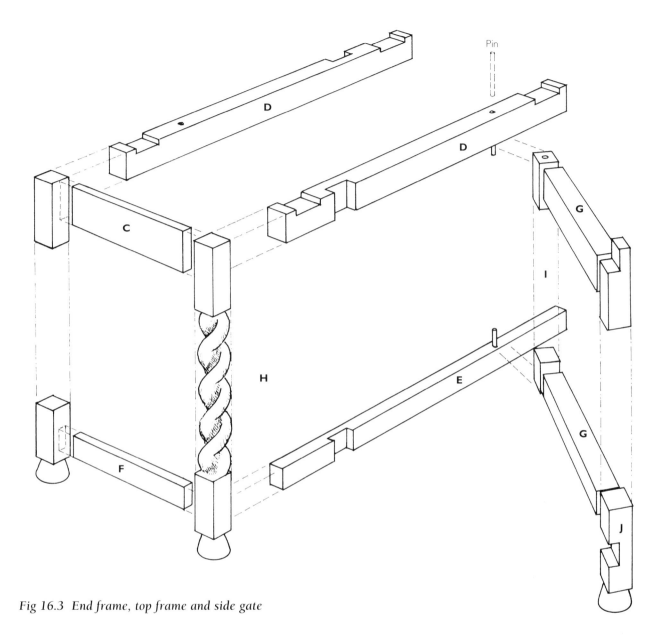

Fig 16.3 End frame, top frame and side gate

7 Lay the table top face down and offer up the framework to check that nothing binds when the gates are opened out and that the top surface of the outer leg of the gate is flush with the underside surface of the table.

8 When you are satisfied, carefully glue the table top to the framework.

FINISHING

Make sure that no glue has seeped out of the joints before you apply a varnish. The one I used was a mahogany varnish but a wax would be appropriate provided the surfaces are treated in the same way as described for the Extendable Dining Table in Chapter 15.

SOFA TABLE

These tables had a relatively short life, spanning from 1790–1820. The one shown here was originally made in 1815. There are many variations of design to be found and the one I have chosen for this model is of the more aesthetic type. To enhance the look of the model, lyre-ended splay legs have been included and, though not shown, the feet can be fitted with castors. It will be observed that the drawers have false fronts to give the impression that they can open either way, though in practice, they can only open as indicated by the arrows. As these tables were of dark colour originally I decided to use mahogany: walnut would have been my second choice.

FRONT AND PLAN VIEWS

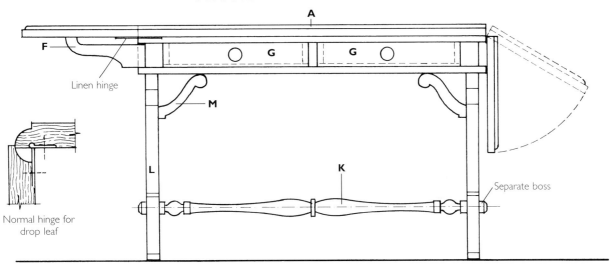

Front view

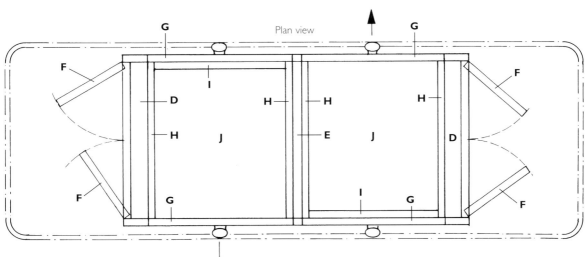

Fig 17.1a Sofa Table: Plan - *continued over*

CUTTING LIST

Mahogany or walnut.

A Table top (including drop-leaves) (1) 155 × 52 × 3mm ($6\frac{1}{8}$ × $2\frac{1}{8}$ × $\frac{1}{8}$in)

B and **C** (2) from 2: 95 × 45 × 2mm ($3\frac{3}{4}$ × $1\frac{3}{4}$ × $\frac{3}{32}$in)

D (6) from 2: 45 × 6 × 5mm ($1\frac{3}{4}$ × $\frac{1}{4}$ × $\frac{3}{16}$in) + from 4: 7 × 6 × 2mm ($\frac{9}{32}$ × $\frac{1}{4}$ × $\frac{3}{32}$in)

E (1) 45 × 6 × 2mm ($1\frac{3}{4}$ × $\frac{1}{4}$ × $\frac{3}{32}$in)

F Drop-leaf supports (1) 100 × 10 × 2mm (4 × $\frac{3}{8}$ × $\frac{3}{32}$in)

G Fronts of drawer (4) 160 × 6 × 2mm ($6\frac{3}{8}$ × $\frac{1}{4}$ × $\frac{3}{32}$in)

H Sides of drawer (4) 160 × 5 × 1mm ($6\frac{3}{8}$ × $\frac{3}{16}$ × $\frac{1}{32}$in)

I Backs of drawer (2) 70 × 5 × 2mm ($2\frac{3}{4}$ × $\frac{3}{16}$ × $\frac{3}{32}$in)

J Bases of drawer (2), thin ply, 80 × 40mm ($3\frac{3}{16}$ × $1\frac{5}{8}$in)

K Cross rail (1), dowel, 5mm diameter ($\frac{3}{16}$in)

L Legs (2) 100 × 45 × 3mm (4 × $1\frac{3}{4}$ × $\frac{1}{8}$in)

M Leg supports (see text) (2) 40 × 5 × 3mm ($1\frac{5}{8}$ × $\frac{3}{16}$ × $\frac{1}{8}$in)

Sizes allow for wastage during cutting and fitting.

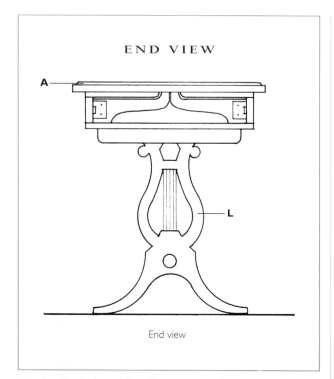

END VIEW

A

L

End view

Fig 17.1b Sofa Table: Plan - continued

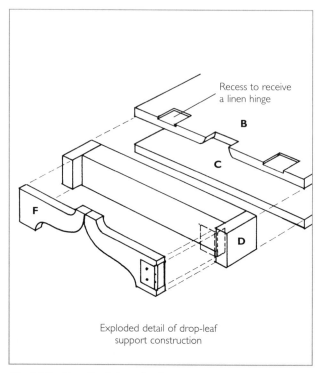

Recess to receive
a linen hinge

B

C

F

D

Exploded detail of drop-leaf
support construction

Fig 17.2 Detail of drop-leaf support

PREPARATION
AND CONSTRUCTION

TABLE TOP A Prepare the table top and drop leaves in accordance with the profile shown on the front and plan views. On this model a groove was made along the top edge using a chisel but if this doesn't appeal to you then all you need to do is to round off the top edge. Once the groove or the rounded edge is complete, the surface of the table can be scraped and rubbed down with a fine abrasive paper and wire wool ready to receive the finish. Linen hinges can be glued to the underside surface as indicated on the front view and the exploded detail.

PARTS B AND C These are simple rectangular strips of timber which need no special surface treatment other than perhaps a brief rub down with abrasive paper to take away the roughness. Part B is to have a notch cut out as shown in Fig 17.2 and the end view in Fig 17.1b. It will also require a pair of shallow chases to be cut out with a chisel to house the linen hinges. Make sure that these do, in fact, line up with the hinges on the table. You can glue the linen hinges into the chases at this stage.

PARTS D These are made up from three pieces of timber as shown, the recess being deep enough to house the drop-leaf supports when the leaves are in the down position. (*See* Fig 17.2.)

As brass hinges are used for the drop-leaf supports, you will only need to superglue the return leg of the hinge to part D as can be seen in the exploded detail. Care must be exercised to avoid getting any glue on the hinge joints otherwise they will seize up. The best way to tackle this is to put a layer of grease across each side of the hinge knuckle before you glue.

Linen hinges are not suitable for this exercise because of the rigidity required for the supports when in the open position. An alternative method is shown in Fig 17.3, but here again, great care is needed when it comes to drilling through part B, the drop-leaf support and part C in one go. It is certainly worth serious consideration though. If you do decide on this method, remember to round off the vertical edges of each support to prevent any tendency for the support to bind.

PART E This is just a simple rectangular cross section of timber whose ends should be made flush with the edges of parts B and C.

DROP-LEAF SUPPORTS F Trace the shape of these onto the timber surface using carbon paper and then cut them out with a knife. Carve all four supports from one piece of timber before separating the parts as this makes for easier handling.

DRAWERS: PARTS G, H, I AND J The sizes and construction can be ascertained from the plan and front views in Fig 17.1a. The drawer fronts can then be prepared as for the table top, by scraping, and then rubbing down with a fine abrasive paper and wire wool, before the components are glued together.

Drill the front panels with a drill bit of the size required to accommodate the brass drawer pull as a tight fit. If the fit is not tight enough, you will have to use superglue or turn some more drawer pulls from timber.

LEGS L Trace the shape from Fig 17.1b onto the timber surface, using carbon paper, and then drill small holes in the central areas that are to be removed. Insert the jigsaw blade and carefully cut around the inner profile of these shapes.

Drill a 1mm ($\frac{1}{32}$ in) diameter hole to receive the cross rail in the position shown and then cut around the outside profile with a fret saw and knife. Be extra careful during this operation since it is easy to break the feet no matter which way the grain travels. It would, of course, be sensible to allow the grain to travel from top to bottom to make sure that the bowed legs do not snap.

Prepare the surfaces by rubbing down with abrasive paper and wire wool.

Now comes the really tricky bit. The five vertical lines indicated on the end view, which are made from gold-coloured thread, are to be constructed as shown in Fig 17.4. It is quite difficult to position them in the space within the leg and a great deal of patience is called for. When you have succeeded in obtaining the right height, by manipulation of the threads, then glue the thin ply ends to the legs.

LEG SUPPORTS M Trace both the leg supports onto a single piece of timber and cut out the shapes with a knife. You may like to use a slightly longer piece of timber than that stipulated, for ease of handling during carving.

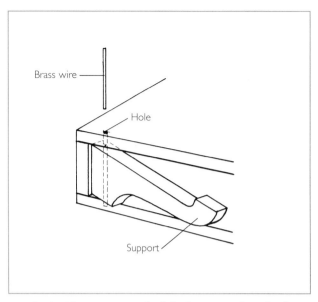

Fig 17.3 *Alternative method for hingeing drop-leaf supports*

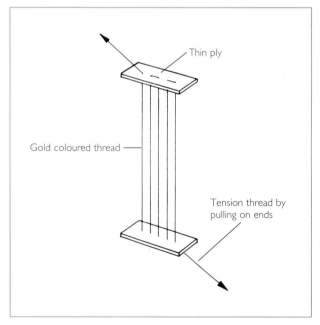

Fig 17.4 *Construction of gold thread assembly for the lyre-ended legs*

CROSS RAIL K This has to be turned from the dowel as indicated on the front view in Fig 17.1a. Use the method described for the Rocking Chair (*see* Legs and stiles in Chapter 8), remembering to turn the two ends down to 1mm ($\frac{1}{32}$ in) diameter to fit into the holes in the legs. The two small bosses can be turned from the same material and then glued onto the surface of the leg, in line with the cross rail.

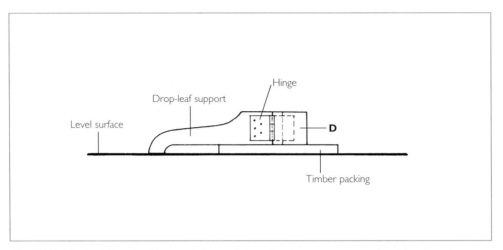

Fig 17.5 Method for checking positions of drop-leaf supports on underside of table

ASSEMBLY

1 Glue drawer components together. *Ensure that they are perfectly square in all directions before the glue has time to set.*

2 Glue part E to underside of part B and at right angles to the edge of part B.

3 Lay the two drawers on each side of part E in order to locate the exact positions of parts D. Now glue parts D to part B. *Remove the drawers as soon as you can so that the glue does not adhere to them.*

4 Glue part C to parts D and E.

5 If brass pins are used as pivots to the drop-leaf supports, now is the time to insert them. The hinges for the supports can now be glued and pinned, but to do this you must make sure that the supports are in the correct position relative to the underside surface of the table top. This can be done by the method shown in Fig 17.5.

6 Glue table top to part B.

7 Glue cross rail to legs. *Ensure that the legs are parallel to each other by separating them during gluing with a block of timber of the right thickness, and with parallel sides.*

8 Glue legs to part C.

9 Glue leg supports to parts C and to legs.

FINISHING

The exposed surfaces should by now be ready to receive the finish of your choice. If varnish is used, beware of the dreaded glue lines, and remove all traces of glue first.

A high polish can be obtained by rubbing down the surfaces between each application of varnish. It is imperative that you allow the varnish to rest between coats and the longer the better. Overnight would be recommended.

Between each coat, when the varnish has dried, rub down with a fine abrasive paper followed by wire wool to get as smooth a surface as possible before the next coat of varnish is added. Always apply the varnish by travelling along the grain of the timber.

OCCASIONAL TABLE

This model would look good in a Georgian setting even though it can be dated as late as a seventeenth century piece of furniture which came into existence during the William and Mary era. It is a very delicate piece having a generally slender appearance and this should be borne in mind when constructing the model. The original table was probably made in oak but would look just as well in mahogany or walnut. I used mahogany myself.

FRONT, END AND PLAN VIEWS

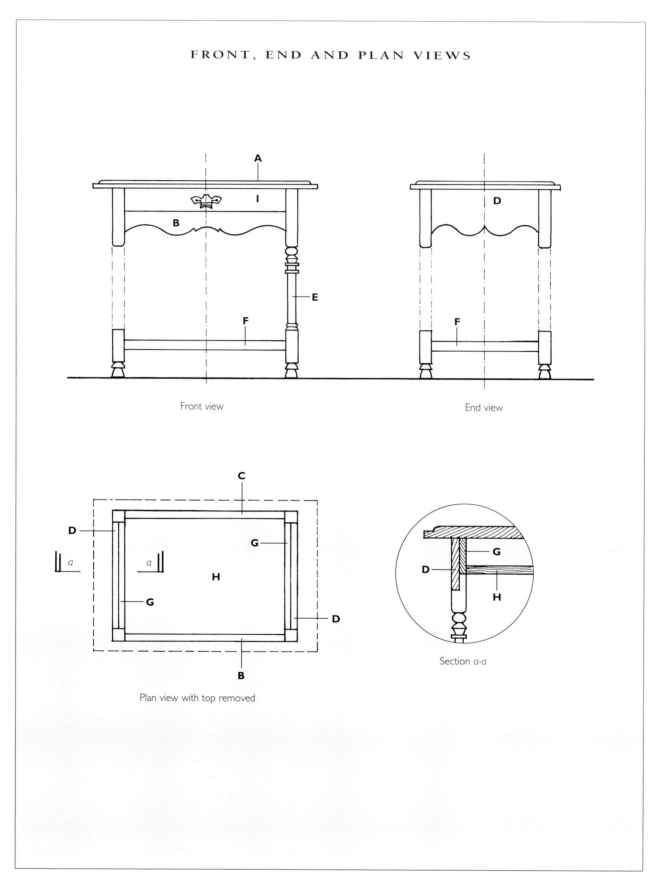

Front view

End view

Plan view with top removed

Section *a-a*

Fig 18.1 Occasional Table: Plan

CUTTING LIST

Oak, mahogany or walnut.

A Table top (1) 60 × 40 × 2mm (2⅜ × 1⅝ × ³⁄₃₂in)

B Front panel (1) 45 × 10 × 1.5mm (1¾ × ⅜ × ¹⁄₁₆in)

C Back panel (1) 45 × 15 × 1.5mm (1¾ × ⅝ × ¹⁄₁₆in)

D Side panels (2) from 2: 30 × 15 × 1.5mm (1¼ × ⅝ × ¹⁄₁₆in)

E Legs (4), cross section, from 3 × 3mm (⅛ × ⅛in)

F Rails (4), strip, from 2: 45 × 2.5 × 1.5mm (1¾ × ⅛ × ¹⁄₁₆in)
     + from 2: 30 × 2.5 × 1.5mm (1¼ × ⅛ × ¹⁄₁₆in)

G (2) from 2: 30 × 8 × 1.5mm (1¼ × ⁵⁄₁₆ × ¹⁄₁₆in)

H (1) 44 × 31 × 1.5mm (1¾ × 1¼ × ¹⁄₁₆in)

I Front of drawer (1) 45 × 6 × 1.5mm (1¾ × ¼ × ¹⁄₁₆in)

J Back of drawer (1) 42 × 5 × 1.5mm (1¾ × ³⁄₁₆ × ¹⁄₁₆in)

K Sides of drawer (2) 70 × 5 × 1.5mm (2¾ × ³⁄₁₆ × ¹⁄₁₆in)

L Base of drawer (1), thin ply, 45 × 35mm (1¾ × 1½in)

It is assumed that you will cut the rails to length from the strip and that the legs will be longer than shown since you will always incur waste when using the lathe.

PREPARATION AND CONSTRUCTION

TABLE TOP A The size given in the cutting list is the actual size and only requires rubbing down along the edges. You may observe that the top edges have been recessed. This can be done with abrasive paper wrapped around a block of scrap timber. However, if you have a steady hand, you could achieve a better and cleaner effect by using a knife against a steel straightedge. The top surface of the table can now be scraped and then rubbed down with a fine abrasive paper and wire wool, ready to accept the finish.

FRONT B, BACK C AND SIDE PANELS D
These can be traced onto the timber surface, using carbon paper, and then cut out to shape with a knife. Prepare the surface that will be exposed in the same way as you did the table top.

LEGS E Turn these from the strip of timber, allowing enough length at each end for fitting into the lathe. For each leg a length of 75mm (3in) should be adequate. Use the procedure described for the Rocking Chair for transferring the measurements from the drawing onto the timber surface once the central cylindrical portion has been gouged down to size. (*See*

Legs and stiles in Chapter 8.) The top and bottom parts are to be left square in order to receive the panels and rails.

RAILS F Cut these out to the same length as the front and side panels.

PARTS G These are pieces that ensure the free movement of the drawer and are to be fitted into the gap behind the side panels as indicated on the plan view. Therefore, they are to be of the same length as the side panels.

ASSEMBLY
At this stage it would be advisable to glue the front, back and side panels and the rails to the legs. Make sure that they are all mutually perpendicular to each other before the glue has time to set. Now check that parts G fit snugly into the space provided and that the faces are flush with the faces of the legs so that the drawer will eventually be in contact with the legs during its operation.

PART H This should be cut to fit into the space provided within the framework and when it is glued in position you must make sure that it lies parallel to the top edge of the framework. I suggest that you

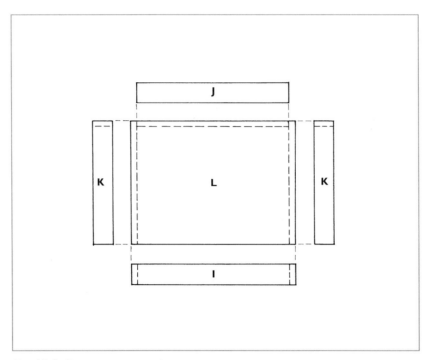

Fig 18.2 Drawer construction

make up a block of scrap timber of the right depth
and with an even thickness so that, with the
framework placed over it and with its top edge resting
on a level surface, part H can then be positioned
accurately whilst the glue is still tacky.

DRAWER I, J, K, AND L The construction is as
shown in Fig 18.2 and the parts should be cut out in
accordance with the details, ready for assembly.

The base must be of sufficient width to enable it to
slide easily between the surfaces of parts G. The length
of the front panel can then be made to the same
dimension as the width of the base. The length of the
base should be such that it touches the rear face of the
back panel, but is short enough to permit the front
panel of the drawer to butt up against it in such a way
that the front surface of the drawer is flush with the
face of the front panel. You may need to rub the pieces
down with a sanding block in order to get them to fit:
beware that you don't lose the parallelism of the base
in so doing.

The sides are then cut to the length of the base, and
the back panel cut to fit between the side panels.
These are then glued onto the top of the base as
indicated by the chain-dotted line shown on the
drawer construction details.

ASSEMBLY

1 Glue the parts I, J, K and L together, ensuring that
each part is both parallel and perpendicular to its
adjacent part. *Check that it fits in the space between
the legs and that it moves freely into place. If it
doesn't, you only have to rub down those parts that
are binding.*
2 Glue the table top to the framework. *Again, check
that the drawer moves freely.*
3 The final touch is to attach the drawer pull and as
these come in a variety of styles, depending upon
the authenticity you desire, you may need to order
it specially from a mail order supplier.

FINISHING

The parts requiring a finish should have been
prepared by this stage, so all you need to do is apply a
varnish or wax. Remember to rub down between
applications and give each one time to dry thoroughly
before subsequent coats are added. Also watch out for
any ugly glue lines and get rid of them before you
varnish. A wax finish, whilst quite good, will not give
the same gloss as that obtained by the proper
application of varnish.

PEMBROKE TABLE

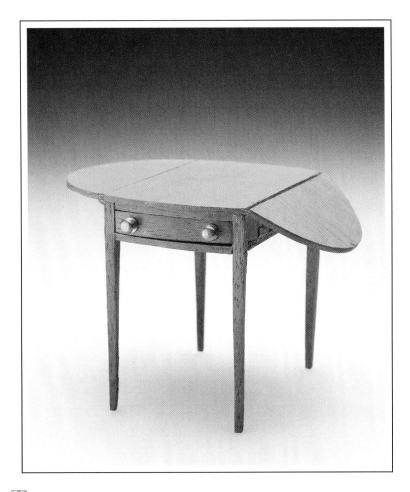

These were popular in the reign of George III and were generally used as a breakfast table. They can be found with ornamental embellishments such as inlays and exotic veneers.
For this model I used my old favourite mahogany but walnut would look just as good.

PLAN, FRONT AND SIDE VIEWS

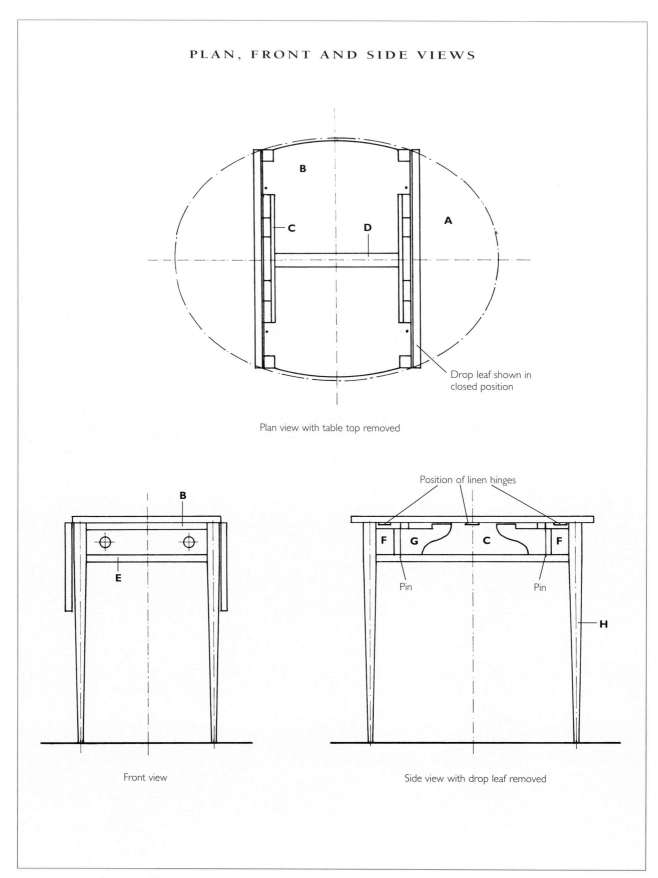

Drop leaf shown in closed position

Plan view with table top removed

Position of linen hinges

Pin

Pin

Front view

Side view with drop leaf removed

Fig 19.1a Pembroke Table: Plan - *continued over*

CUTTING LIST

Mahogany or walnut.

A Table top (including drop leaves) (1) 90 × 70 × 2mm (3⅝ × 2¾ × 3/32in)

B (1) 65 × 40 × 2mm (2⅝ × 1⅝ × 3/32in)

C (2) from 2: 35 × 10 × 1mm (1½ × ⅜ × 1/32in)

D (1) 35 × 4 × 4mm (1½ × ¼ × ¼in)

E (1) 65 × 40 × 2mm (2⅝ × 1⅝ × 3/32in)

F (4) 28 × 10 × 2mm (1⅛ × ⅜ × 3/32in)

G Drop-leaf supports (4) 80 × 8 × 2mm (3⅛ × 5/16 × 3/32in)

H Legs (4) 240 × 3 × 3mm (9½ × ⅛ × ⅛in)

I Fronts of drawers (2) 70 × 6 × 5mm (2¾ × ¼ × 3/16)

J Base of drawers (2), thin ply, 60 × 35mm (2⅜ × 1½in)

K Sides of drawers (4) 100 × 5 × 1.5mm (4 × ¼ × 1/16in)

L Backs of drawers (2) 60 × 5 × 1.5mm (2⅜ × ¼ × 1/16in)

Sizes given allow for some wastage during rubbing down and fitting.

ELEVATED VIEW

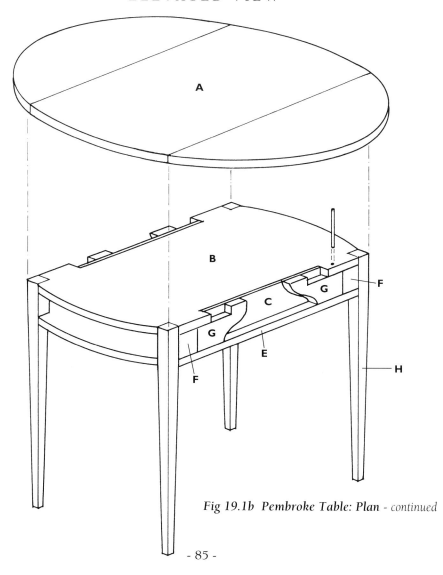

Fig 19.1b Pembroke Table: Plan - continued

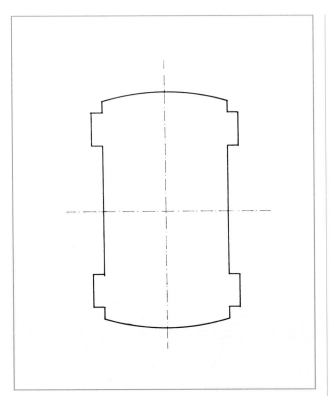

Fig 19.2 Detail of part B

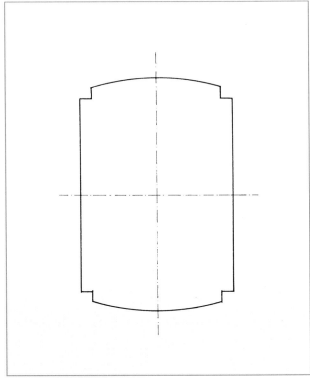

Fig 19.3 Detail of part E

PREPARATION AND CONSTRUCTION

TABLE TOP A Using carbon paper, trace the outline of the profile, shown as a chain-dotted line on Fig 19.1a, from the drawing onto the timber surface, with the grain of the timber travelling from back to front. Carefully cut around the outline using either a fret saw or a knife and round off the top edge with abrasive paper.

Now, using a bead saw or a straightedge and knife, cut out the centre portion to the width shown on the front view. The next thing to do is to prepare the top surface by scraping and then rubbing down with a fine abrasive paper and wire wool, ready to receive the finish. Turn the table top and drop leaves onto their faces and attach, by means of glue, the linen hinges referred to on the side view. Put aside until needed.

PARTS B AND E Trace these onto their respective timber surfaces from Figs19.2 and 19.3, and cut out the shapes with either a fret saw or a bead saw and knife. Check that the corner slots match up with each other as this is where the legs are to fit.

PARTS D AND F Cut these out to the lengths shown in Fig 19.1a but slightly oversize so that you can adjust the lengths later when fitting things together.

PART C The length of this piece (*see* Fig 19.4) should fit into the central gap along the side of part B and the depth will be such that it will eventually rest on part E and touch the underside surface of the table top.

DROP-LEAF SUPPORTS G Trace all four of these from Fig 19.1a onto the one piece of timber and carefully cut out the shapes with a bead saw and knife. Finish off by rubbing down with abrasive paper. Remember to round off the vertical edges near the pivot point.

LEGS H Cut and shape these in the same way as described for the Dining Table (*see* Legs: parts F in Chapter 14) but with a different jig this time. Check that they are each of the same length.

DRAWERS I, J, K AND L The construction and assembly arrangement of each of the two drawers is shown on Fig 19.5. The front panels should be traced onto the timber indicated in the cutting list and cut out by the method described for the Modern Dining Chair. (*See* Back rail in Chapter 13: *see also* Fig 13.3.)

The front face of the drawers can be rubbed down to receive the finish but more importantly, to ensure that the curve of the face coincides with the curvature of parts B and E, since they must be flush when assembled.

The bases are to be shaped to fit the profile of the inner curve of the front panels, against which they are to butt.

Drill the front of each drawer where shown, using a drill bit commensurate with the shank of the drawer pulls so that the latter will fit tightly in the holes. If they don't, you will have to resort to superglue.

ASSEMBLY

1 Glue part B to legs, one at a time, ensuring that each leg is vertical.
2 With part B face down on a flat surface, glue into it parts C, making sure that they are at right angles to part B.
3 Glue parts F to part B and to legs.
4 Glue part E to parts C and F and to legs.
5 Place drop-leaf supports into position within the space provided and drill 1mm ($^1/_{32}$ in) diameter holes through part B drop-leaf supports and part E to receive the brass wire which is to act as a pivotal pin. *Since this is a very tricky operation I suggest that you practice on some scrap timber of the same thickness until you are happy enough to try it on the actual supports. With the pins inserted, check that the supports move freely and when they do, put a blob of glue on the underside face of part E to prevent the pin from falling out.*
6 Finally, glue the table top to part B.

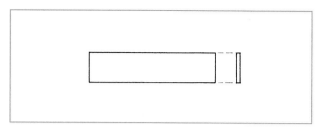

Fig 19.4 Detail of part C

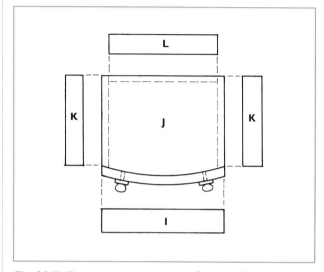

Fig 19.5 Drawer construction and assembly

FINISHING

The parts, having been prepared, can now receive the finish.

If varnish is to be applied, let it dry off overnight before rubbing down with a fine abrasive paper and wire wool ready for the next coat. Get rid of any glue lines before the first coat goes on and if you want a good glossy finish, then you will have to exercise some patient waiting between varnish applications.

Wax is a bit easier to apply but lacks the glossiness created by a good varnish.

BUREAUX

BUREAU

As soon as I saw a photograph of this in a magazine I simply had to make it, so the following drawings are my representation of the bureau and the model has certainly lived up to expectations. The model was made entirely in beech since it is a relatively modern piece of furniture.

FRONT, SIDE AND SECTIONAL VIEWS

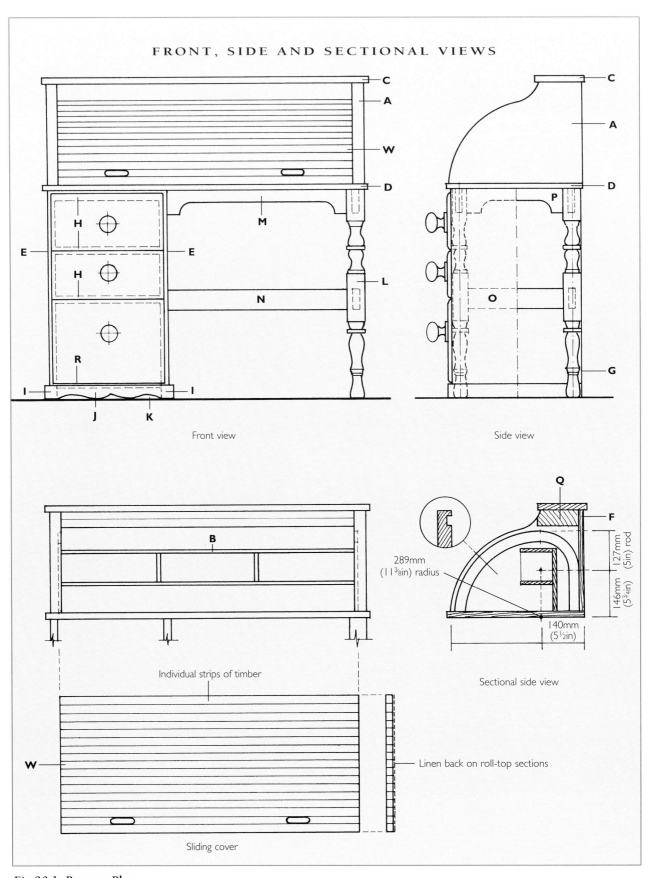

Front view

Side view

Individual strips of timber

Linen back on roll-top sections

Sliding cover

289mm
(11³⁄₈in) radius

127mm
(5in) rod

146mm
(5³⁄₄in)

140mm
(5¹⁄₂in)

Sectional side view

Fig 20.1 Bureau: Plan

CUTTING LIST

Beech.

A Grooved side panels (2) 40 × 30 × 3mm
($1^5/8$ × $1^1/4$ × $^1/8$in)

B Shelf unit (1) 180 × 10 × 0.75mm ($7^1/8$ × $^3/8$ × $^1/32$in) +
80 × 20 × 0.75mm ($3^1/8$ × $^7/8$ × $^1/32$in)

C Top panel (1) 90 × 15 × 1.5mm ($3^5/8$ × $^5/8$ × $^1/16$in)

D Desk top panel (1) 90 × 40 × 1.5mm ($3^5/8$ × $1^5/8$ × $^1/16$in)

E Side panels to drawer unit (2) 110 × 35 × 2mm
($4^3/8$ × $1^3/8$ × $^3/32$in)

F Rear panel (1) 80 × 30 × 1.5mm ($3^1/4$ × $1^1/4$ × $^1/16$in)

G Rear panel (1) 55 × 30 × 1.5mm ($2^1/4$ × $1^1/4$ × $^1/16$in)

H Drawer dividers (3) 90 × 35 × 2mm ($3^5/8$ × $1^3/8$ × $^3/32$in)

I Pedestal sides (2) from 2: 35 × 3 × 3mm ($1^1/2$ × $^1/8$ × $^1/8$in)

J Pedestal front (1) 35 × 3 × 3mm ($1^1/2$ × $^1/8$ × $^1/8$in)

K Pedestal back (1) 30 × 3 × 3mm ($1^1/4$ × $^1/8$ × $^1/8$in)

L Legs (2), strip, 5 × 5mm ($^3/16$ × $^3/16$in)

M and **N** Stiles (2) 100 × 6 × 1.5mm (4 × $^1/4$ × $^1/16$in)

O and **P** Stiles (2) 60 × 12 × 1.5mm ($2^3/8$ × $^1/2$ × $^1/16$in)

Q Timber block (1) 80 × 15 × 4mm ($3^1/4$ × $^5/8$ × $^3/16$in)

R Drawer assembly base (1) 35 × 30 × 0.75mm
($1^3/8$ × $1^1/4$ × $^1/32$in)

S Fronts of drawers

  S1 (1) 30 × 15 × 1mm ($1^1/4$ × $^5/8$ × $^1/32$in)

  S2 (1) 30 × 14 × 1mm ($1^1/4$ × $^9/16$ × $^1/32$in)

  S3 (1) 30 × 23 × 1mm ($1^1/4$ × 1 × $^1/32$in)

T Sides of drawers

  T1 (2) from 2: 35 × 11 × 1mm ($1^1/2$ × $^1/2$ × $^1/32$in)

  T2 (1) 35 × 21 × 1mm ($1^1/2$ × 1 × $^1/32$in)

U Backs of drawers (3) 50 × 30 × 1mm (2 × $1^1/4$ × $^1/32$in)

V Bases of drawers (3) 90 × 35 × 0.75mm ($3^5/8$ × $1^1/2$ × $^1/32$in)

W Sliding cover (1), strip, 2 × 1mm ($^3/32$ × $^1/32$in)

Sizes given allow for some wastage when rubbing down
and fitting.

PREPARATION AND CONSTRUCTION

GROOVED SIDE PANELS A Trace the outlines and the grooves from Fig 20.1 onto the timber surface using the method shown in Fig 20.2 and begin by cutting out the grooves. This is achieved by the method shown in Fig 20.3, using a great deal of care to ensure that the groove is of even depth and width and that it 'flows' without any kinks forming. A check for conformity with the drawing will be made later when the sliding cover has been made up. Now cut carefully around the profile and rub down the edges with abrasive paper. Finish the outer faces by scraping and then rubbing down with abrasive paper and wire wool, ready to receive the final coats of varnish, or wax.

SHELF UNIT B Cut out the component parts of this unit, taking your measurements from the front view (with sliding cover open) and the sectional side view. You can, at this stage, glue the elements together taking care to see they are at right angles to each other. Now glue the back panel to the shelf unit. Check from the drawing that the finished unit does not encroach upon the groove in the side panel. As the space available is very restricted, you may have to do a certain amount of rubbing down to get the unit to fit. Check that the shelf unit, sliding cover and side panels conform to the front view by holding them all together loosely at first, and then try to see if the sliding cover moves reasonably smoothly along the groove by clamping the side panels to the shelf unit. Do not glue yet.

TOP PANEL C AND DESK TOP PANEL D Cut out these two rectangular pieces of timber which are to be exactly the same length as each other and prepare the upper surfaces by scraping and then rubbing down with abrasive paper and wire wool, ready to receive the finish.

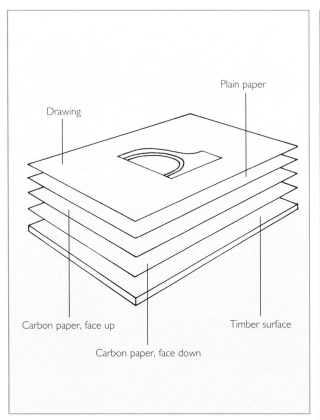

Fig 20.2 Method for tracing outlines and grooves onto timber

SIDE PANELS E TO DRAWER UNIT Cut these out to the length shown on the front view and to the width extrapolated from the side view, bearing in mind that they will be as wide as the overall width of the legs. Prepare the outer faces, ready for the finish.

REAR PANELS F AND G Cut these out and rub down the edges with abrasive paper. Note that part F butts up to the inside faces of the side panels A and that part G does the same between parts E. The faces can now be prepared for the finish as described earlier.

DRAWER DIVIDERS H Cut these out (from the outline indicated on the front view) using a Minicraft bench saw, if possible, to maintain consistency of width. Without the bench saw you will have to make sure that the strip from which these dividers are to be cut, is of even width throughout.

PEDESTAL UNIT PARTS I, J and K Parts I butt into part J and overlap part K. Part J is the only one that is to be carved to the profile shown on the front view. The exposed faces of all parts can be prepared for the final finish.

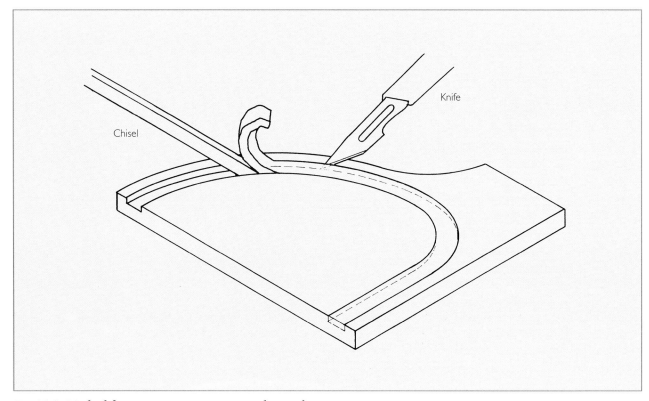

Fig 20.3 Method for cutting out grooves on side panel

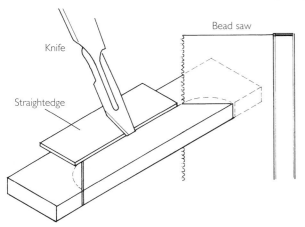

Fig 20.4 Method for shaping stiles

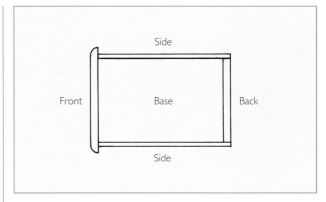

Fig 20.5 Drawer construction (not to scale)

LEGS L A minimum length of 80mm (3¼ in) will be required in order to fit into the lathe. Mark the principal points onto the timber surface as described in Fig 10.4, after you have roughed down the cylindrical portions. Do the roughing-down after you have marked out where the square portions are to be situated so that you don't interfere with them when using the chisel.

When you have obtained two identical legs, the next task is to cut out the slots where shown to receive the stiles, M, N, O and P. Do not penetrate right through the legs. The whole operation is best done with a miniature chisel, after you have pre-drilled the holes to the required depth. Should you feel that this is taxing your patience too far, glue the stiles directly to the legs later.

STILES M, N, O AND P Cut these pieces from the timber, noting that there are two parts M. Shape parts M and P as shown in Fig 20.1, using a bead saw, knife and straightedge. (*See* Fig 20.4.) The curved bits can be done using some abrasive paper wrapped around a scrap piece of dowel or pencil. Now prepare the faces to receive the finish.

TIMBER BLOCK Q Cut out this piece, which is to butt in between the faces of parts A, and is consequently exactly the same length as the shelf unit B. The curved edge shown on section *a-a* is obtained by rubbing down with abrasive paper wrapped around a suitable piece of dowel and should meet up with the upper curve of parts A. You can leave the finishing touches to this work until the sliding cover is installed if you wish.

DRAWER ASSEMBLY BASE R This is a simple rectangular piece of timber which is to be let into the pedestal unit and upon which the drawer is to slide. When it comes to gluing it in place, you will need a flat piece of timber of the right thickness placed underneath it to make certain that it is fixed in the correct position.

DRAWERS S, T, U AND V After you have cut out the component parts with a Minicraft bench saw or from a prepared strip of consistent width, make up the drawers as shown in Fig 20.5. Note the variation in the drawer fronts shown on Fig 20.6. When it comes to gluing the parts together, it would be as well if the sides, back and base for each drawer are assembled first. The fronts can be fixed on later.

Now construct and glue the drawer dividers H to the side panel E in the way shown in Fig 20.7. When completed and with the pedestal in place, see if the incomplete drawers fit into the spaces provided.

You can now think about attaching the front panels of each drawer. To do this, I suggest that you first place a thin strip of timber, of a size less than the

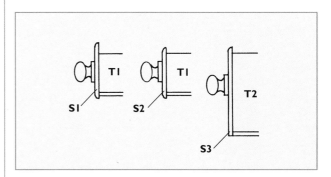

Fig 20.6 Detail of drawer fronts

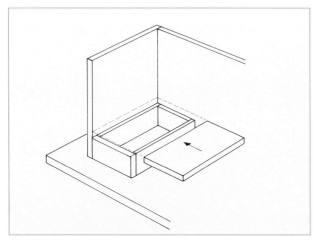

Fig 20.7 *Determine the correct position of the dividers from the spacing of the drawers*

dimensions of the hole, into the hole and resting against the inner face of part G so that it forms a pack. Then you can put the incomplete drawers in place where it will be seen that they stand proud of the edges of the framework. This is so that when the glue is applied to the edges of the drawers, it will not come into contact with the framework, otherwise you won't get the drawers out again.

Now carefully place each drawer front into position as shown on the front view and allow the glue to set. The drawer fronts are to be drilled to accept the drawer pulls which are to be made from 5mm ($^3/_{16}$ in) diameter dowel. The size of drill bit will need to be 1.5mm ($^1/_{16}$ in) diameter.

SLIDING COVER W This is to be made up from thin strips of timber as shown on the plan. These can be cut out slightly longer than indicated so that you can trim the sides down to the actual length later. The strips are laid side by side on a piece of linen which has been coated with glue. Make sure that the individual strips are not glued together where the glue from the linen may have seeped through. This can be done by running a thin knife blade between them, very carefully.

Cut one edge of the sliding cover at right angles to the length and check that it moves freely in the appropriate groove. Now check the overall length required by laying the sliding cover on the plan, and cut it at right angles to its length. Check that it moves freely in its groove.

When you are satisfied, clamp the two ends A to the shelf unit with the sliding cover in place and see if it still moves smoothly. If not, rub down the edges, slightly round off the top edges and try again before the parts are assembled. Cut out the finger grooves as shown, or attach some small pieces of timber to the surface. Finally, prepare the face ready to receive the finish.

ASSEMBLY

1 Glue drawer unit to desk top D.
2 Glue front stile M to desk top and drawer unit.
3 Glue front leg to stile M and desk top. *Make sure that the desk top stands proud of the face of the leg as shown on the side view.*
4 Glue stile P to desk top and front leg.
5 Glue stile O to front leg.
6 Glue rear stile M to desk top and drawer unit.
7 Glue rear leg to parts M, N and desk top. *Check the positioning of each part whilst the glue is still tacky and make sure that they are at right angles to each other.*
8 Glue shelf unit B to one side of unit A. *Check that they are at right angles to each other.*
9 Glue timber block Q to the same face of part A.
10 With the sliding cover in position, clamp the other side panel A to the assembly to do a final check that the cover moves freely. When it does, remove the clamp and glue the end of the shelf unit to A. *Make sure that the two ends A are at the same relative position to each other and to part B.*
11 Glue side panels A and bottom edge of shelf unit B to desk top to line up with the unit under the desk top.
12 Glue rear panel F to parts C, D and A. *Check that it does not encroach upon the groove.*
13 Glue top panel C to parts Q, A and F.

FINISHING

If you have prepared all necessary surfaces properly, then all you need is some clear polyurethane varnish to finish, after first removing any glue lines. If you feel that more coats are required, remember to allow the first coat to harden overnight and to then rub down the surface ready for the next coat.

OFFICE BUREAU

I first saw this piece of furniture in the *Antiques Roadshow* programme on BBC television and decided that it would look good in model form. Little did I know how difficult it would be to work out the details. Well, as you can see, it became possible. I would add that I have no idea as to its original use and the title here is my own invention, given simply because it is a self-contained office which takes up little room. The details worked out in the method of construction are entirely from my own imagination, so don't be afraid to amend them if you feel that improvements can be made. As far as timber is concerned, it would look good in any of the popular hardwoods. I chose walnut because, like many close-grained timbers, it lends itself to easy carving and to the attainment of fine detail.

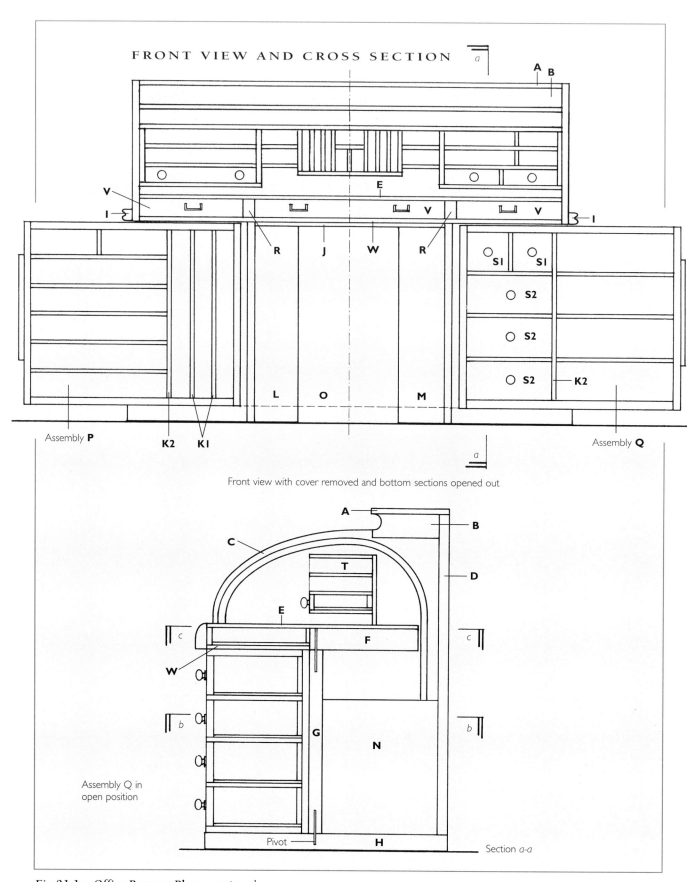

FRONT VIEW AND CROSS SECTION

Assembly **P**

K2   K1

Front view with cover removed and bottom sections opened out

Assembly **Q**

Assembly Q in
open position

Pivot

Section *a-a*

Fig 21.1a Office Bureau: Plan - *continued over*

CROSS SECTIONS

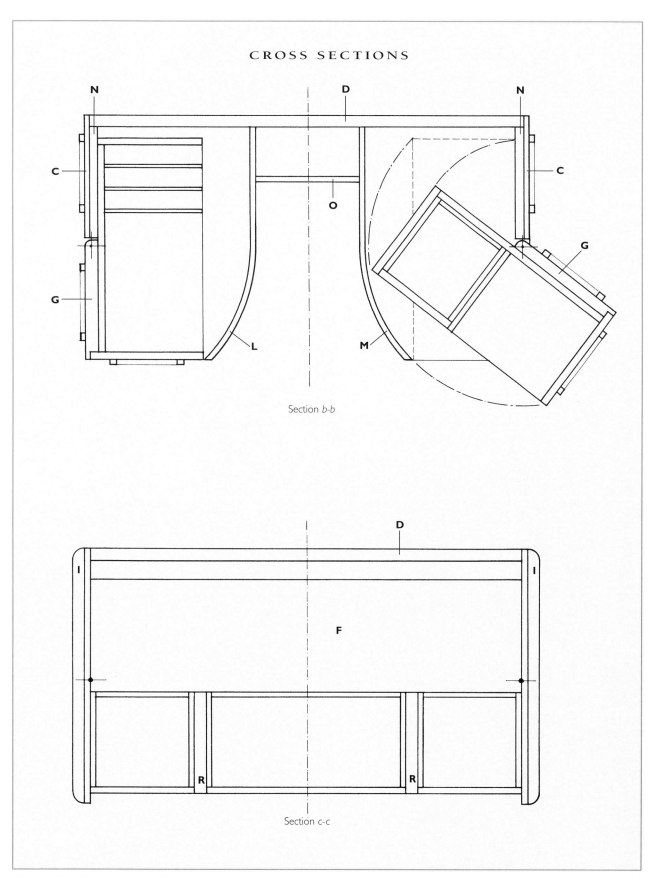

Section *b-b*

Section *c-c*

Fig 21.1b Office Bureau: Plan - *continued*

CUTTING LIST

Any hardwood.

A Top panel (1) 115 × 21 × 1.5mm (4⅝ × 1 × ¹⁄₁₆in)

B Block (1) 115 × 18 × 6mm (4⅝ × ¾ × ¼in)

C Side panels (2) from 90 × 65 × 2mm (3⅝ × 2⅝ × ³⁄₃₂in)

D Rear panel (1) 115 × 85 × 3mm (4⅝ × 3⅜ × ⅛in)

E Desk top panel (1) 115 × 57 × 1mm (4⅝ × 2¼ × ¹⁄₃₂in)

F Block (1) 115 × 30 × 6mm (4⅝ × 1¼ × ¼in)

G Panels (2) 100 × 35 × 3.5mm (4 × 1½ × ⅛in)

H Pedestal (1) 120 × 65 × 4mm (4¾ × 2⅝ × ³⁄₁₆in)

I Trims (2) 140 × 3 × 3mm (5½ × ⅛ × ⅛in)

J Panel (1) 50 × 50 × 1mm (2 × 2 × ¹⁄₃₂in)

K Dividers (4) from 4: 45 × 26 × 0.75mm (1¾ × 1¹⁄₁₆ × ¹⁄₃₂in)

L and **M** Panels (2) 55 × 70 × 0.75mm (2¼ × 2¾ × ¹⁄₃₂in), grain in 55mm direction.

N Pack (2) 35 × 30 × 1.5mm (1½ × 1¼ × ¹⁄₃₂in)

O Panel (1) 55 × 30 × 0.75mm (2¼ × 1¼ × ¹⁄₃₂in)

P and **Q** Filing assemblies

tops and bottoms (4) 250 × 27 × 2mm (10 × 1⅛ × ³⁄₃₂in)

sides (4) 200 × 30 × 2mm (8 × 1¼ × ³⁄₃₂in)

backs (2) 115 × 50 × 1.5mm (4⅝ × 2 × ¹⁄₁₆in)

dividers (excluding dividers K) (13) from 2: 250 × 27 × 0.75mm (10 × 1⅛ × ¹⁄₃₂in)

R Dividers (2) from 2: 30 × 5 × 3mm (1¼ × ³⁄₁₆ × ⅛in)

S Drawers in assembly Q

fronts (5) 100 × 10 × 2mm (4 × ⅜ × ³⁄₃₂in)

backs (5) 100 × 10 × 1.5mm (4 × ⅜ × ¹⁄₁₆in)

sides (10) 250 × 10 × 1.5mm (10 × ⅜ × ¹⁄₁₆in)

bases (5) 100 × 25 × 0.75mm (4 × 1 × ¹⁄₃₂in)

T Pigeon-hole assembly

shelves, dividers and spacers (29) 300 × 20 × 0.75mm (12 × ⅞ × ¹⁄₃₂in)

back panel (1) 115 × 20 × 0.75mm (4⅝ × ⅞ × ¹⁄₃₂in)

U Drawers in pigeon-hole assembly

fronts (3) 60 × 5 × 1.5mm (2⅜ × ³⁄₁₆ × ¹⁄₁₆in)

backs (3) 60 × 5 × 0.75mm (2⅜ × ³⁄₁₆ × ¹⁄₃₂in)

sides (6) 120 × 5 × 0.75mm (4¾ × ³⁄₁₆ × ¹⁄₃₂in)

bases (3) 65 × 20 × 0.75mm (2⅝ × ⅞ × ¹⁄₃₂in)

V Drawers under desk top panel

fronts (3) 110 × 5 × 1.5mm (4⅜ × ³⁄₁₆ × ¹⁄₁₆in)

backs (3) 110 × 5 × 0.75mm (4⅜ × ³⁄₁₆ × ¹⁄₃₂in)

sides (6) 180 × 5 × 0.75mm (7⅛ × ³⁄₁₆ × ¹⁄₃₂in)

bases (3) 110 × 30 × 0.75mm (4⅜ × 1¼ × ¹⁄₃₂in)

W Panel (1) 115 × 30 × 1mm (4⅝ × 1¼ × ¹⁄₃₂in)

X Exterior panel trims (2) 320 × 1.5 × 1.5mm (12⅝ × ¹⁄₁₆ × ¹⁄₁₆in)

Y Sliding cover (1) from 26: 115 × 2 × 1mm (4⅝ × ³⁄₃₂ × ¹⁄₃₂in)

Sizes in general allow for some waste due to fitting requirements.

PREPARATION
AND CONSTRUCTION

TOP PANEL A   Cut this out from the outline shown in Fig 21.1a and prepare the upper surface by scraping and then rubbing down with a fine abrasive paper and with wire wool ready to receive the finish.

BLOCK B   Cut out and chase out a groove, using a saw or chisel, to the profile indicated on section *a-a*, Fig 21.1a. This can be done now or later, when panel C has been made, so that the shapes coincide. The final rubbing can be done with some abrasive paper wrapped around a pencil.

SIDE PANELS C   Trace the shape from Fig 21.2 using the method shown in Fig 20.2, and chase out the groove in which the sliding cover is to move. This is done by the method shown in Fig 20.3, taking care to ensure that the groove is of even depth and width and that no kinks form. Since the panels are relatively thin, great care is needed to arrive at a depth which can accommodate the sliding cover without the latter

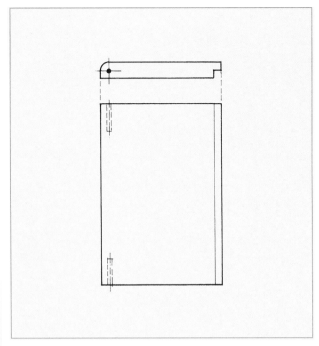

Fig 21.3 Detail of panels G

slipping out. The checks made during the construction of the sliding cover will verify your efforts. Now cut around the external profile with a fret saw and rub down with abrasive paper. Check that both panels C are identical. Having done this, prepare the faces as for top panel A, ready to receive the finish.

REAR PANEL D   Cut the panel out and prepare the outer surface, ready for the finish.

DESK TOP PANEL E   Cut the panel out and prepare the top surface, ready for the finish.

BLOCK F   Cut out to the details shown in section *c-c*, Fig 21.1b, noting that this block is to be exactly the same length as panels D and E.

PANELS G   These can be cut out now or left until the assemblies P and Q have been constructed, since these panels are to be the same length as the side panels of the assemblies. Note the detail and the shaping required as shown on Fig 21.3. The edge groove can be cut out by using a knife and straightedge and the top and bottom drilled as shown, with a 1mm ($^1/_{32}$ in) diameter drill bit. The depth of the holes is unimportant but their position is. Round

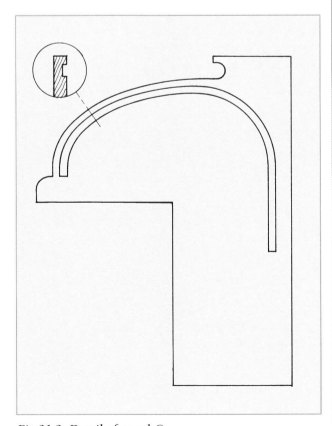

Fig 21.2 Detail of panel C

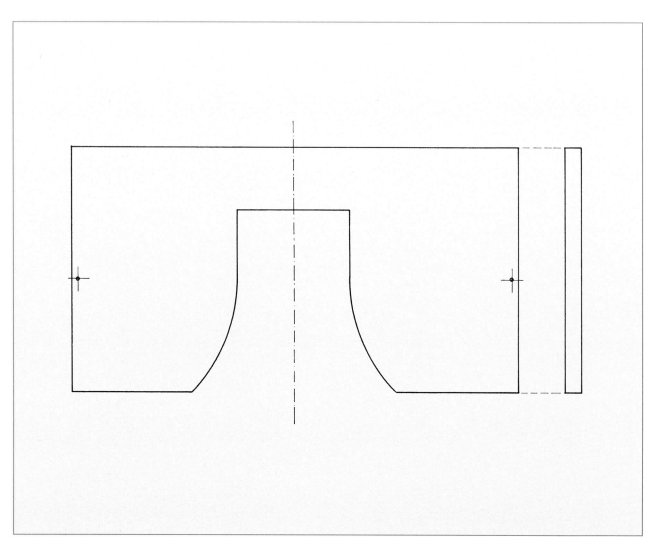

Fig 21.4 Detail of pedestal H

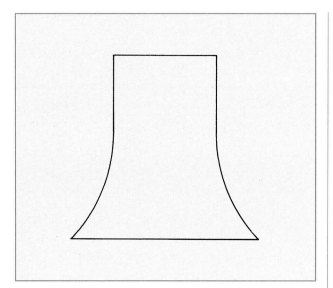

Fig 21.5 Detail of panel J

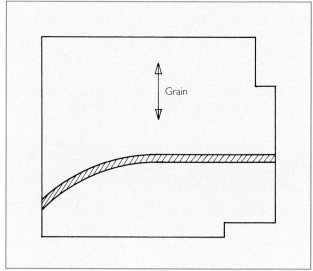

Fig 21.6 Detail of panel M (panel L is its mirror image)

Fig 21.7 Detail of panel O

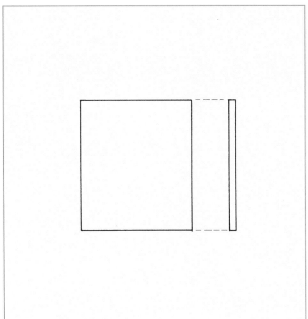

Fig 21.8 Detail of pack N

off the edge as indicated to enable the assemblies to rotate easily, without binding. The outer surface can now be prepared for the finish, as for top panel A, and the trims can be cut out and glued in position for the panelling effect.

PEDESTAL H Trace the details given in Fig 21.4 onto the timber surface, using carbon paper, and then cut out the shape inside the knee hole with a fret saw.

PANEL J When tracing this shape onto the timber surface (*see* Fig 21.5), allow a little bit extra around the curved parts so that you will be able to rub them down later when the parts are assembled, to obtain a good fit.

The purpose of this panel is to maintain the top edges of panels L and M in their final positions during and after the gluing operation.

PANELS L AND M An elevation of these is shown on their details. (*See* Fig 21.6.) The width as indicated is, of course, not the true width of the panels because of the curvature as shown by the cross-hatched area on the detail. Therefore, when you trace the shape of these panels onto the timber surface, allow a bit extra on the left-hand edge so that when it is eventually curved to fit, it will be a relatively simple matter to

trim the edge. Allowance has been made for this in the cutting list.

Prepare the outer surface of each panel as for top panel A, ready for the finish.

PANEL O This is shown on the detail in Fig 21.7 and extends, on the finished model, from the underside of panel J to the underside of pedestal H. Cut out and prepare its face, ready for the finish.

PACK N Cut this out to the shape shown in Fig 21.8 and check its length against side panel C. It should extend from the end of the groove to the bottom edge of panel C. (*See* section *b-b*, Fig 21.1b.)

The partially exploded view in Fig 21.9 gives some idea of how the pieces fit together. The purpose of pack N is to act as a stop for the sliding cover and also as a stop for the revolving assemblies P and Q.

FILING ASSEMBLY P This is to be made up from rectangular strips for the shelving and thicker rectangular pieces for the carcass. Cut out the shelving with a Minicraft bench saw, if possible, so that you can be assured of the consistency of width required throughout. The vertical pieces must wait until the top and bottom panels have been glued into the side panels. Cut out the side panels in such a way that they

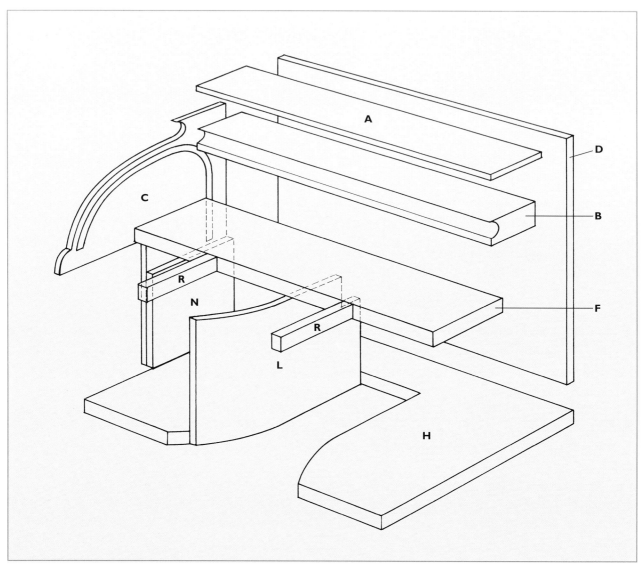

Fig 21.9 Partially exploded view of bureau

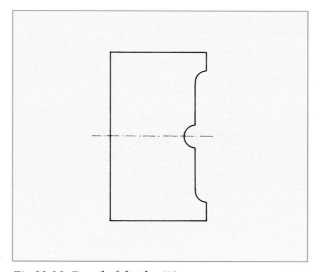

Fig 21.10 Detail of divider K1

fit snugly into the gap in panel C. Be careful not to undercut these, or the assembly, when made, will be a sloppy fit. Once you are satisfied with these side panels, begin to glue the assembly together in the way shown in Fig 20.7, except that here you must prepare a piece of scrap timber to the thickness you will need between the shelving instead of using the drawers in the aforementioned method. Note the position of the back panel relative to the side panels on section *b-b*, Fig 21.1b.

DIVIDERS K The dividers K can now be cut to fit the space available and dividers K1 can be cut to the shape shown in Fig 21.10: dividers K2 are not shaped. Trace the shape for dividers K1 onto the timber surface and cut it out with a knife, finishing off by rubbing the curved portions with abrasive paper wrapped around a pencil. Now prepare those surfaces that will be on display to receive the finish and then cut out and glue the trims onto the outer face to give the panelling effect.

FILING ASSEMBLY Q AND DRAWERS S This is a mirror image of assembly P as far as the carcass is concerned, and the method described for the construction of that assembly can be applied here for the shelving.

To construct the drawers, butt the front panel to the edge of, and at right angles to, the base panel. Follow this with each side panel, which should be glued to the top surface of the base panel and butted and glued to the front panel. Now glue the back panel inside the side panels and on top of the base panel.

Use the drawers to place the dividers in their correct position and at the spacing to suit the drawers. Begin at the top of the assembly so that the vertical divider can be glued in position first of all, and then follow the method suggested in Fig 20.7 for placing the rest of the dividers. Once they are in place, the vertical divider can be glued in position and the rest of the shelves can follow. To make sure they line up with the drawer dividers, you can use the drawers as spacers.

The front panels of the drawers should now be prepared by scraping and then rubbing down with abrasive paper and wire wool, ready for the finish to be applied.

PIGEON-HOLE ASSEMBLY T AND DRAWERS U The exploded view of this assembly in Fig 21.11 will give you some idea as to how the elements are to fit together and as these are all of the same width, the Minicraft bench saw can provide you with consistency of length where repetitive parts are required. When all the parts are ready for assembly, start by gluing the end pieces to the back panel, making sure that they are at right angles to each other. Now glue the shelving above the drawers to the side and back panels, followed by the two vertical pieces

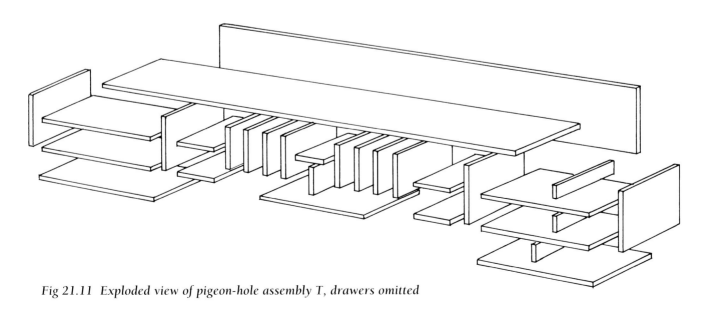

Fig 21.11 Exploded view of pigeon-hole assembly T, drawers omitted

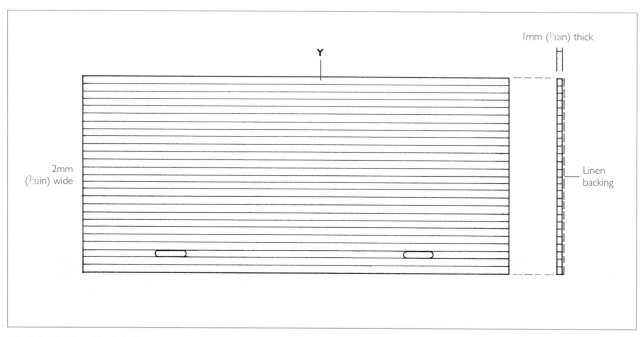

Fig 21.12 Detail of sliding cover

whose faces abutt the edges of the shelves. This done, you can make the drawers, as shown on the front view and in section *a-a*, Fig 21.1a, to fit into the space provided. (*See also* Fig 18.2.) Carry on gluing the rest of the elements in position, checking with the drawing at each stage and making sure that all parts are at right angles to each other.

DRAWERS V UNDER DESK TOP PANEL These are to be made up to the depth allocated for the parts R and block F. The overall length when placed next to parts R should be exactly the same length as for the pigeon-hole assembly.

You will see that these drawers are fitted with brass drawer pulls which can be applied when the surface of the timber has been prepared, ready to receive the finish.

PANEL W This will become the bottom panel of the desk top drawer unit, as shown on the front view and section *a-a*, Fig 21.1a, and will be exactly the same length as the desk top panel E.

TRIMS I These are simply strips of timber used to finish off the exterior appearance of the side panels C. To give them a bit of character, I cut a groove along their length and rounded off the ends as indicated on section *c-c* in Fig 21.1b, Fig 21.13 and the front view.

SLIDING COVER Y If you have managed to get the strips mentioned in the cutting list to be 2mm (³/₃₂ in) wide throughout their length, then it is a relatively simple matter to construct this cover.

Cut out 26 strips of timber to the length indicated in Fig 21.12. Lay a sheet of linen on a flat surface and coat it with glue. Whilst the glue is still tacky, lay the strips of timber side by side and touching each other, until you have reached the extent required.

Now trim the area with a knife and check that the strips have not stuck together anywhere. If they have, ease them apart with a thin knife blade.

Trim one edge to be perfectly square with the adjacent edges and check that the cover will move smoothly along the groove in panel C. Now judge the overall length from the front view and trim the edge to suit. Again, check that this end will run smoothly in its appropriate groove and then, with the pigeon-hole assembly and the cover in place, clamp the two side panels C in position, checking at the same time that the cover still moves easily. If it doesn't, trim the edges to suit.

EXTERIOR PANEL TRIMS X Cut these out to the lengths shown in Fig 21.13 and carefully glue them in position, making sure that they look rectangular and are not askew.

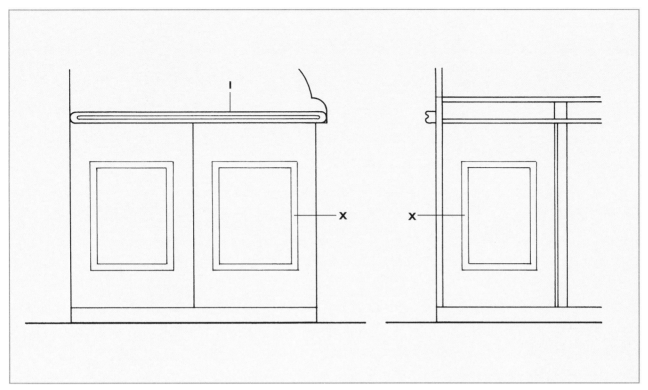

Fig 21.13 Detail of panelling on side panels

ASSEMBLY

Before you begin, ensure that parts A, B, E, F and W, together with the pigeon-hole assembly, are all of identical length, then proceed as follows:

1 Glue panel A to panel C, one end only.
2 With panel D fitted loosely in position, glue block B to A and C. *Make sure that the bottom edge does not encroach upon the sliding cover groove.*
3 Remove panel D.
4 Glue panel W to panel C.
5 Glue block F to panel C.
6 Place the end drawer under the desk top, loosely in position, then locate and glue the divider R to block F and panel W. Remove the drawer to prevent the glue sticking to it and when the glue has set, place the middle drawer in position and locate and glue the other divider R to block F and panel W. Remove the drawer.
7 Glue desk top panel E to panel C, dividers R and block F.
8 Glue pigeon-hole assembly to panel C, noting the position from section *a-a*, Fig 21.1a, so that it does not interfere with the groove.

9 With the sliding cover in place, glue the second end panel C to the ends of parts A to W, inclusive. *Check the movement of the sliding cover before the glue has time to set in case you need to make any last minute adjustments to the ends of the cover. Check also that the drawer at the end fits into the space provided and moves easily.*

10 Now comes a tricky operation. That is to drill 1mm ($\frac{1}{32}$ in) diameter holes in the positions shown on section *c-c*, Fig 21.1b. To locate the holes, place the assemblies P and Q, with their brass wires in place, into their relative positions regarding the panels C, and mark off where the holes are required. Check the distance in from the outside face of panel C to locate the position of the hole in that direction. If you have managed to do that, see if assemblies P and Q move as they should. *If, by any chance, you cannot drill easily from underneath the desk unit, you may have to resort to some other method of forming the required hole. You may find that a 1mm ($\frac{1}{32}$ in) diameter steel rod made red hot will do to penetrate the timber. After all, you don't have to go too far in order to provide a hole into which the brass-wire pivots are to operate.*

11 Locate the holes in the pedestal H and drill them part way through as indicated on section *a-a*, Fig 21.1a. With the assemblies P and Q in place, put the pedestal into its final position. *Check that the assemblies still move easily and are not too slack. Should they be slack, adjustment can be made to the end of panel C.*

12 With the assemblies P and Q in place, glue the pedestal to panels C.

13 Glue rear panel D to panel A, block B, pedestal H and panels C. *Check that the back face is flush with the outer edges of the panels.*

14 Glue panels L and M to the underside of panel W and to the sides of the pedestal H as shown on the front view. These must then be kept in place by holding them against the pedestal until the glue has set. At the same time and whilst the glue is still tacky, glue panel J to panel W. This helps to trap the top edge of panels L and M and helps to form the curved portion of these panels. *Should the panels spring away from the pedestal, you may have to use either superglue or some fine pins to secure them. I had no trouble with the first method. One suggestion that could prevent such a thing happening is if you pre-form the curves using steam or by some other method.*

15 Glue panel O to panels L, M and J. You will have to tuck panel O up behind panel J and against the face of the pedestal H.

16 Glue trims I to sides of panels C.

FINISHING

The finish can be either clear polyurethane varnish, mahogany varnish, or wax.

Varnish finishes require plenty of time between applications, preferably overnight, and before each coat is added, the surface must be rubbed down with fine abrasive paper and wire wool.

If all surfaces on display have been prepared as for panel A, you may find that you have a very smooth finish to start with and may only need a beeswax finish to complete the job. If so, then it should be applied with wire wool and left for at least three hours before it is polished. There is less trouble when applying a wax finish, but it won't give you the glossy effect of a varnish.

CHIPPENDALE-STYLE BUREAU

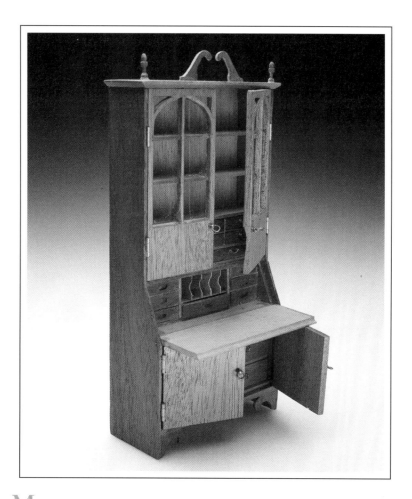

Many of the bureaux of this type are attributed to Chippendale. It is mainly the interior arrangement of the drawers and pigeon holes that differs from the original design.

The model shown here was made in beech, but if it is authenticity that you require then mahogany or walnut are the timbers to give it that period look.

FRONT VIEW AND CROSS SECTION

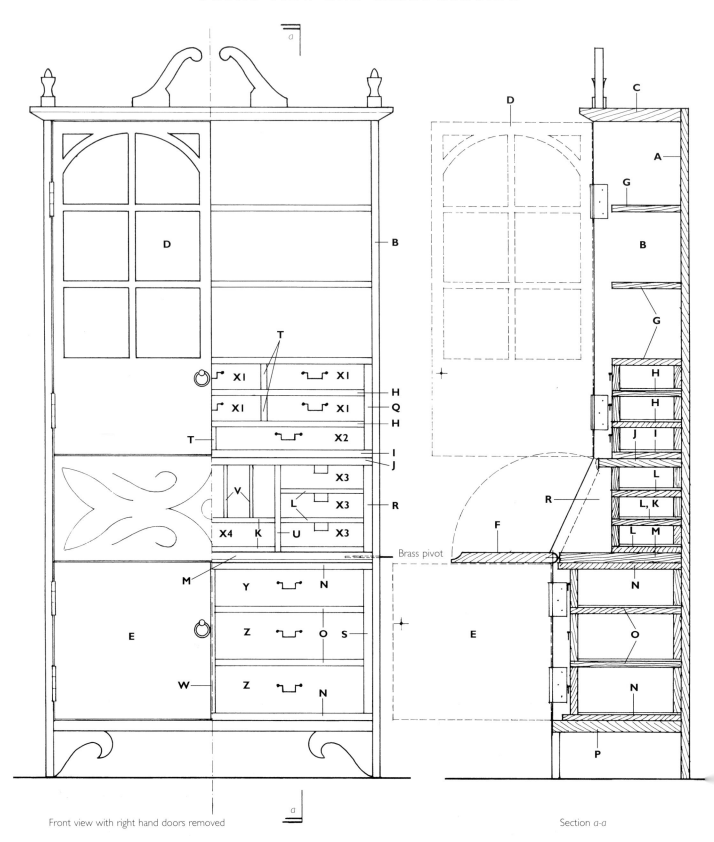

Front view with right hand doors removed

Section *a-a*

Fig 22.1 Chippendale-style Bureau: Plan

CUTTING LIST

Beech, mahogany or walnut.

A Rear panel (1) 180 × 86 × 2mm (7$\frac{1}{8}$ × 3$\frac{1}{2}$ × $\frac{3}{32}$in)

B Side panels (2) 175 × 40 × 2mm (7 × 1$\frac{5}{8}$ × $\frac{3}{32}$in)

C Top panel (1) 100 × 26 × 3mm (4 × 1$\frac{1}{8}$ × $\frac{1}{8}$in)

D and **E** Doors (4) 270 × 45 × 3mm (10$\frac{5}{8}$ × 1$\frac{3}{4}$ × $\frac{1}{8}$in)

F Desk flap (1) 90 × 30 × 3mm (3$\frac{5}{8}$ × 1$\frac{1}{4}$ × $\frac{1}{8}$in)

G Shelves (3) 270 × 20 × 1.5mm (10$\frac{5}{8}$ × $\frac{7}{8}$ × $\frac{1}{16}$in)

H Separators (2) 90 × 20 × 1.5mm (3$\frac{5}{8}$ × $\frac{7}{8}$ × $\frac{1}{16}$in)

I Separators (1) 90 × 20 × 2mm (3$\frac{5}{8}$ × $\frac{7}{8}$ × $\frac{3}{32}$in)

J Separators (1) 90 × 25 × 2mm (3$\frac{3}{4}$ × 1 × $\frac{3}{32}$in)

K Separators (6) 25 × 20 × 1.5mm (1 × $\frac{7}{8}$ × $\frac{1}{16}$in)

L Separators (2) 40 × 20 × 1.5mm (1$\frac{5}{8}$ × $\frac{7}{8}$ × $\frac{1}{16}$in)

M Desk top (1) 90 × 35 × 3mm (3$\frac{5}{8}$ × 1$\frac{3}{8}$ × $\frac{1}{8}$in)

N and **O** Separators (6) 360 × 35 × 1.5mm (14$\frac{1}{4}$ × 1$\frac{3}{8}$ × $\frac{1}{16}$in)

P Base (1) 90 × 35 × 3mm (3$\frac{5}{8}$ × 1$\frac{3}{8}$ × $\frac{1}{8}$in)

Q Packs (2) 25 × 20 × 1.5mm (1 × $\frac{7}{8}$ × $\frac{1}{16}$in)

R and **S** Packs (4) 130 × 35 × 1.5mm (5$\frac{1}{8}$ × 1$\frac{3}{8}$ × $\frac{1}{16}$in)

T and **U** Dividers (7) 90 × 20 × 1.5mm (3$\frac{5}{8}$ × $\frac{7}{8}$ × $\frac{1}{16}$in)

V Divider (4) 60 × 20 × 0.75mm (2$\frac{3}{8}$ × $\frac{7}{8}$ × $\frac{1}{32}$in)

W Divider (1) 40 × 35 × 3mm (1$\frac{5}{8}$ × 1$\frac{3}{8}$ × $\frac{1}{8}$in)

X1 to **X4** Drawers

   fronts (15) 410 × 6 × 2mm (16$\frac{1}{8}$ × $\frac{1}{4}$ × $\frac{3}{32}$in)

   backs (15) 410 × 6 × 1.5mm (16$\frac{1}{8}$ × $\frac{1}{4}$ × $\frac{1}{16}$in)

   sides (30) from 2: 300 × 6 × 1.5mm (12 × $\frac{1}{4}$ × $\frac{1}{16}$in)

   bases (15) from 2: 240 × 17 × 0.75mm (9$\frac{1}{2}$ × $\frac{3}{4}$ × $\frac{1}{32}$in)

Y Drawers

   fronts (2) 90 × 10 × 2mm (3$\frac{5}{8}$ × $\frac{1}{2}$ × $\frac{3}{32}$in)

   backs (2) 90 × 10 × 1.5mm (3$\frac{5}{8}$ × $\frac{1}{2}$ × $\frac{1}{16}$in)

   sides (4) 60 × 10 × 1.5mm (2$\frac{3}{8}$ × $\frac{1}{2}$ × $\frac{1}{16}$in)

   bases (2) 90 × 30 × 0.75mm (3$\frac{5}{8}$ × 1$\frac{1}{4}$ × $\frac{1}{32}$in)

Z Drawers

   fronts (4) 180 × 15 × 2mm (7$\frac{1}{8}$ × $\frac{5}{8}$ × $\frac{3}{32}$in)

   backs (4) 180 × 15 × 1.5mm (7$\frac{1}{8}$ × $\frac{5}{8}$ × $\frac{1}{16}$in)

   sides (8) 120 × 15 × 1.5mm (4$\frac{3}{4}$ × $\frac{5}{8}$ × $\frac{1}{16}$in)

   bases (4) 180 × 30 × 0.75mm (7$\frac{1}{8}$ × 1$\frac{1}{4}$ × $\frac{1}{32}$in)

Sizes throughout allow for some wastage during cutting and fitting.

PREPARATION AND CONSTRUCTION

REAR PANEL A It is a good idea to begin with this because it will form the foundation upon which the rest of the elements are to be built. It is a simple rectangular panel whose size can be obtained from Fig 22.2. Cut it out with a straightedge and knife or, if possible, use a minicraft bench saw so that you can get clean cut edges that are not only square but parallel. This is to allow the side panels B to butt up against the edges without leaving gaps.

Rub down the outer surface with a scraper, followed by fine abrasive paper and wire wool to prepare for the finish.

SIDE PANELS B The sizes of this panel can be obtained from Fig 22.2. Cut it out with a knife and straightedge. The inside face of each panel must be chased out to accommodate the brass hinges in the positions shown, following the method described under Hingeing in Chapter 2.

Prepare the outer faces as for the rear panel, ready for the finish to be applied.

TOP PANEL C A plan view is shown on Fig 22.3. The cut away portion is to be such that the rear panel A will fit snugly inside, with the back face flush with the edges. The chamfer can then be cut, using a knife and straightedge, with the bottom of the chamfer coinciding with the widths of the side panels and the

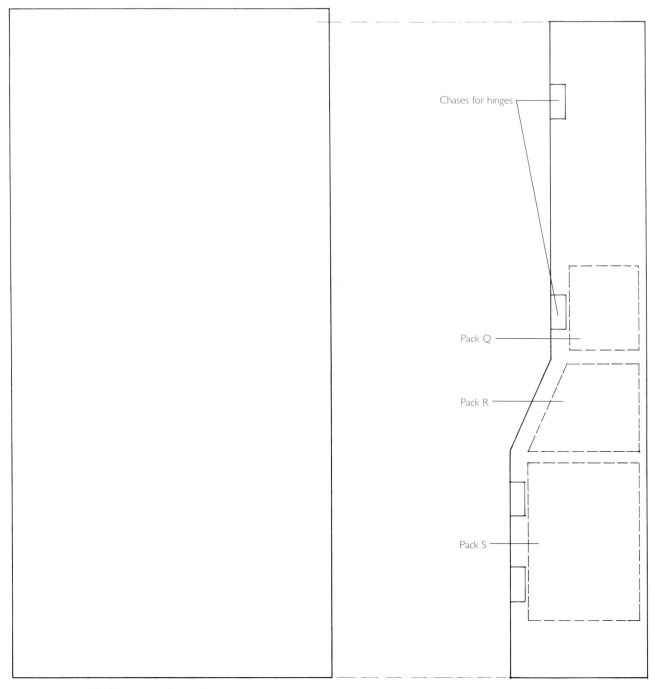

Fig 22.2 Detail of rear panel A and side panels B

rear panel, as can be seen on the front view and on section *a-a*, Fig 22.1.

SHELVING G Their lengths are to be the same as the width of the rear panel A.

DOORS D Trace the 'windows' from Fig 22.4 onto the timber surface, using carbon paper, and drill a small hole in or near the corner of each pane, through which to feed the fret saw blade. Cut out the shapes indicated with care. Rub down the front edges to form a chamfer as shown and then glue a sheet of thin perspex to the inside face of each hole. An alternative would be to cut out the basic inside shape where the windows are to fit and then make up the mullion and cross members of each window using thin strips of timber with a piece of perspex sandwiched between them as shown in Fig 22.4. The windows can then be

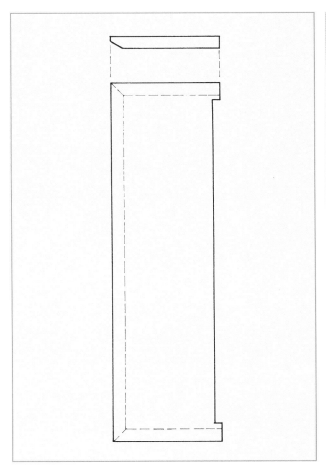

Fig 22.3 Detail of top panel C

the separator I is in its correct position as indicated on section *a-a*.

Prepare the drawer fronts ready to accept the finish by rubbing down once again, with a scraper, abrasive paper and wire wool.

Drill the necessary holes required for the drawer pulls using a 1mm ($\frac{1}{32}$ in) diameter drill bit.

DIVIDERS T These are to be to the same depth as the drawer fronts and cut out to the length indicated by section *a-a*. A Minicraft bench saw will ensure that the lengths are maintained.

PACKS Q, R AND S These are to be cut out to the shapes shown in Fig 22.2.

It is worth noting that when pack R is eventually glued in position, its sloping edge will act as a stop for the desk flap and should, therefore, be parallel to the sloping portion of the side panels, and be the thickness of the desk flap away, so that the face of the flap is flush with the edge of the side panels B. This can be readily seen in section *a-a*.

DIVIDERS U These should be cut out to the same depth as pack R, so it may be as well if you wait until this depth can be ascertained during assembly. You

fitted and glued into the door frame. If you adopt this latter method, be sure to check that the horizontal members are in accord with the drawing.

The hinges will need recessing, as explained under Hingeing in Chapter 2, and a 1mm ($\frac{1}{32}$ in) diameter hole drilled where indicated to receive the door pulls.

Prepare the outer surface, rubbing down with a scraper, abrasive paper and wire wool, ready to accept the finish.

DRAWERS X1 AND X2 Make these up as indicated on the front view, section *a-a* and Fig 22.5, but before cutting out the drawer fronts, you should determine the length of each piece by the method shown in Fig 22.6. This will ensure that when assembly takes place, the drawers will fit comfortably into the spaces provided.

The height of each drawer front can be treated in the same manner but using separators H instead of the dividers and packs in Fig 22.6. This is to be sure that

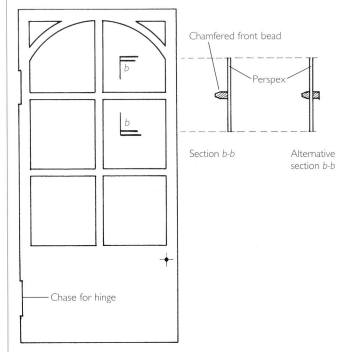

Fig 22.4 Detail of door and alternative 'window' construction

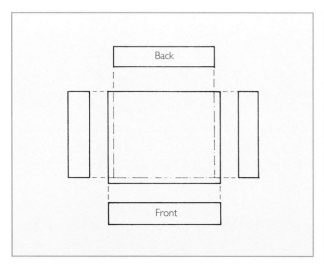

Fig 22.5 Typical drawer construction

can, of course, cut them out using the front view as a guide, and fit them later.

DIVIDERS V These are to be cut out to the depth of two drawer fronts X3 plus one separator L and then shaped as shown in Fig 22.7 using a bead saw, a knife and a piece of abrasive paper wrapped around some dowel. To make life a bit easier, and in order to make sure that they are all identical, it would be best if,

before you shape them, you clamp all of them together and then cut them to shape.

DIVIDER W This is to be cut out to the size indicated on the front view.

SEPARATORS L These are to be the same length as drawers X3 and the same width as separators H.

SEPARATORS K These are to be the same length as drawer X4 and the same width as separator L.

DRAWERS X3 AND X4 The shapes for these drawer fronts are shown on Fig 22.7 together with the cutouts for the finger recesses along the top edges. These can be cut out with a bead saw and miniature chisel.

The fronts can now be prepared, ready to receive the finish.

DESK TOP M This is a simple, rectangular piece of timber of the same overall length as the width of the rear panel, and should have perfectly square edges to butt into the side panels B. Prepare the top face, ready to receive the finish.

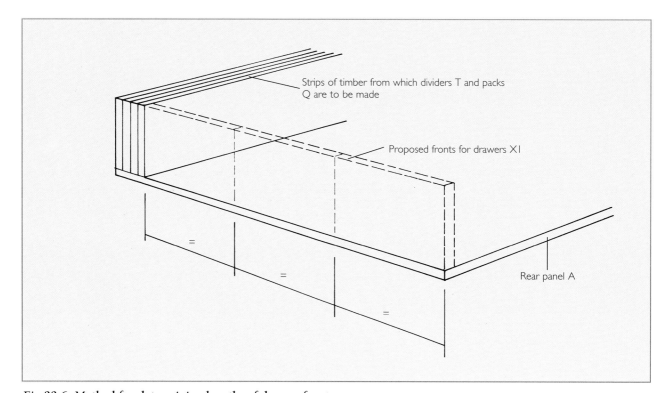

Fig 22.6 Method for determining lengths of drawer fronts

DESK FLAP F If you have managed to obtain the overall depth of the drawer units X3 and their separators L in accordance with the drawing, then the desk flap will be the same width as shown on section *a-a*. If this is not so, adjustments will need to be made to the flap in order for it to fit properly in its closed position. The overall length of the flap is the same as the width of the rear panel A.

Shape the top edge as shown in section *a-a*, so that when the flap is in the closed position it will fit onto the edge of separator J and be flush with the edge of the side panel B.

When you have reached these objectives, the next thing to do is to decorate the face of the flap. The design I have used is my own invention. You may like to try your skill in some other way.

Now prepare the surface, using a scraper, abrasive paper and wire wool, ready to accept the finish.

SEPARATORS N These two separators are to be cut to the same length as the width of the rear panel A and to the widths shown on section *a-a*.

DRAWERS Y AND Z The drawer fronts are to be as shown in Fig 22.7 and their lengths should be checked by a similar method to that shown in Fig 22.6.

The surfaces should be prepared, ready to receive the finish, and then holes are to be drilled to accept the drawer pulls as indicated on the front view.

SEPARATORS O The lengths and widths of these four separators are to be exactly the same as the length and width of the drawers adjacent to them.

DOOR E Cut both leaves as shown in the front view and when placed side by side, they should be of the same overall size as the width of the rear panel A. Chase out the recesses for the hinges in the positions shown (*see* Hingeing in Chapter 2) and drill holes 1mm ($^{1}/_{32}$ in) diameter for the door pulls where indicated.

Prepare the outer face, ready to accept the finish, by first scraping, and then rubbing down with a fine abrasive paper and wire wool.

Check that the depth of each leaf is the same as the depth of the drawers Y and Z, two separators O and two separators N. If not, trim the door to suit. The top edge of each leaf acts as a stop for the desk flap so be sure that it is at the right level when it comes to fixing it in position.

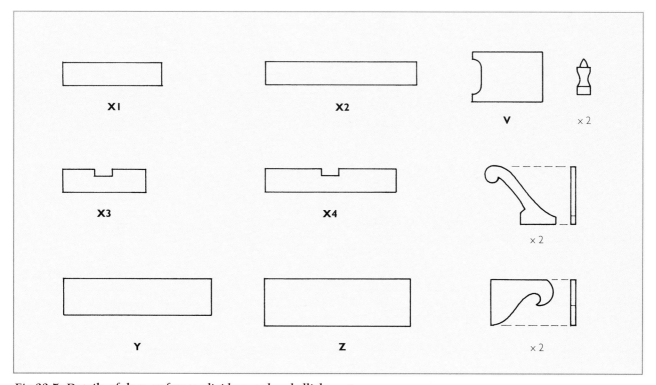

Fig 22.7 Details of drawer fronts, dividers and embellishments

EMBELLISHMENTS These are shown in Fig 22.7 and, with the exception of the turned finials, can be traced from the drawing onto the surface of some scrap pieces of timber and cut out with a fret saw. The finials can be turned by the method described in Fig 10.5.

BASE P This is a simple rectangular piece of timber whose length is identical to the width of the rear panel. It should have square edges to fit into the side panels without any gaps showing.

ASSEMBLY

1 Glue side panels B to rear panel A.

2 Glue top panel C to side and rear panels.

3 Glue shelves G to side and rear panels. *Make sure of their final position by placing the door leaves D loosely in place and checking that the shelves coincide with the horizontal members of the window frames.*

4 With doors D in place, position separator J so that it touches the underside of the door panel as shown on section *a-a*. Glue the separator to the side and rear panels. *Check that all parts are at right angles to each other.*

5 Glue pack Q to side panel, rear panel and shelf G.

6 Turn the bureau upside down and position the dividers T by placing drawers X1 alongside and then glue the dividers to the underside face of the shelf and to the rear panel A. *Remove the drawers before the glue has time to set.*

7 Glue separator H to dividers T, packs Q and rear panel.

8 Repeat for the next layer of drawers.

9 Turn the bureau the right way up and place separator I on top of separator J. *Check that the dividers T and the drawers will fit into the available space. Some rubbing down may be required for the drawers to move freely.*

10 Remove the drawers and glue the separator I to the side panels, divider T, packs Q and rear panel A.

11 Glue packs R to side panels, separator J and rear panel.

12 Glue desk top M to packs R, side panels and rear panel. *Make sure it is at right angles to its adjacent parts.*

13 Glue separator N to underside of desk top M, side panels and rear panel.

14 Glue packs S to side panels and top separator N, and to rear panel.

15 Using the method shown in Fig 20.7, determine the position of the drawer separators O and glue them to the packs S and rear panel.

16 Position divider W so that it is central in the width of the rear panel and glue to the ends of separators O, separator N (top one only) and rear panel. *Check that the drawers Y and Z fit into the spaces provided.*

17 Glue separators O into place. (*See* Fig 20.7.)

18 Glue bottom separator N to divider W, packs S and rear panel.

19 Glue base P to bottom separator N, side panels and rear panel. *Check that the bottom drawers fit into the available space and adjust where necessary.*

20 Glue finials and other embellishments in the positions shown on the front view and section *a-a*.

21 Now that the gluing is completed, the time has come to fit the doors and the desk flap. Attach hinges to doors first and offer them up to side panels where indicated. *If you find that the doors don't operate as they should, then refer to the method of hingeing as shown on Fig 2.12 and when ready, superglue the hinges to the side panels and then pin them.*

22 Place desk flap in its final closed position and whilst holding it in place, drill through the side panels and into the edges of the flap from each side using a 1mm ($^1/_{32}$ in) diameter drill bit. You will have to do this with bated breath, a steady hand and with fingers crossed. When you are sure you have managed that, insert the brass wire into each hole. *Check that the flap not only moves as it should but that when it is in the open position, it is level with the desk top M as can be seen in section *a-a*.*

FINISHING

By now, all exposed parts should have been prepared, so all that is required is a coat of varnish which can be either clear polyurethane, mahogany varnish if mahogany has been used, or a clear varnish if beech has been used. Remember to allow sufficient time between each application and to rub down well between coats with wire wool.

BUREAU BOOKCASE

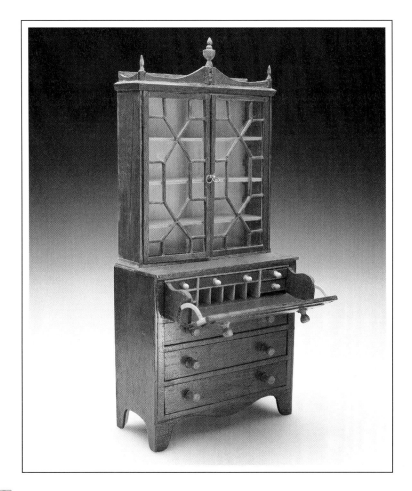

This can only be described as a pseudo Federal/Georgian-style bureau since the top, or what is properly called a 'pediment', is of Federal origin whereas the arrangement of the glass panels is typically Georgian in design. Mahogany was used for the majority of the model and lime for the drawer pulls.

FRONT AND SIDE VIEWS

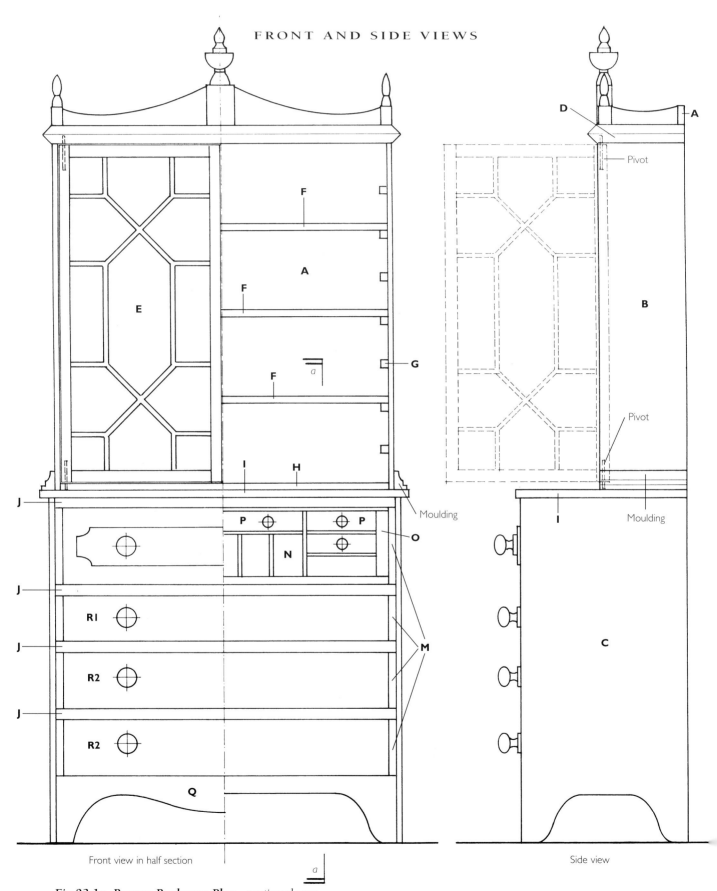

Front view in half section

Side view

Fig 23.1a Bureau Bookcase: Plan - *continued over*

CROSS SECTION

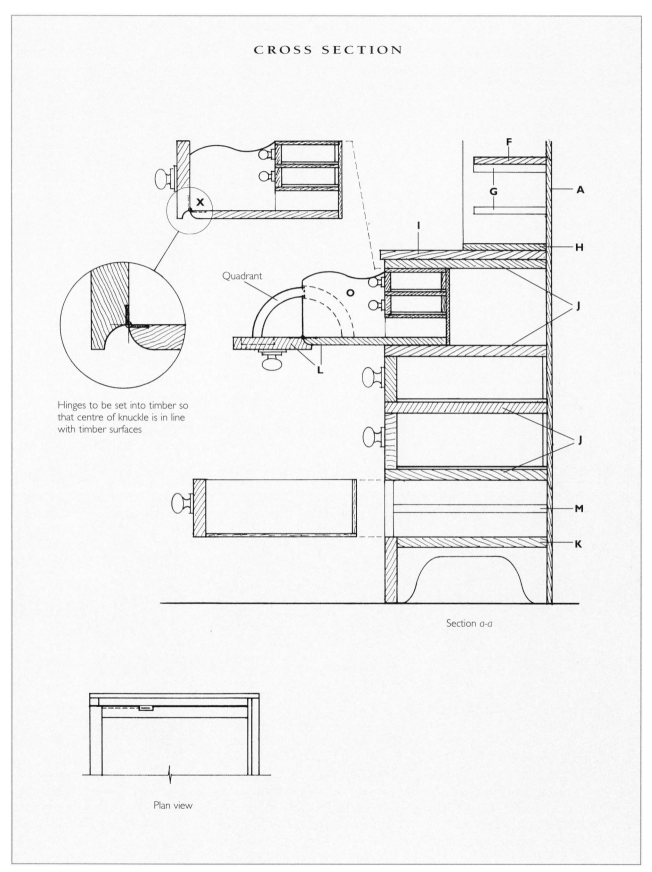

Quadrant

Hinges to be set into timber so
that centre of knuckle is in line
with timber surfaces

Section *a-a*

Plan view

Fig 23.1b Bureau Bookcase: Plan - *continued*

CUTTING LIST

Mahogany; lime.

A Rear panel (1) 200 × 95 × 1.5mm (8 × 3¾ × ¹/₁₆in)

B Side panels (2) 190 × 25 × 1.5mm (7½ × 1 × ¹/₁₆in)

C Side panels (2) 190 × 45 × 1.5mm (7½ × 1¾ × ¹/₁₆in)

D Top panel (1) 95 × 25 × 5mm (3¾ × 1 × ³/₁₆in)

E Doors (2) from 2: 300 × 3 × 2mm (12 × ⅛ × ³/₃₂in) +
from 2: 300 × 1.5 × 1.5mm (12 × ¹/₁₆ × ¹/₁₆in)

F Shelves (3) 270 × 20 × 2mm (10⅝ × ⅞ × ³/₃₂in)

G Shelf supports (14) 280 × 3 × 2mm (11 × ⅛ × ³/₃₂in)

H Panel (1) 90 × 22 × 2mm (3⅝ × 1 × ³/₃₂in)

I Panel (1) 100 × 46 × 2mm (4 × 2 × ³/₃₂in)

J Separators (4) 360 × 45 × 3mm (14¼ × 2 × ⅛in)

K Base (1) 90 × 40 × 3mm (3⅝ × 1⅝ × ⅛in)

L Desk top (1) 90 × 40 × 2mm (3⅝ × 1⅝ × ³/₃₂in) +
90 × 20 × 4mm (3⅝ × 1 × ³/₁₆in)

M Side pieces (14) 410 × 2 × 2mm (16⅛ × ³/₃₂ × ³/₃₂in)

N Pigeon-hole assembly (12) 290 × 16 × 1mm
(11½ × ⅝ × ¹/₃₂in) + 90 × 20 × 1mm (3⅝ × 1 × ¹/₃₂in)

O Pigeon-hole sides (2) 40 × 20 × 3mm (1⅝ × 1 × ⅛in)

P Drawers in pigeon hole

fronts (5) 125 × 5 × 1.5mm (5 × ¼ × ¹/₁₆in)

backs (5) 125 × 5 × 1mm (5 × ¼ × ¹/₃₂in)

sides (10) 150 × 5 × 1mm (6 × ¼ × ¹/₃₂in)

bases (5) 125 × 16 × 0.75mm (5 × ⅝ × ¹/₃₂in)

Q Pedestal front panel (1) 95 × 20 × 3mm (3¾ × 1 × ⅛in)

R Main drawers

fronts (3) 90 × 45 × 3mm (3⅝ × 1¾ × ⅛in)

backs (3) 90 × 45 × 1mm (3⅝ × 1¾ × ¹/₃₂in)

sides (6) 90 × 40 × 1mm (3⅝ × 1⅝ × ¹/₃₂in)

bases (3) 270 × 40 × 0.75mm (10⅝ × 1⅝ × ¹/₃₂in)

Pediment can be made from scrap pieces of timber.
Moulding can be obtained by mail order.
Sizes given allow for cutting and fitting.

Fig 23.2 Detail of rear panel A

PREPARATION AND CONSTRUCTION

REAR PANEL A Cut this out to the shape shown on Fig 23.2 and make the edges square since they are to butt up to the faces of the side panels and so avoid unsightly gaps when assembled.

SIDE PANELS B AND SHELF SUPPORTS G
The side panels are plain rectangular pieces of timber as can be seen on the side view. Cut them out and then cut, fit and glue the shelf supports in the positions indicated on the front view and section *a-a*, Fig 23.1b. Match the spacing on the opposite side panel and check that they are parallel to the top edges and to each other. As the rear panel A will be fixed inside the side panels and its face flush with the edges, it means that the shelf supports are to be set in from the back edge of the side panel. The best way to make sure of this is to lay the rear panel on a flat surface, butt the side panel up against it, then locate the shelf supports. Cut the shelf supports to the lengths shown on section *a-a* and glue them to the side panels B in the positions indicated on the front view. Remove the rear panel before the glue sets.

Prepare the surface to receive the finish by scraping and then rubbing down with fine abrasive paper and wire wool.

SIDE PANEL C Trace the shape of this panel from the side view, using carbon paper, and then cut out the profile with a fret saw.

Prepare the outer surface to receive the finish, as for the side panels, above.

TOP PANEL D Cut out to the shape shown in Fig 23.3, with a bead saw and knife. The chamfers shown on the three sides can be roughly shaped with a knife and steel straightedge, and then rubbed down with abrasive paper wrapped around a block of timber, making sure that the bottom edge is coincident with the overall width of the bureau and side panels as shown on the front and side views. (*See* Assembly of doors regarding the drilling for the wire pivots.)

PANEL H This is the same length as the width of the rear panel and the same width as the width of panel B. (*See* Assembly of doors regarding the drilling for the wire pivots.)

SHELVES F These are to be the same length as the width of the rear panel and the same width as that shown on section *a-a*, Fig 23.1b. It will be noticed that the front edge is set back to accommodate the thickness of the door frames.

ASSEMBLY OF DOORS E

1 Lay a thin sheet of perspex over the front view.
2 Cut out sides of frames and glue to perspex.
3 Cut out, fit and glue top and bottom pieces of frame to perspex and to side pieces. The frame should now correspond exactly with the drawing.
4 Cut out interior pane dividers and fit and glue to perspex.
5 Repeat steps 1 to 4 for other door.
6 When the glue has set, trim perspex to frame size. *Check that the two doors, when laid side by side, correspond to the width of the rear panel A.*

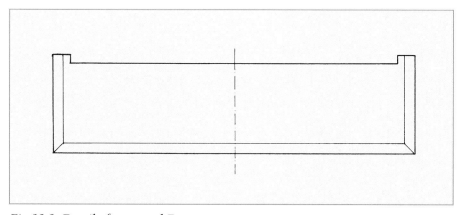

Fig 23.3 Detail of top panel D

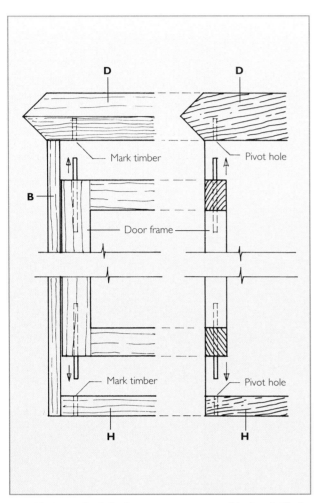

Fig 23.4 Method for locating positions of holes drilled to receive brass wire pins

7 Round off vertical edge of each leaf adjacent to side panels B, so that when the door swings open it will not bind.

8 Carefully drill into the ends of vertical side pieces of each door, to receive the brass wire pins which are to act as pivots. A 1mm ($^1/_{32}$ in) diameter hole will be needed and as the frame member is so very thin, the greatest possible care is required, together with a steady hand.

9 Insert brass wire in the top and bottom holes and using them, locate the position of the hole required in top panel D as shown on the front and side views. Do this by placing the door frame in the position shown in Fig 23.4 and mark off where the pivot touches the top panel.

10 Drill the hole part way through. Locate the holes required in panel H by the method shown in Fig 23.4.

11 Drill 1mm ($^1/_{32}$ in) diameter holes in the face of each leaf to accommodate the door pulls. Make sure the pulls are a tight fit. If they aren't, you can use superglue.

PANELS I The shape of this panel can be obtained from Fig 23.5. Cut out the shape with a bead saw and knife.

Prepare the upper surface using a scraper, abrasive paper and wire wool, ready to receive the finish.

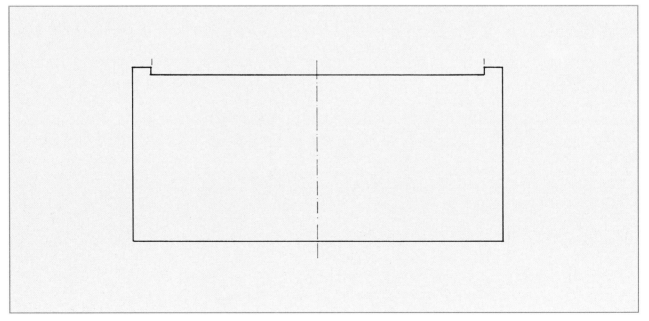

Fig 23.5 Detail of panel I

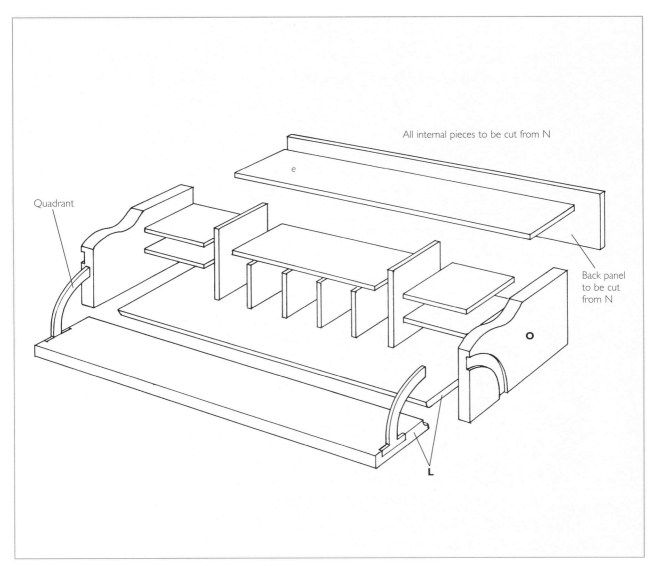

Quadrant

All internal pieces to be cut from N

e

Back panel
to be cut
from N

L

Fig 23.6 Exploded view of pigeon-hole assembly N

SEPARATORS J For consistency in the length and
width of these panels, a Minicraft bench saw is a must.
It also gives the square edges needed.

BASE K Use the bench saw, with the length set for
the separators J, to cut this panel and then adjust
when cutting the width to that shown on section *a-a*,
Fig 23.1b.

PEDESTAL FRONT PANEL Q Trace this shape
onto the timber surface using carbon paper, as shown
in Fig 2.1. Cut out the profile with a fret saw and
check that the overall length corresponds to the width
of the rear panel A.

Prepare the outer face, ready to receive the finish.

PIGEON-HOLE ASSEMBLY N Cut out the width
of the partitions to that shown on section *a-a*,
Fig 23.1b, and the exploded view, using the bench
saw for consistency in size, and cut the back panel to
the height shown on section *a-a*. The length of the
back panel will be the same as the width of the rear
panel A.

The exploded view of the pigeon-hole assembly
(*see* Fig 23.6) will help you to visualise how the
components fit together.

DESK TOP L This is made up of two rectangular
pieces of timber of different thicknesses as can be seen
in section *a-a*. The lengths of each are the same and
correspond to the length of the main drawer fronts.

The detail of joint X (*see* section *a-a*, Fig 23.1b) indicates how the edges of the two panels are to be shaped so that when the desk flap is in the open position, its top face is flush with the panel at its rear and when closed, it will fit snugly into the gap between separators J. It also demonstrates how the hinges are to be let into the surface so that the centre of the knuckle is coincident with the upper surface of the desk top. The ends of the desk flaps are to be chased out with a small chisel to receive the cross bar of the quadrants as shown on section *a-a*.

The front of the desk flap, when in the closed position, is to have a decorative strip of timber glued to its surface. The shape of the strip can be seen on the front view.

Prepare both surfaces ready to receive the finish.

SIDE PIECES M These are short lengths of timber which will be glued to the side panels B and to the separators J when the latter are fixed in position. Cut them to the lengths shown on the front elevation and section *a-a*, Figs 23.1a and 1b, and glue them to the side panels C in the positions indicated. Notice, from section *a-a*, how the strips are at right angles to the vertical strips. This is to make sure that the drawers do not slip sideways when moved in and out.

SIDES O Using carbon paper, trace the shapes shown in Fig 23.7, including the grooves, onto the timber surface. Now cut out the profile with a fret saw and chase out the grooves with a miniature chisel and knife as indicated in Fig 20.3. It should be noted that the depth of the grooves must be to the thickness of the quadrant so that when the pigeon-hole assembly is closed up, the quadrants do not catch on the sides of

the side pieces M. Both faces of sides O are to be prepared to receive the finish, by using a scraper and then rubbing down with abrasive paper and wire wool.

ASSEMBLY OF PIGEON-HOLE UNIT

1 Glue the sides O onto the top side of the desk top L. *Make sure that they are at right angles to the desk top. Check that the desk top fits into the space allocated for it by laying the rear panel A on a flat surface and loosely assembling the side panels B and side pieces M as shown in Fig 23.8.*

2 Glue the back panel to the ends of sides O so that the ends overlap as can be seen on section *a-a*.

3 Glue the topmost piece *e*, as shown on the exploded view, onto the tops of each side piece O and to the back panel.

4 Glue the horizontal drawer dividers to the sides O and to the back panel. (*See* Fig 23.9.) *Remove the drawer before the glue sets.*

5 Repeat step 4 for the next drawer divider.

6 Glue the vertical dividers to the ends of the horizontal dividers, the panel *e* and the back panel.

7 Follow the same procedure for the other dividers.

8 Fit and glue the central horizontal divider to the vertical dividers and the back panel. *Check that all the drawers will fit into the spaces provided.*

9 Make up the drawers, ensuring that all of their component parts are at right angles to each other. *When this is done, check again that they have free movement in their respective holes. If they are tight, rub down the parts with abrasive paper until they do move smoothly. Note that the face of the drawer fronts are to be flush with the edges of the dividers.*

10 Fit and glue in place the four vertical dividers so that they are parallel to each other and at right angles to the adjacent surfaces. *You will need a pair of tweezers for this exercise and a piece of paper marked out as shown in Fig 23.10.*

11 Hinge the desk flap to the desk top L, as shown in section *a-a*, and superglue and pin the hinges in position.

12 A thin layer of Leatherette can be glued to the top of the desk top L and extended over the desk flap upper surface, when in the open position. (*See* Fig 23.11.)

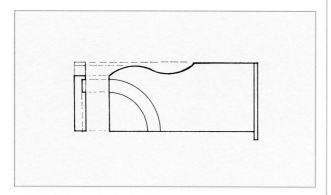

Fig 23.7 Detail of sides O

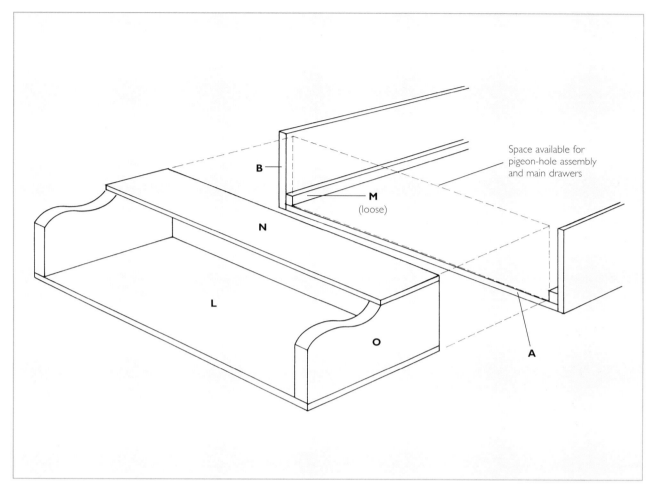

Fig 23.8 Method for checking fit of desk top and length of drawer fronts

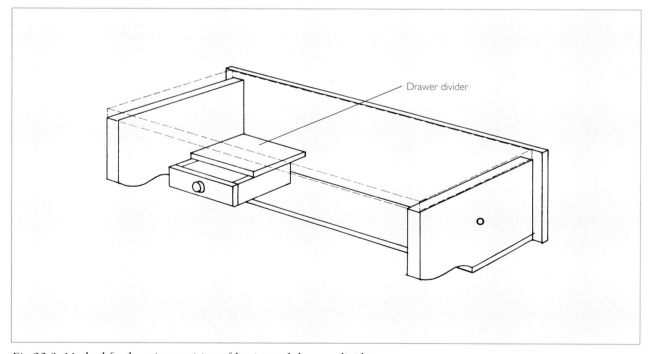

Fig 23.9 Method for locating position of horizontal drawer dividers

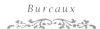

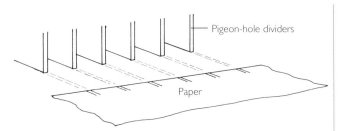

Fig 23.10 *Use marked paper to ensure correct positioning of vertical dividers*

Fig 23.12 *Detail of quadrant*

13 Make the quadrants from either brass or thin ply. (*See* Fig 23.12.) I used ply but would prefer thin brass sheet. My reason for choosing ply, however, is that it is easier to glue to the sides of the desk flap. If you would like to use brass, you will have to drill two small holes in the crosspiece, which fits into the chases formed in the sides of the desk flap, and then superglue and pin them in position. *When the quadrants are in place, check that they move easily in the grooves provided. Check also that when the desk flap is in the closed position, you cannot see the bottom edge of desk top L. If you have kept closely to the details given, the front face of the flap when closed should be flush with the edge of the separator J and the faces of side pieces M.*

MAIN DRAWERS R Using the method shown on Fig 23.8, mark out the length of each drawer front. The heights of the drawer fronts vary, so when it comes to determining them, use the method suggested in Fig 23.13. Drill the fronts of each drawer, including the desk flap, in the locations indicated using a 2mm (^{3}/$_{32}$ in) diameter drill bit. Turn the knobs to fit, and glue them in place after the surface of the drawer front has been prepared to receive the finish.

Cut out and assemble the sides, backs and bases of each drawer and glue them together, making sure that all components are at right angles to each other.

MOULDING Cut out and glue the two strips of moulding to the side panels B and panel I.

PEDIMENT This can be made up from thin strips of scrap timber as indicated on the front and side views, and turned finials can be made from dowel and glued to square sectioned bases.

ASSEMBLY

1 Glue the side panels B to the edges of the rear panel A and at right angles to it.
2 Glue panel H to the side and rear panels.

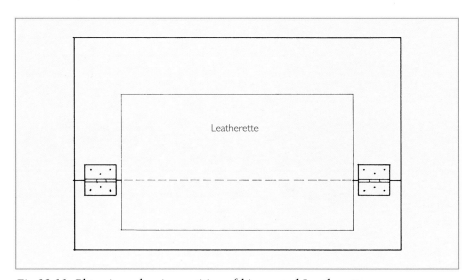

Fig 23.11 *Plan view, showing position of hinges and Leatherette*

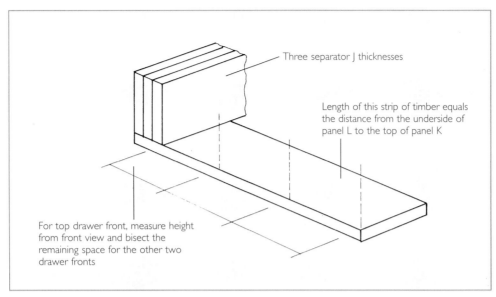

Three separator J thicknesses

Length of this strip of timber equals the distance from the underside of panel L to the top of panel K

For top drawer front, measure height from front view and bisect the remaining space for the other two drawer fronts

Fig 23.13 Method for measuring height of drawer fronts

3 Put the shelves in position and insert the lower pivots into their respective holes in panel H, with the doors attached to the pivots. *Check that the doors fit snugly between the side panels B and are flush with their edges. If not, rub down the side of each door panel with abrasive paper.*

4 With the doors in place, glue the top panel D to the top edges of side panels B and to the inside face of the rear panel A. The pivots in the doors should be engaged in their holes. *Make sure that the doors are not glued to the top panel by periodically moving the door leaves to and fro until the glue has set.*

5 Glue panel I to the side and rear panels and to the underside face of panel H.

6 Glue the side panels C to panel I and the edges of rear panel A, at right angles to it.

7 Glue the top separator J to the underside of panel I and to the side and rear panels.

8 Put the pigeon-hole assembly loosely in position and locate the position of the separator J underneath. Glue the separator to the side and rear panels. *Check that the pigeon-hole assembly not only moves easily, but that the desk flap, when in the closed position, fits into the space between the separators. Remove the assembly when satisfied.*

9 Glue the remaining separators J in place, using the method suggested in Fig 20.7.

10 Glue the base panel to the side and rear panels.

11 Glue the pedestal front panel to the side panels and to the front edge of the base panel K, so that its top edge is flush with the top face of panel K. Any height adjustments to the pedestal panel can be made later by rubbing down with abrasive paper.

12 With the pigeon-hole assembly in place, fit and glue the side pieces M to the side panels and separators so that their front faces are flush with the edges of the side panels C and the separators J. *Check that the drawers fit between them and adjust, where necessary, by rubbing down the side faces of the drawers with abrasive paper.*

13 Assemble the parts forming the pediment to check that they conform to the drawing, and then glue them together and to the top panel D as shown on the front and side views. *Should any adjustments be necessary, this can be taken up on the thin strips of timber, which are shown curved on elevation, before the glue is applied.*

FINISHING

All exposed parts, having been prepared in advance, now only require a varnish finish. I used a mahogany varnish to help darken the appearance of the timber. Remember to remove any glue lines before you varnish, to leave up to eight hours between each coat, and to rub down with fine abrasive paper and wire wool before applying the next coat.

DAVENPORT

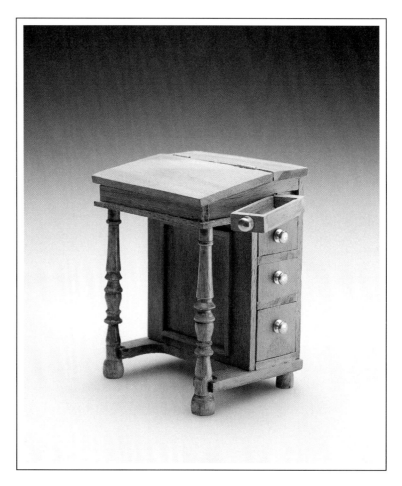

I came across this Davenport on a visit to Kendal in the Lake District. The original was designed by Gillow of Lancaster. Because of the intricacy of certain embellishments that would be difficult to scale down, the model has been somewhat modified. Also, as I didn't have time to study all aspects of the design, or see inside the desk, the result is perhaps not quite as Gillow intended. I have adopted some features from other Davenport designs, of which there are many. The drawer P, shown on the exploded view in Fig 24.2, had internal partitions on the original to accommodate the odd bits of office paraphernalia that people acquire. If you fancy adding these partitions then have a go. The timber I chose for the model was walnut.

SIDE, FRONT AND PLAN VIEWS

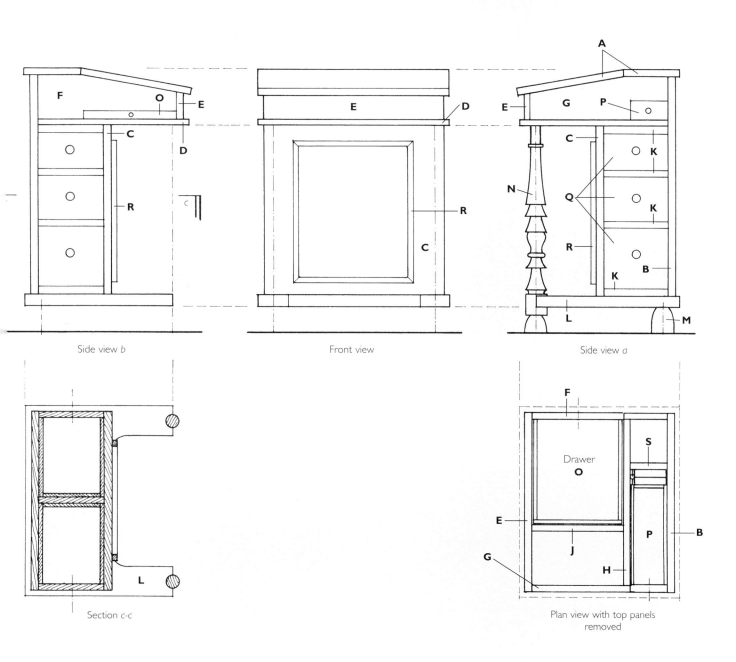

Side view *b*

Front view

Side view *a*

Section c-c

Plan view with top panels
removed

Fig 24.1 Davenport: Plan

CUTTING LIST

Walnut.

A Desk-top panels (2) 51 × 45 × 2mm (2 × 1¾ × ³⁄₃₂in)

B Rear panel (1) 60 × 50 × 2mm (2³⁄₈ × 2 × ³⁄₃₂in)

C Front panel (1) 50 × 45 × 2mm (2 × 1¾ × ³⁄₃₂in)

D Panel (1) 51 × 40 × 1.5mm (2 × 1⁵⁄₈ × ¹⁄₁₆in)

E Front piece (1) 50 × 7 × 1.5mm (2 × ⁵⁄₁₆ × ¹⁄₁₆in)

F and **G** Side panels (2) 40 × 30 × 1.5mm
(1⁵⁄₈ × 1¼ × ¹⁄₁₆in)

H Divider (1) 45 × 12 × 1.5mm (1¾ × ½ × ¹⁄₁₆in)

I Panel (1) 30 × 25 × 0.75mm (1¼ × 1 × ¹⁄₃₂in)

J Drawer stop (1) 25 × 3 × 1.5mm (1 × ⅛ × ¹⁄₁₆in)

K Drawer separators (4) 200 × 20 × 2mm (8 × ⅞ × ³⁄₃₂in)

L Base panel (1) 51 × 40 × 3mm (2 × 1⁵⁄₈ × ⅛in)

M Feet (2), dowel, 7mm (⁹⁄₃₂in) diameter

N Legs (2), dowel, 7mm (⁹⁄₃₂in) diameter

O Drawer

front (1) 25 × 2 × 2mm (1 × ³⁄₃₂ × ³⁄₃₂in)

back (1) 25 × 3 × 1mm (1 × ⅛ × ⅛in)

sides (2) 60 × 2 × 1mm (2³⁄₈ × ³⁄₃₂ × ¹⁄₃₂in)

base (1) 30 × 25 × 0.75mm (1¼ × 1 × ¹⁄₃₂in)

P Drawer

front (1) 10 × 5 × 2mm (½ × ¼ × ³⁄₃₂in)

back (1) 12 × 10 × 2mm (½ × ½ × ³⁄₃₂in)+ 10 × 5 × 1mm
(½ × ¼ × ¹⁄₃₂in)+ 10 × 5 × 2mm (½ × ¼ × ³⁄₃₂in)

sides (2) 60 × 5 × 1mm (2³⁄₈ × ¼ × ¹⁄₃₂in)

base (1) 30 × 10 × 0.75mm (1¼ × ½ × ¹⁄₃₂in)

Q Main drawers

fronts (6) 80 × 20 × 2mm (3⅛ × 1 × ³⁄₃₂in)

backs (6) 80 × 20 × 1mm (3⅛ × 1 × ¹⁄₃₂in)

sides (12) 90 × 80 × 1mm (3⅝ × 3⅛ × ¹⁄₃₂in)

bases (6) 60 × 45 × 0.75mm (2³⁄₈ × 1¾ × ¹⁄₃₂in)

R Strip on front panels 150 × 1.5 × 1.5mm (6 × ¹⁄₁₆ × ¹⁄₁₆in)

S Drawer stop (1), timber offcut, 2mm (³⁄₃₂in) square

Some allowance has been made in these sizes for wastage
and fitting, but check with the drawing before cutting out
the parts.

PREPARATION AND CONSTRUCTION

REAR PANEL B The size for this can be obtained
from the plan and side views in Fig 24.1. Cut it out as
accurately as possible so that you end up with square
corners and parallel sides. Prepare the one face by
scraping and then rubbing down with fine abrasive
paper and wire wool ready to receive the finish.

FRONT PANEL C AND STRIP R This is the same
width as panel B. The height can be obtained from the
side view.

Prepare the surface to receive the finish, as for
panel B. Now prepare the framework of timber strip

R, by mitreing each corner as you would for a picture
frame, and glue it to the panel as shown on the front
view.

PANEL D Cut this out to the sizes obtained from the
front and side views. Instructions for the two holes
indicated on the exploded view in Fig 24.2 are given
later, before all the parts are glued together.

FRONT PIECE E The length of this is identical to
the width of the front panel C. Cut it out to the sizes
obtained from the front and side views, noting that the
top edge is slightly chamfered to accommodate the
desk top when in the closed position.

Prepare the surface, ready to receive the finish.

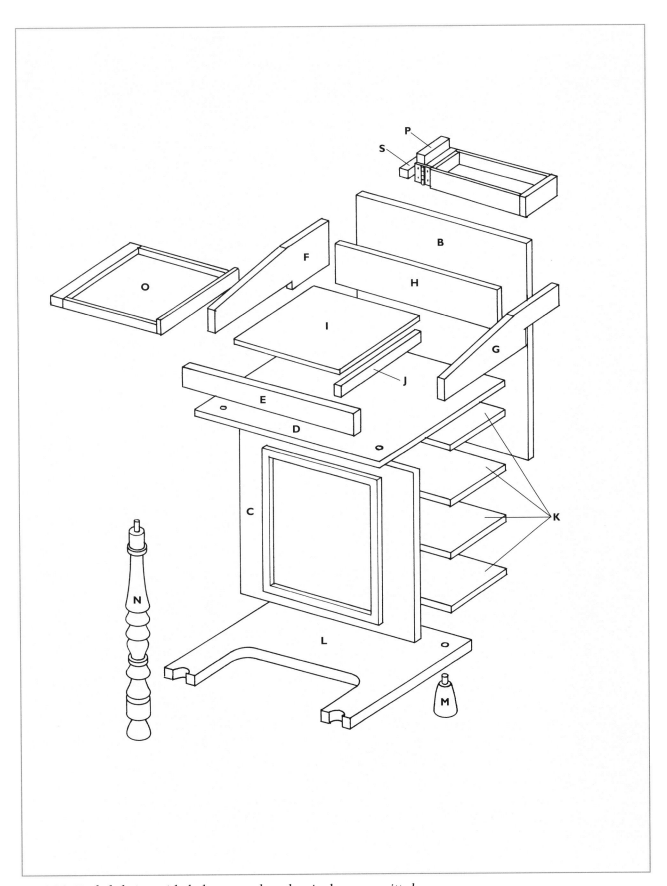

Fig 24.2 Exploded view with desk-top panels and main drawers omitted

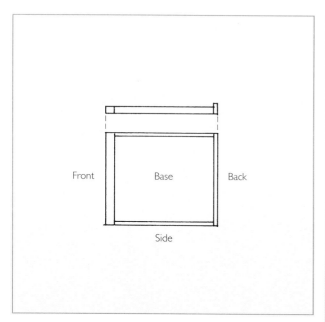

Fig 24.3 Construction of drawer O

SIDE PANELS F AND G Trace or measure the shapes of these and cut out the chamfer with a knife and straightedge, and the slots with a bead saw and knife. Make sure that the edges of the slots are at right angles to their faces since the fronts of drawers O and P are to fit into the slots.

Prepare the outer surfaces, ready to receive the finish.

DRAWER O Make this up from the information contained in Fig 24.3. The side pieces are extremely thin and need careful handling if they are to look right when glued in position. Note that the back piece is slightly deeper than the front. This is because it is to act as a stop against the inside face of the side panel F when the drawer is open.

The drawer front must be made to fit into the slot formed in panel F and its surface then prepared to receive the finish. A small brass nail can be partially inserted in the front face to act as a drawer pull.

DRAWER STOP J Cut this to the length shown in Fig 24.1. Its location can be ascertained from the plan view and Fig 24.2.

DIVIDER H The length is identical to the width of the rear panel B, minus the thickness of the side panels F and G. (*See* Fig 24.2 for clarification.) The height of the divider can be obtained from the side views. It will extend from the top of panel D to the underside face of the desk-top panel. The thickness of this divider is important, as an inspection of the plan view will show. One face will coincide with the edge of the slot for drawer O, whilst the other face will coincide with the edge of the slot for drawer P, the sides being parallel to the rear panel B.

To check that this is so, stand the panels F and G on a flat surface, with their backs against a straightedge and offer up the divider between them. Remember, it must be parallel to the straightedge and meet the other conditions specified. If these criteria are not met, it may be that the divider is too thick. If this is so, rub it down with abrasive paper until it fits. Don't interfere with the slots if you can help it because this will have repercussions on the drawers O and P.

DRAWER P The construction of this needs very careful attention because when in operation and in the open position, the drawer has to rotate through 90° and end up parallel to the side panel G. This requires a hinge mechanism and enough space to be allowed for the knuckle of the hinge to be flush with the face of the side panel of the drawer. (*See* Fig 24.4.) The back panel of the drawer is made up from three pieces: a thin piece for making up the drawer itself, followed by two thicker pieces of different heights, the smaller of which is glued to the thin back piece. Fixing the hinge can be a pain, the problem being that the width of the hinge leaves may be wider than the thickness of the timber to which they are attached, but with perseverance and patience, it's amazing what one can do. Some filing will be required and possibly some drilling for the pin holes that are needed, together with superglue when they are attached. To prevent the superglue from seeping into the hinge's knuckle, it is advisable to smear some grease over the knuckles beforehand.

To assemble the parts, place the completed drawer on a flat surface and glue the first timber block to the back panel of the drawer. Offer up the second timber block and clamp it to the first block. Now try to fix the hinge and make sure that it does not extend beyond the overall depth of the drawer. Check that the drawer front still fits into its slot in panel G.

Further adjustments may be necessary during the construction phase.

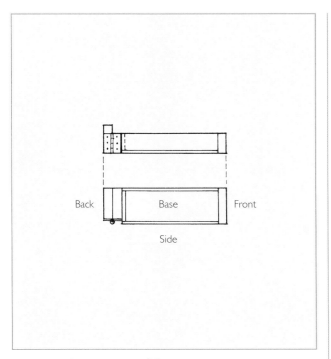

Fig 24.4 Construction of drawer P

DRAWER STOP S This need only be a very short length of 2mm ($^3/_{32}$ in) square timber offcut and need not necessarily fill the entire width of the space available.

PANEL I This is as wide as the slot in panel F and extends from the inside face of panel F to the outer face of the drawer stop J. The length can be obtained from the plan view.

DRAWER SEPARATORS K These are best cut out with a Minicraft bench saw, to maintain consistency of width. The length of these separators is identical to the width of the front and rear panels. On section *c-c* you will see a timber spacer between the drawers. This can be made up from any scrap of timber and not necessarily to the same length as shown, since it is only to act as a stop.

MAIN DRAWERS Q These comprise three sets of drawers, each side of the Davenport. It will be seen that the drawers are of different heights, the sizes of which can be obtained from the side views.

Cut out the parts and glue them together in accordance with the details shown on section *c-c*, maintaining right angles to all adjacent parts. As the

width of the drawer fronts are identical, it would be best to cut these out using a Minicraft bench saw. When the drawers are completed, lay them on the rear panel B in their closed position and check the space between them into which the stop is to fit.

Prepare the drawer fronts, ready to receive the finish, and then drill 1mm ($^1/_{32}$ in) diameter holes as shown on the side views, to accommodate the brass drawer pulls. Don't put the drawer pulls in until you are satisfied that the drawer fronts are flush with the edges of the front and rear panels.

BASE PANEL L This is to be cut out to the shape shown on section *c-c*. It can be traced onto the timber surface using carbon paper, or measured from the drawing. The curved portions, which are to receive the legs N, can be roughly cut out with a knife and finished off with abrasive paper wrapped around some dowel of suitable diameter.

The position of the holes near the back edge can be obtained from the front and side views and should be large enough to accommodate the spigot on the feet M. For clarification, see Fig 24.2.

Now lay the panel L onto a flat surface and then lay panel D on top of it such that the rear panel B butts up to its edge and leaves a slight projection beyond panel L as indicated on the side views. Clamp the two panels L and D together and turn them over.

Now mark off the position of the holes required in panel D to receive the spigots of the legs N and drill panel D to suit the intended diameter of the spigots. This will ensure that, when constructed, the legs N will be parallel to each other and to the front panel C.

FEET M AND LEGS N Turn these by the method described under Stiles, legs and arm rest supports in Chapter 10, (*see also* Fig 10.5) and form their respective spigots to fit the holes in panels D and L.

DESK-TOP PANELS A The overall sizes of each part can be obtained from the front and side views. Cut them out and prepare the surfaces ready to receive the finish. Note that the adjoining edges of these panels have a slight chamfer which can be shaped with some abrasive paper. Also, notches have to be chased out along these edges to accommodate the hinges.

ASSEMBLY

1 Glue the bottom separator K to the rear panel and at right angles to it.

2 Glue the other three separators K to the rear panel, using the method described in Fig 20.7.

3 With one of each of the main drawers placed loosely in the closed position, locate and glue the small drawer stop to separator K, then remove the drawer before the glue sets. *Check that the drawer opposite fits into its space properly. The front faces of all the drawers should be flush with the edges of the front and rear panels, if not rub down. You can now fit the drawer pulls into their holes.*

4 Glue front panel C to separators K. *Make sure drawers can move easily in spaces provided.*

5 Glue panel D to the rear panel, separator K and the top edge of the front panel C. *Make sure that the panel is symmetrically disposed about the centreline of the front view.*

6 Glue front piece E to the top edge of panel D and at right angles to it. *Check that the chamfer along the top edges of front piece E is the correct way around.*

7 Loosely position drawers O and P in their closed position to check that divider H does not hinder their movement, then glue the divider in place and remove the drawers before the glue sets. *If the divider does interfere, rub down the offending part until the drawers move freely, because once the top is glued on there is no way to make adjustments for this.*

8 Place drawers O and P loosely in position when divider H is fixed and the glue has set so that you can locate and glue in place the drawer stops J and S.

9 Find a scrap of timber as thick as stop J and lay it on top of panel D to act as a spacer whilst you glue panel I to divider H, front piece E and the top of stop J. *Remove the spacer before the glue sets.*

10 Place drawers O and P into their respective spaces and locate side panels F and G to check that they fit snugly between front piece E and rear panel B

and that the drawer fronts fit into their slots without unsightly gaps around their edges. Adjust as necessary and even remake the side panels where adjustment is futile. Glue the side panels to front piece E, rear panel B, the ends of divider H and the top of panel D. Side panel F will also need to be glued to the edge of panel I. *Check that drawers O and P move easily in their spaces and that drawer P can move through 90° in the open position. If it doesn't, you may have to remove the side panel G to carry out any adjustments.*

11 When all is as it should be, check that the desk-top panels fit on top of the exposed edges of the surrounding panels and if they do, fit the hinges so that the desk-top flap ends up touching the side panels and the front piece E. If you find it sits awkwardly, remove one leaf of each hinge and make the chamfer along the edge of the panel a bit more pronounced. Return the hinges, superglue them in place and then apply pins for added security. Carefully glue the top portion of the desk-top panels to the rear panel, side panels and divider H.

12 Base panel L should now be located as accurately as possible. To ensure that this is so, place the spigots of legs N into the holes in panel D and check that they are parallel to the front face by offering the base panel up to them so that the legs fit comfortably into the curved spaces provided. Now mark the position of base panel L and glue it onto the underside of separator K, and the front and rear panels.

13 Glue the feet in place.

FINISHING

The exposed faces should now be ready to accept the finish. In this case, I suggest you use a clear polyurethane varnish after first removing any glue lines. Allow the varnish time to dry (at least eight hours), and then rub down the surfaces with wire wool before applying the next and subsequent coats.

MISCELLANEOUS

WELSH DRESSER

This makes a fine addition to a modern dolls' house when
made in lighter timber. The timber I chose for this model was beech.

FRONT VIEW

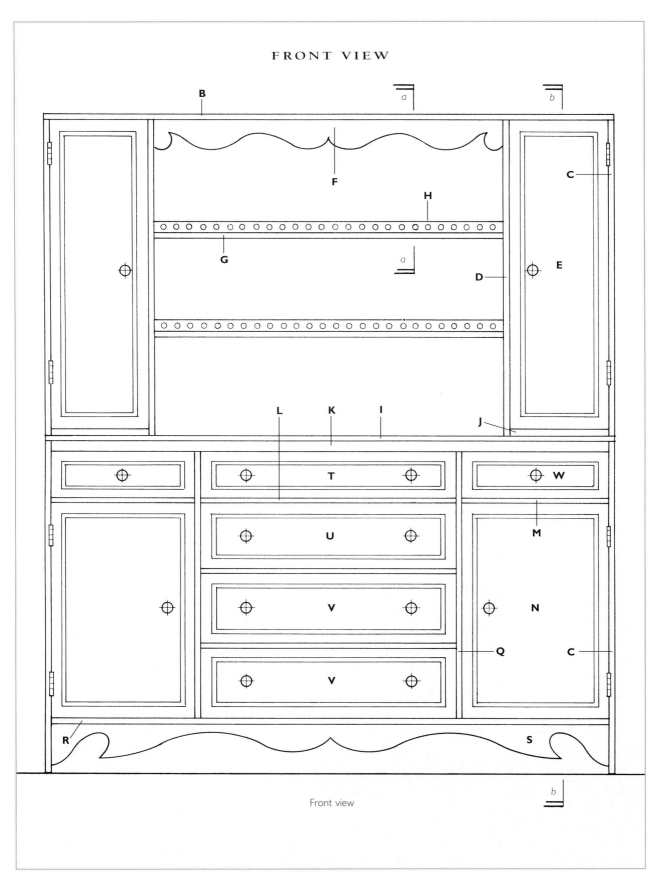

Front view

Fig 25.1a Welsh Dresser: Plan - *continued over*

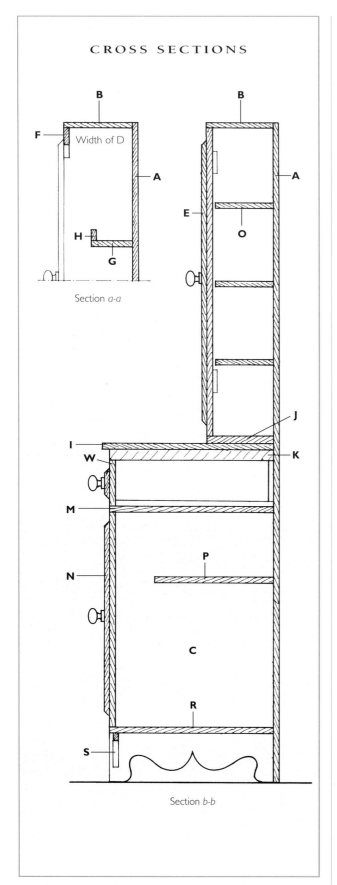

CROSS SECTIONS

Section *a-a*

Section *b-b*

Fig 25.1b Welsh Dresser: Plan - continued

PREPARATION AND CONSTRUCTION

On this model, no finish was applied, but if it is your desire to have one, each individual piece must be prepared as you go, by scraping and then rubbing down with fine abrasive paper and wire wool.

REAR PANEL A This is a rectangular panel which will butt in between the side panels C. It extends from the top to the bottom, as shown in section *b-b*, and needs to be cut out as accurately as possible in order to establish square corners and thereby parallel sides. (*See* Fig 25.1b.)

TOP PANEL B This is a rectangular panel whose sizes can be obtained from the front view and section *b-b*, Figs 25.1a and 1b respectively. Again, accuracy is called for when cutting out. The width can be guaranteed when using a Minicraft bench saw and the ends can be cut either on the bench saw or with a knife and try square.

SIDE PANELS C Cut out the shape shown on Fig 25.2, remembering that there are two panels. The outline can be traced onto the timber surface, using carbon paper, and the upper portions can then be cut out with a knife and straightedge and the curved bits at the bottom can be cut out with a fret saw. Where the worktop is to be located, the use of a try square and knife will ensure that the return is at right angles to the panel sides.

Also, there are four chases to be cut out on each side panel to receive the hinges. Great care is required in this operation as the side panels are so thin. This is best done with a miniature chisel to the depth suggested in Figs 25.2.

CUPBOARD SIDES D The sizes of these panels can be obtained from the front view and section *a-a* in Figs 25.1a and 1b. They should be cut out with a bench saw where possible, to make sure that the sides are parallel and the edges square.

DOORS E These are to be made up from two panels, the sizes of which can be obtained from Fig 25.3. They comprise the main panel and a fascia panel (*see* front view and section *b-b*, Figs 25.1a and 1b).

CUTTING LIST

Beech.

A Rear panel (1) 175 × 150 × 1.5mm (7 × 6 × $\frac{1}{16}$in)

B Top panel (1) 153 × 18 × 1.5mm (6 × $\frac{3}{4}$ × $\frac{1}{16}$in)

C Side panels (2) 174 × 47 × 1.5mm (7 × 2 × $\frac{1}{16}$in)

D Cupboard sides (2) 84 × 18 × 1.5mm (3$\frac{3}{8}$ × $\frac{3}{4}$ × $\frac{1}{16}$in)

E Doors (2) 165 × 27 × 1.5mm (6$\frac{1}{2}$ × 1$\frac{1}{8}$ × $\frac{1}{16}$in) +
155 × 23 × 1mm (6$\frac{1}{8}$ × 1 × $\frac{1}{32}$in)

F Valance (1) 95 × 10 × 1.5mm (3$\frac{3}{4}$ × $\frac{3}{8}$ × $\frac{1}{16}$in)

G Shelves (2) 190 × 11 × 1.5mm (7$\frac{1}{2}$ × $\frac{1}{2}$ × $\frac{1}{16}$in)

H Plate racks (2) 190 × 5 × 1.5mm (7$\frac{1}{2}$ × $\frac{3}{16}$ × $\frac{1}{16}$in)

I Worktop (1) 153 × 46 × 1.5mm (6 × 2 × $\frac{1}{16}$in)

J Cupboard bases (2) 60 × 18 × 1.5mm (2$\frac{3}{8}$ × $\frac{3}{4}$ × $\frac{1}{16}$in)

K Panel (1) 150 × 45 × 3mm (6 × 1$\frac{3}{4}$ × $\frac{1}{8}$in)

L Separators (3) 210 × 45 × 1.5mm (8$\frac{1}{4}$ × 1$\frac{3}{4}$ × $\frac{1}{16}$in)

M Separators (2) 80 × 45 × 1.5mm (3$\frac{1}{4}$ × 1$\frac{3}{4}$ × $\frac{1}{16}$in)

N Doors (2) 120 × 40 × 1.5mm (4$\frac{3}{4}$ × 1$\frac{5}{8}$ × $\frac{1}{16}$in) +
110 × 35 × 1mm (4$\frac{3}{8}$ × 1$\frac{1}{2}$ × $\frac{1}{32}$in)

O Shelves (6) 180 × 16 × 1.5mm (7$\frac{1}{8}$ × $\frac{5}{8}$ × $\frac{1}{16}$in)

P Shelves (2) 80 × 32 × 1.5mm (3$\frac{1}{4}$ × 1$\frac{1}{4}$ × $\frac{1}{16}$in)

Q Dividers (2) 145 × 45 × 1.5mm (5$\frac{3}{4}$ × 1$\frac{3}{4}$ × $\frac{1}{16}$in)

R Base panel (1) 150 × 45 × 1.5mm (6 × 1$\frac{3}{4}$ × $\frac{1}{16}$in)

S Pedestal front (1) 150 × 15 × 1.5mm (6 × $\frac{5}{8}$ × $\frac{1}{16}$in)

T Drawer

front (1) 68 × 12 × 1.5mm (2$\frac{3}{4}$ × $\frac{1}{2}$ × $\frac{1}{16}$in)

fascia (1) 63 × 7 × 1mm (2$\frac{1}{2}$ × $\frac{5}{16}$ × $\frac{1}{32}$in)

sides (2) 90 × 11 × 1mm (3$\frac{5}{8}$ × $\frac{1}{2}$ × $\frac{1}{32}$in)

back (1) 68 × 11 × 1mm (2$\frac{3}{4}$ × $\frac{1}{2}$ × $\frac{1}{32}$in)

base (1) 68 × 45 × 0.75mm (2$\frac{3}{4}$ × 1$\frac{3}{4}$ × $\frac{1}{32}$in)

U Drawer

front (1) 68 × 18 × 1.5mm (2$\frac{3}{4}$ × $\frac{3}{4}$ × $\frac{1}{16}$in)

fascia (1) 63 × 12 × 1mm (2$\frac{1}{2}$ × $\frac{1}{2}$ × $\frac{1}{32}$in)

sides (2) 90 × 17 × 1mm (3$\frac{5}{8}$ × $\frac{3}{4}$ × $\frac{1}{32}$in)

back (1) 68 × 17 × 1mm (2$\frac{3}{4}$ × $\frac{3}{4}$ × $\frac{1}{32}$in)

base (1) 68 × 45 × 0.75mm (2$\frac{3}{4}$ × 1$\frac{3}{4}$ × $\frac{1}{32}$in)

V Drawers

fronts (2) 140 × 19 × 1.5mm (5$\frac{1}{2}$ × $\frac{3}{4}$ × $\frac{1}{16}$in)

fascias (2) 130 × 13 × 1mm (5$\frac{1}{8}$ × $\frac{1}{2}$ × $\frac{1}{32}$in)

sides (4) 90 × 40 × 1mm (3$\frac{5}{8}$ × 1$\frac{5}{8}$ × $\frac{1}{32}$in)

backs (2) 68 × 40 × 1mm (2$\frac{3}{4}$ × 1$\frac{5}{8}$ × $\frac{1}{32}$in)

bases (2) 140 × 45 × 0.75mm (5$\frac{1}{2}$ × 1$\frac{3}{4}$ × $\frac{1}{32}$in)

W Drawers

fronts (2) 80 × 12 × 1.5mm (3$\frac{1}{4}$ × $\frac{1}{2}$ × $\frac{1}{16}$in)

fascias (2) 70 × 7 × 1mm (2$\frac{3}{4}$ × $\frac{5}{16}$ × $\frac{1}{32}$in)

sides (4) 180 × 12 × 1mm (7$\frac{1}{8}$ × $\frac{1}{2}$ × $\frac{1}{32}$in)

backs (2) 80 × 12 × 1mm (3$\frac{1}{4}$ × $\frac{1}{2}$ × $\frac{1}{32}$in)

bases (2) 80 × 45 × 0.75mm (3$\frac{1}{4}$ × 1$\frac{3}{4}$ × $\frac{1}{32}$in)

Sizes generally allow for cutting and fitting.

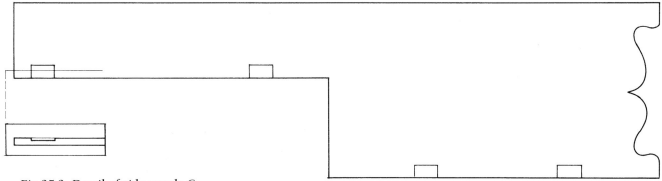

Fig 25.2 Detail of side panels C

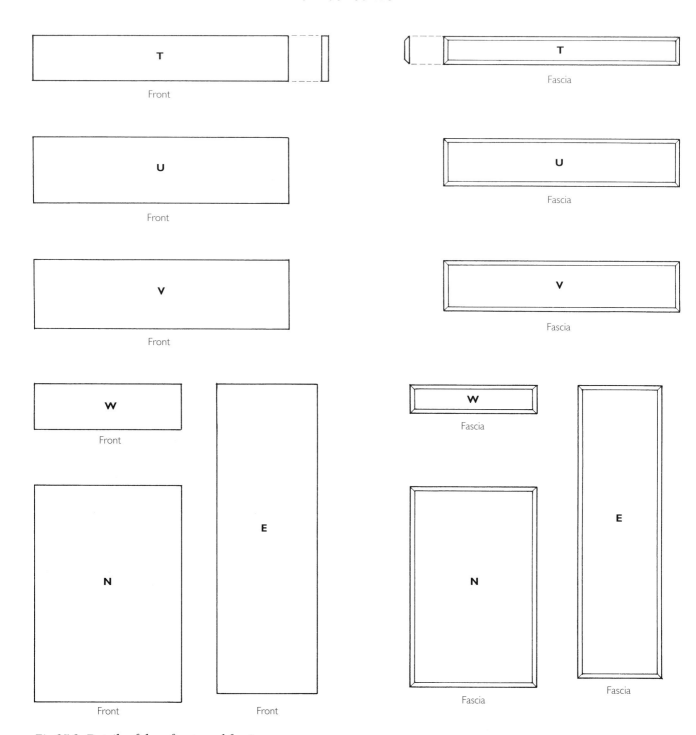

Fig 25.3 Details of door fronts and fascias

Note how the fascia panel is to have a chamfered edge which can be achieved by the method shown in Fig 25.4. This applies to all fascias on doors and drawers.

The edges of the main panel will need chasing out to receive the hinges as shown in Fig 25.5 and this can be done with a bead saw and miniature chisel. To remind you not to cut too deeply, have another look at the hingeing methods in Fig 2.12. Also, when determining the position of the hinge recesses, refer to the side panels C and note that the top edge of the door is coincident with the top edge of panel C.

Drill 1mm ($^1/_{32}$ in) diameter holes in the door panels, when the fascias have been glued on, to accept

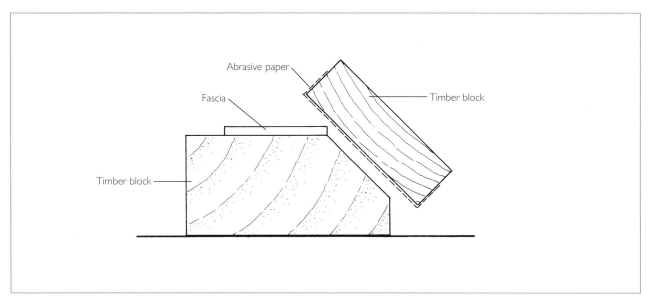

Fig 25.4 Abrasive paper wrapped around a timber block can be used to create a chamfered edge

the brass door knobs. Incidentally, when you glue the fascia panel to the main panel, it would be advisable to clamp the panels between two blocks of timber to make sure that they do not try to separate, or that the combined panels do not try to buckle due to the moisture contained in the glue. Leave them clamped until the glue has hardened.

VALANCE F Trace the shape of this from the front view in Fig 25.1a onto the timber surface, using carbon paper, and cut out the profile with a fret saw or knife, whichever you find the most convenient. Leave a little bit extra on the length to enable you to 'fit' it in place later.

SHELVES G When cutting these shelves to the sizes obtained from the front view and section *a-a* (see Figs 25.1a and 1b), allow a bit extra in the length to assist when it comes to fitting in place.

PLATE RACKS H Cut out these strips to the length shown on the front view, allowing a little extra to help with fitting later. Mark out the position of the holes, using a paper template or a rule, and make an incision with an awl to help locate the drill bit. Now drill the holes with a 1.5mm ($1/16$ in) diameter drill bit. When you are satisfied that the holes are in line and evenly spaced, you can then rub down the edges with abrasive paper around a block of timber until the depth shown on the front view has been reached.

WORKTOP I Trace the shape of this panel from Fig 25.6 and cut out as accurately as possible, using a bead saw for the return portions and a knife and straightedge, or bench saw, for the remainder.

CUPBOARD BASES J Cut these out to the sizes obtained from the front view and section *b-b*, Fig 25.1b, noting that they are of the same width as door E.

PANEL K Cut this out to the sizes obtained from the front view and section *b-b*, Figs 25.1a and 1b, using a bench saw for preference since it needs to be as square as possible in all directions.

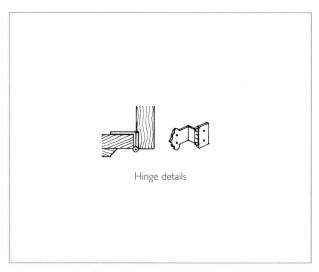

Fig 25.5 Detail of hinge

Fig 25.6 Detail of panel I

SEPARATORS L AND M Cut these out to the sizes obtained from the front view and section *b-b*, Figs 25.1a and 1b, making sure that all edges are perfectly square, since they will be on view.

DOORS N The size of these doors and their fascias can be obtained from Fig 25.3. Cut them out and follow the directions given for chamfering and gluing under Door E. (*See* Fig 25.4.)

The edge of each door requires a chase for the hinges and this can be done with a bead saw and miniature chisel, taking care not to cut too deeply. (*See* Fig 2.12.) However, before you commit yourself to chasing out for the hinges, it may be as well if you leave this task until the construction of the dresser reaches its conclusion.

SHELVES O Cut these six shelves out to the depth shown on section *b-b*, Fig 25.1b, and to a length equal to the width of door E.

SHELVES P Cut out these two shelves to the depth shown on section *b-b* and to a length equal to the width of door N.

DIVIDERS Q Cut out these two panels to the length shown on the front view and to a width equal to that of the width of panel K shown on section *b-b*.

BASE PANEL R Cut out this panel to the sizes obtained from the front view and section *b-b*.

PEDESTAL FRONT S Trace the shape of this panel onto the timber surface, using carbon paper, and cut it out with a fret saw or knife. Allow a little extra in the length to enable fitting later.

DRAWERS T, U, V AND W The sizes of the fronts and fascias of these drawers can be obtained from Fig 25.3. Cut them out with a Minicraft bench saw where possible to ensure squareness and equality of size. As mentioned earlier, it is a good practice, when gluing the fascia panel to the main panel, to clamp the panels between two blocks of timber to avoid separation or buckling that may be caused by moisture in the glue.

The sides of drawers T and W extend from inside face of the drawer front to the inside face of the rear panel A, and their depths from the top of the drawer front to the top face of the drawer base.

Drawers U and V have sides extending as for the drawers T and W but with a depth that can be obtained from the front view less the thickness of the drawer base in each case.

The backs of all drawers butt into the sides and rest on the bases.

The bases butt into the drawer fronts and extend to the face of the rear panel A as shown on section *b-b*.

ASSEMBLY

1 With the rear panel A laid on a flat surface, glue the side panels C to its outer edges, making sure that the parts are at right angles to each other.

2 Glue the top panel B to the top edges of the side panels C and to the inside face of the rear panel A as shown on section *b-b*, Fig 25.1b.

3 Glue the worktop I to the side and rear panels so that the edges of the front section are flush with the side panels.

4 Position shelves O and glue them to the side and rear panels, making sure that they are at right angles to the adjacent panels.

5 Glue panels J to worktop I.

6 Glue cupboard sides D to the ends of shelves O and to top panel B, rear panel A and worktop I.

7 Fit valance F into the space provided and glue to top panel B and cupboard sides D as shown on the front view and section *a-a*, Fig 25.1b.

8 Position shelves G and fit them into the space provided. Glue them to rear panel A and to cupboard sides D.

9 Fit plate racks H to shelves G and glue in place.

10 Glue panel K to worktop I, using clamps to ensure even contact of the parts along their length.

11 Assemble drawers T, U, V and W and glue all component parts together, making sure that they are all at right angles to each other. Then drill the front panels after the fascias have been attached in the way described under Doors E. *Check that drawers T, U, V are of the same width and adjust where necessary by rubbing down the sides with abrasive paper. Drawers W should also be the same width as each other.*

12 Working from either side, place drawer W in position and locate separator M which should then be glued to the rear and side panels. Remove the drawer before the glue sets.

13 Locate divider Q and glue it to the underside of panel K, the end of separator M and to rear panel A. To be sure it is parallel to the side panel, check to see if drawer W will fit in at the lower end of divider Q.

14 Locate separators L by the method shown in Fig 20.7, starting from the top with drawer T in position. Work progressively towards the bottom

with the use of drawers U and V. Glue the separators to divider Q and to rear panel A, removing each drawer before the glue sets.

15 Glue the other divider Q to the ends of separator L, the underside of panel K and to rear panel A.

16 Check to see if the other drawer W fits into the space provided and adjust where necessary by rubbing down the sides with sandpaper. Fit and glue separator M in place whilst the drawer is in position and then remove the drawer before the glue sets.

17 Fit and glue shelves P in place and at right angles to the rear and side panels.

18 Glue base panel R to the side and rear panel and to the ends of dividers Q. *Check that the bottom drawer V moves freely in the space provided and adjust where necessary by rubbing down the edges with abrasive paper.*

19 Fit and glue the pedestal front S in the position shown on the front view and section *b-b*, Fig 25.1b.

20 Fix the hinges to doors E with superglue and pins, putting a thin layer of grease over the knuckles to prevent glue seeping into them. *Check that the doors operate properly. If they tend to bind on their surrounds, rub down the offending edges with abrasive paper.*

21 Superglue and pin the hinge leaf to the side panel.

22 At this point, you should mark off the position of the chases required in doors N to receive the hinges. These can be cut out, being careful not to cut out too deeply, using a bead saw and miniature chisel.

23 When all is as you would wish, repeat the instructions stated for doors E, above.

FINISHING

It should be noted that the faces of the doors and drawers in the bottom portion of the dresser, and the doors in the upper portion, are to be flush with the front edges of their surrounds. If they are not, try to correct it since it will otherwise be quite noticeable. No finish was applied to this model, but if you would like one, each piece must be scraped down and rubbed with abrasive paper and wire wool, during the preparation stage. A clear polyurethane varnish is all that is required to preserve the timber.

STEPLADDER

If you wish to add a touch of realism to your dolls' house accoutrements, these ladders look great and are a delight to see in their own right. The model shown here was made in beech.

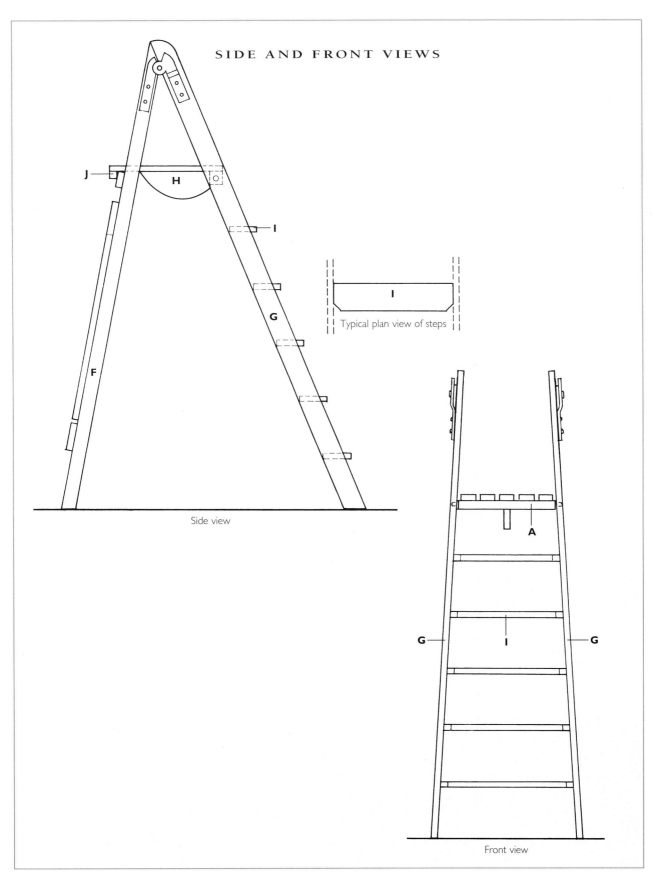

SIDE AND FRONT VIEWS

Typical plan view of steps

Side view

Front view

Fig 26.1a Stepladder: Plan - *continued over*

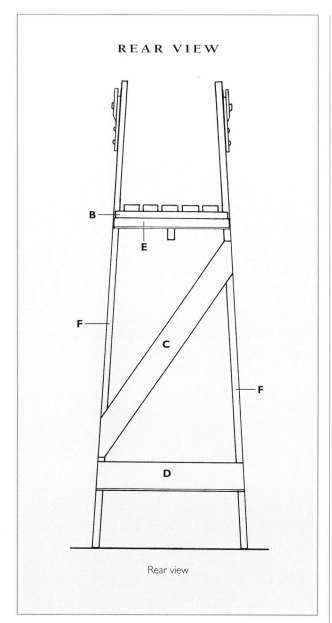

REAR VIEW

Rear view

Fig 26.1b Stepladder: Plan - continued

PREPARATION AND CONSTRUCTION

PART A Cut this out to the length obtained from Fig 26.2 and then, using a knife, carefully shape the spigots on each end to approximately 1.5mm (¹/₁₆ in) diameter.

PART B Cut this out to the length shown on Fig 26.2.

PLATFORM J This is made up from five identical strips of timber which are then glued to parts A and B in the positions indicated.

CAM H Trace the shape of this from Fig 26.3 onto the timber surface, using carbon paper, and cut it out with a knife. Rub down the edges with abrasive paper until you achieve a nice smooth curve. Glue the cam to the central strip of timber on the platform and to part A as shown on Fig 26.2.

PARTS G Trace the shape onto the timber surface, marking the position of the hole required to receive the spigot on the end of part A, and cut out the shape with a knife and a bead saw where appropriate. To make sure the holes are in the same position, it is advisable to clamp the two parts G together and then drill through them both with a 2mm (³/₃₂ in) drill bit. Check that the spigots on parts A fit easily in the holes and adjust them if you find they bind in any way.

PARTS F Trace the shape onto the timber surface and cut out with a bead saw. Make sure that both parts are identical by clamping them together and rubbing down the combined edges with a sanding block.

HINGES These were made from sheet aluminium. Trace the shapes onto the metal surface using carbon paper and cut out the profiles roughly, with snips and

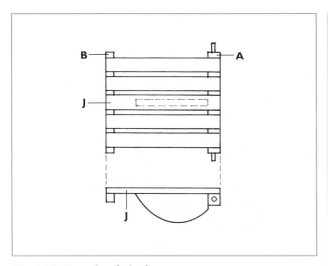

Fig 26.2 Details of platform

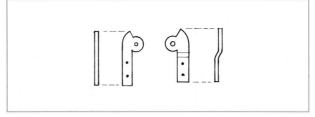

Fig 26.4 Detail of hinge

ground. To make sure this is so, lay the assembly so far constructed on top of the drawing to check the relative extent of the parts F and G and the spigots on part A, then mark off on parts F the position of part E. Transfer the assembly onto the rear view to enable you to check the distance between the feet of the ladder.

When you are happy with this, glue part E in place. Don't worry if the ends overlap the sides of parts F, since it is an easy matter to trim them with a bead saw.

PARTS C AND D The size for parts C and D can be ascertained from Fig 26.1b. Locate and glue part D in position and follow this with part C, trimming the ends with a bead saw so that they are flush with the faces of parts F.

STEPS I The steps will now have to be fitted. To do this, it would be as well if you marked off the position of the steps from the drawing onto a strip of paper and then transferred the marks onto the inner faces of parts G. Now it becomes a case of judging the distance between the faces of parts G into which the steps must fit. This can be done using a separate strip of paper, or card, onto which is marked the length required for each of the five steps and then transferring this information onto the timber strip.

The lengths can then be cut out with a bead saw and the ends chamfered very slightly to fit onto the faces of parts G. The plan view of the steps shows a mitred corner at each end and these must be cut out before the steps are glued in place. When gluing does occur, be sure that the steps are parallel to the platform and to each other.

FINISHING

A clear polyurethane varnish is all that is required in order to protect the timber surface.

a metal saw. Drill 2mm ($^3/_{32}$ in) diameter holes through the leaves thus formed.

Use a pin vise for the final shaping, filing down the curved parts around the holes as accurately as possible and forming a kink in one leaf as shown in Fig 26.4. Drill two extra holes, of 0.5mm ($^1/_{32}$ in) diameter, in the leaves to accommodate the pins needed for fixing them to the parts F and G.

The pivot I made from a child's old dress ring which was manufactured from a very soft metal alloy. First, form a head on the one end of the metal rod whilst holding it in the pin vise and then, after feeding it through the hinge holes, cut off the other end near to the surface of the hinge so that there is enough metal to form the remaining head.

It is best to attach the hinges to parts F and G, checking that they move freely, before the steps are made.

PART E Place the spigots of part A into the holes in part G to enable you to locate part E, which is a simple rectangular piece of timber. The position of part E is shown on the rear view and it will be noticed how, with this in place, the platform is parallel to the

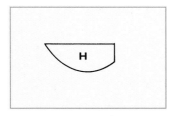

Fig 26.3 Detail of cam

CONVERSATION PIECE

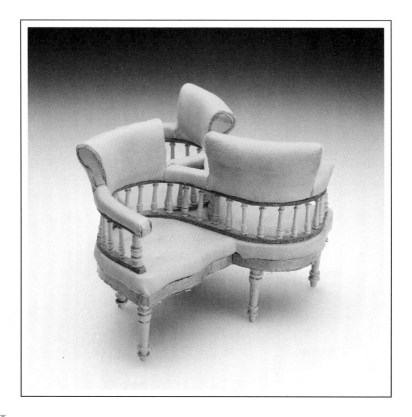

If you are contemplating a Victorian-type setting for your dolls' house then this model would suit the proposed room, assuming you have plenty of space to accommodate it. I have called it a conversation piece because it is the kind of furniture where three people can sit and have a chat together in comfort. The common name for this furniture, which was very popular in the latter part of the nineteenth century, is a sociable.

It is possible to adapt the drawings shown in order to develop a two-seater chair which was, perhaps, more commonly employed in those days.

Most of the timber work will be covered up but that on display is mainly lime for the turned parts and mahogany for parts D. I made part E from oak and the covering to the seat, arm rests and chair back from soft leather.

PLAN VIEW

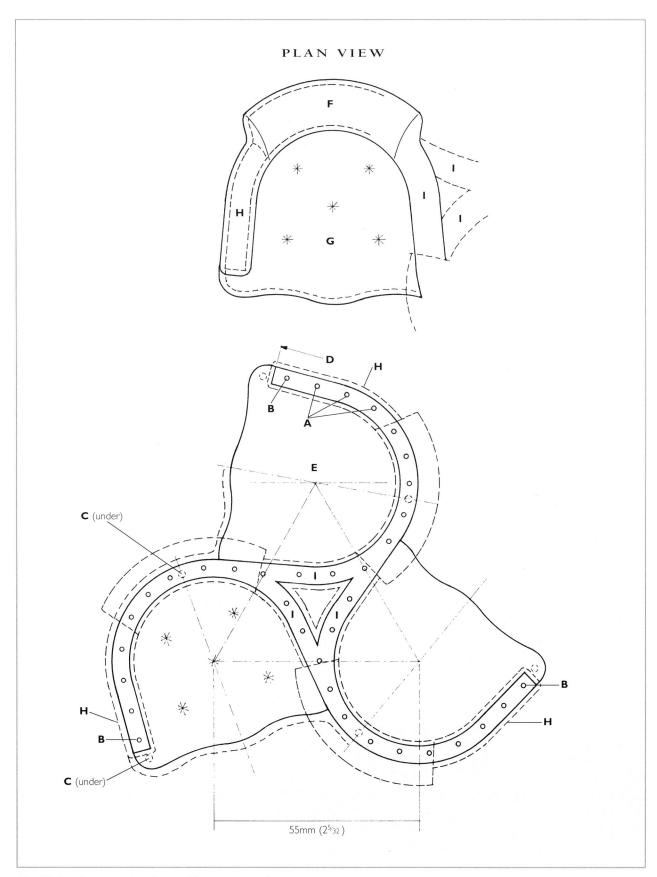

Fig 27.1a **Conversation Piece: Plan** - *continued over*

VIEW ON ELEVATION

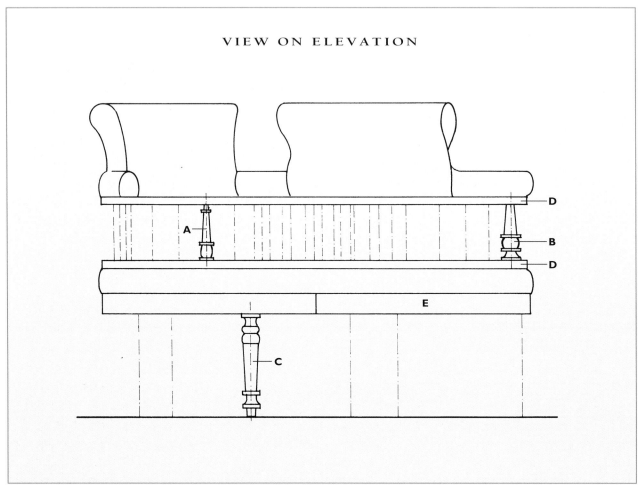

Fig 27.1b   Conversation Piece: Plan - *continued*

CUTTING LIST

Lime; mahogany; oak.

A Supports (36), dowel, from 3: 300 × 5mm diameter (12 × ¼in)

B Supports (3), dowel, 120 × 10mm diameter (4¾ × ⅜in)

C Legs (6), dowel, 300 × 10mm diameter (12 × ⅜in)

D Parts (2) from 2: 120 × 120 × 2mm (4¾ × 4¾ × ³⁄₃₂in)

E Base (1) 120 × 120 × 5mm (4¾ × 4¾ × ³⁄₁₆in)

F Backs (3), balsa, 180 × 30 × 20mm (7⅛ × 1¼ × ¾in)

G Seats (3), polystyrene sheet, 6mm (¼in) thick

H and **I** Arm rests (6), polystyrene sheet, 6mm (¼in) thick

The sizes given allow for cutting, shaping and fitting during construction.

PREPARATION AND CONSTRUCTION

PART D AND BASE E Trace these from the plan view in Fig 27.1a onto the timber surface, using carbon paper, and carefully cut around their profiles with a fret saw. Check that the two parts D are identical and the base E follows the same outer profile. Rub down the edges with abrasive paper to get them smooth. Drill 3.5mm (⅛ in) diameter holes in the underside of base E, in order to receive the spigots of legs C. Refer to the plan view for their positions.

SUPPORTS A AND B AND LEGS C It is essential when turning these, that they appear to be identical to the shapes drawn. This can be achieved through the use of a paper template to mark each of the pieces, as indicated in Fig 8.6. It can be a bit tedious in the case of supports A due to the number involved. It took me seven and a half hours to shape them all on my Minicraft lathe.

SEATS G Cut these from the sheet of polystyrene and shape with a knife. The profile being identical to that of base E, all you need to do is place the base E over the polystyrene sheet and cut around its edge. Drill 4mm (⁵⁄₃₂ in) diameter holes in the seat, where indicated, to help form the dimpling effect when the cover is added later. For this purpose, you will also need to cut out the same shape from some stiff card, onto which will be sewn the thread for the dimpling effect.

ARM RESTS H AND I Cut these individually from the polystyrene sheet to the profile shown in Fig 27.1a. Note that the three arm rests I are smaller than the three arm rests H.

BACKS F These were carved from blocks of balsa to the shape indicated by the dotted lines in Fig 27.1a. You can, if you so wish, drill some holes through the chair backs to create a dimpling effect similar to the seats. However, it is not so easy to conceal the threads at the rear unless you use a stiff card on which to sew them. In this case, you have to sew the threads through the cover, polystyrene and card after which you can wrap the leather over the rear and glue it in place.

ASSEMBLY

1 Cover the seats with the thin leather and place the stiff card underneath the polystyrene sheet. Sew through the leather, the pre-drilled holes in the sheet and through the card. *Don't pull the thread too tight and judge when to stop by eye.*

2 Glue the leather seat cover to the underside of the card and then glue the seat to base E. *Use clamps to make sure it is firmly attached.*

3 Again using clamps, glue the bottom parts D to the top of the seats and check that the seats are of an even thickness all around their edges.

4 Check that the lengths of all supports A and B are the same and if so, glue their bases to the top part of D in the positions indicated on the plan view. *Check that the supports are vertical and parallel to each other. Then, when the glue has set, lay a flat board on top of the supports to see if you can detect any difference in height between them. Adjust where necessary by carefully rubbing down with abrasive paper, carrying out constant checks along the way.*

5 Glue the leather cover to each of the chair backs and then carefully shape the end pieces to fit into the spaces down each side. *Do not get any glue on the face of the leather as it will create a nasty stain.*

6 Glue the chair backs to the other part D in the positions shown and then fit and glue the arm rests in place. When the glue has set, glue the leather cover over them and trim off any excess leather from the backs and arms.

7 Glue the spigots on the legs into the holes in base E and finally cut out some fabric to represent hessian, and glue it to the underside of base E.

FINISHING

It is not all that easy to apply a finish to the parts once they are glued together but if you are careful, a clear polyurethane varnish is all you need. I didn't bother with a finish myself, except around the edge of base E, where I applied a gold coloured enamel for effect.

SPINNING WHEEL

It is quite possible to write an entire book on spinning wheels because of the variety that can be found both here and abroad. The one shown here, I discovered in a museum, and made up the model from a photograph that I took of it. A foundation piece is necessary since the spinning wheel is made up of two parts connected only by the rod that activates the wheel. Whilst most of the older spinning wheels were in a darker timber, I used beech which gives it a light appearance. The reason I chose beech was because it turns well and can be worked to a fine detail. If you want a darker finish you can, of course, stain it later.

SIDE, END AND PLAN VIEWS

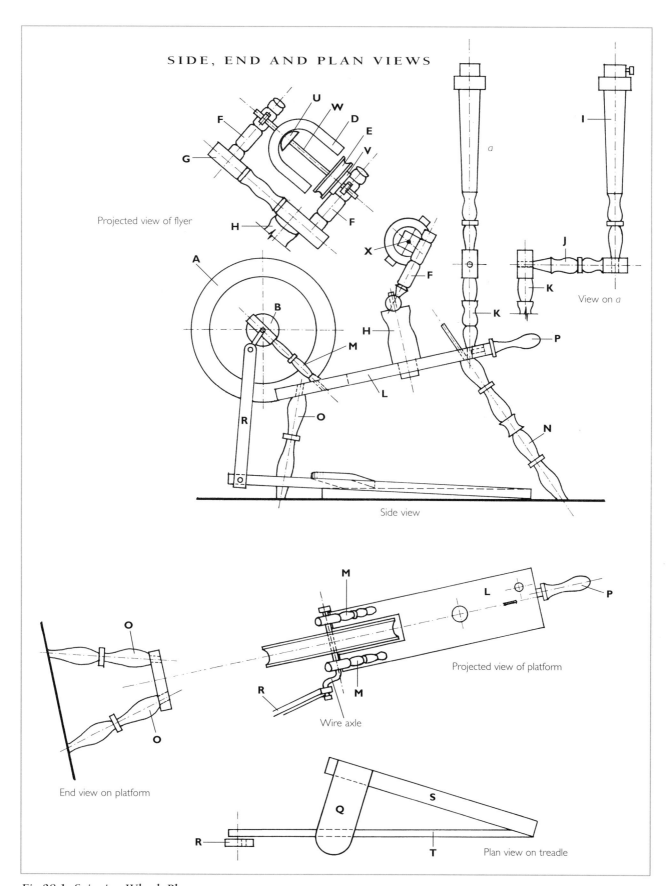

Projected view of flyer

Side view

View on *a*

End view on platform

Projected view of platform

Wire axle

Plan view on treadle

Fig 28.1 Spinning Wheel: Plan

CUTTING LIST

Beech.

A Wheel (1) 50 × 50 × 6mm (2 × 2 × ¼in)

B Wheel hub (1), dowel, 10mm diameter (⅜in)

C Spokes (8), dowel, 5mm diameter (³⁄₁₆in)

D Flyer (1) 20 × 20 × 3mm (1 × 1 × ⅛in)

E Flyer wheel (1), dowel, 3 × 12.5mm diameter (⅛ × ½in)

F Flyer supports (2), dowel, 5mm diameter (¼in)

G Crosspiece (1), dowel, 5mm diameter (¼in)

H Support (1), dowel, 10mm diameter (⅜in)

I Post (1), dowel, 10mm diameter (⅜in)

J Part (1), dowel, 5mm diameter (¼in)

K Part (1), dowel, 5mm diameter (¼in)

L Platform (1) 60 × 16 × 3mm (2⅜ × ¾ × ⅛in)

M Supports (2), dowel, 10mm diameter (⅜in)

N Leg (1), dowel, 10mm diameter (⅜in)

O Legs (2), dowel, 10mm diameter (⅜in)

P Handle (1), dowel, 10mm diameter (⅜in)

Q Treadle foot (1) 25 × 10 × 2mm (1 × ⅜ × ³⁄₃₂in)

R Arm (1) 40 × 3 × 2mm (1⅝ × ⅛ × ³⁄₃₂in)

S Short lever (1) 55 × 4 × 2.5mm (2¼ × ¼ × ⅛in)

T Long lever (1) 80 × 2.5 × 2mm (3¼ × ⅛ × ³⁄₃₂in)

U Mushroom piece (1), dowel, 5mm diameter (¼in)

V Flyer wheel (1), dowel, 10mm diameter (⅜in)

W Spindle (1), dowel or cocktail stick, 5mm diameter (³⁄₁₆in)

X Ends of flyer (2), thin plywood, 5 × 5mm (¼ × ¼in)

Sizes allow for cutting, shaping and fitting during construction.

PREPARATION AND CONSTRUCTION

WHEEL A It is normal to make the wheel from four quadrants which are then spoked and jointed at their rims. If you are a perfectionist you may like to do something similar. For this model, I simply drilled out the wheel using an attachment to the drilling machine which had saw teeth (*see* Fig 28.2). After drilling a pilot hole in the timber, it should be firmly clamped in a vise during the cutting operation.

Chase out the groove around the rim with a knife and a needle file. If you are a competent lathe operator, you may find the manufacture of the wheel easier to achieve.

WHEEL HUB B To make this, turn some 10mm (⅜ in) diameter dowel down to the diameter shown and drill a 1mm (¹⁄₃₂ in) diameter hole along its axis to receive the wire axle.

Carefully mark the position of the spokes out by drawing lines across the end face and drill eight 1mm

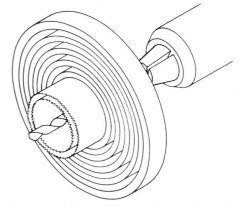

Fig 28.2 A saw-toothed attachment on the drilling machine enables a wheel to be cut out

(¹⁄₃₂ in) holes around the edge and on the centreline, ready to receive the spigot at the end of the spokes.

SPOKES C Turn these from 5mm (³⁄₁₆ in) diameter dowel to the shape shown on Fig 28.3. Place them loosely in the holes around the hub and offer the wheel up to check that the spokes fit snugly to the inside rim. Any adjustment should be taken up at the spigot end. When they fit reasonably well, they can be glued into the hub and to the wheel rim as indicated. Check that the spokes are evenly spaced and in line with the centreline of the width of the rim.

FLYER D Trace the horseshoe shape onto the timber surface, using carbon paper, and carefully cut around the profile with a fret saw. Rub down with a needle file to arrive at the final shape.

MUSHROOM PIECE U This fits inside the flyer and can be made by turning a piece of dowel to the shape shown. A small hole can be drilled in the end if you are careful, ready to receive the spindle.

FLYER WHEEL E Cut this from the dowel or from a piece of timber which has been turned down to 12.5mm (½ in) diameter and whilst it is in the lathe, you can chase out the groove with a needle file. Drill a 1mm (¹⁄₃₂ in) diameter hole along its axis, to receive the spindle.

FLYER WHEEL V This is the wheel next to wheel E and is cut from dowel or from a piece of timber turned down to 8mm (⁵⁄₁₆ in) diameter. As for wheel E, it is drilled to receive the spindle. This wheel has no groove. If you are skilled with the lathe you can, of course, turn both wheels from one piece of timber.

SPINDLE W Make this from dowel or a cocktail stick rubbed down to 1mm (¹⁄₃₂ in) diameter and then cut into two lengths, the longer one passing through the flyer wheel E and terminating at the mushroom piece U, the shorter one extending beyond the horseshoe-shaped piece D as shown on the details of the flyer assembly. A third hand would be useful here to make sure that the spindle is in line and at right angles to the mushroom piece U.

FLYER SUPPORTS F Turn these from 5mm (¼ in) diameter dowel with their bases thinned down to about 1mm (¹⁄₃₂ in) diameter, ready to fit into the holes that will be drilled into the crosspiece G supporting them.

ENDS OF FLYER X Two square tabs X made from thin plywood scraps are to be drilled with a 1mm (¹⁄₃₂ in) diameter hole to receive the spindle and then

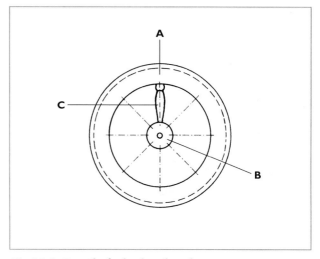

Fig 28.3 Detail of wheel and spoke

glued to the supports F as shown. Make sure that they are in line with each other.

CROSS PIECE G This should be turned from 5mm (¼ in) diameter dowel and drilled to receive the supports F. A further 1mm (¹⁄₃₂ in) diameter hole will be required to receive the spigot from support H. Try your best to maintain the angle shown when drilling, otherwise the flyer may end up fouling the vertical post I, shown on the side view.

SUPPORT H This can be turned to the shape shown on the side view from 10mm (³⁄₈ in) diameter dowel and a spigot formed at each end, the bottom spigot being 5mm (³⁄₁₆ in) in diameter and the top spigot 1mm (¹⁄₃₂ in) in diameter.

POST I Turn this from 10mm (³⁄₈ in) diameter dowel to the shape indicated in the view on *a*. At the top end, you will see what appears to be a small screw. This is made up from odd scraps and glued to post I. Drill a small hole to receive it, if you can, to give it rigidity.

PART J Turn this, from 5mm (¼ in) diameter dowel to the details shown in the view on *a* and drill a 2mm (³⁄₃₂ in) diameter hole in the end to receive post I.

PART K Turn this from 5mm (¼ in) diameter dowel to the details shown on the side view and drill a 2mm (³⁄₃₂ in) diameter hole in the end to receive part J.

PLATFORM L Cut out the basic shape to that shown on the projected view and cut out the slot to house the wheel using a bead saw and chisel.

On the drawing I have moved the support H nearer to the centre rather than in the position indicated on the photograph, since the latter looks a bit too close to part K. I think you will agree.

The drilling of the platform is tricky because of the inclination of the various parts that come into it. I managed to do it by eye, but you may decide to make a card cutout as suggested under Arm rest in Chapter 8. (*See* Fig 8.3.)

Drill the holes on the legs to suit the spigots, or turn the spigots to the size of the hole you wish to drill.

SUPPORTS M Turn these to the details shown on the side view, allowing enough in length to pass through the platform as indicated. Drill a 1mm ($\frac{1}{32}$ in) diameter hole in the sides to accommodate the wire axle.

LEG N Turn this to the details given on the side view and allow an extended length at the top where it passes through the platform. The foot of the leg will need to be chamfered as indicated, as will the top of the shaft where it meets with the underside of the platform. This can be done with a knife.

LEGS O Turn these to the details given on the end view on the platform and note the special chamfer required at each end due to the splaying out of the legs.

HANDLE P Turn this to the detail shown on the side view and note that it is to fit into a pre-drilled hole in the platform. Note also, from the projected view of the platform, that the handle is off centre.

TREADLE Q, S AND T This is made up from three pieces of timber: the treadle foot Q, short lever S and long lever T. Cut them out to the shapes shown on the plan view on the treadle and drill a 1mm ($\frac{1}{32}$ in) diameter hole in the longer piece to receive a connecting pin for arm R.

ARM R Cut this out to the length shown on the side view and drill a 1mm ($\frac{1}{32}$ in) diameter hole at each end as indicated.

ASSEMBLY

1 Pass the spindle of the flyer through the holes in the tabs on supports F and then glue supports F into the holes in the crosspiece G.
2 Glue the spigots of support H into the crosspiece G and the platform respectively, ensuring that the flyer assembly is positioned as shown on the side view.
3 Glue post I into part J and part J into part K, making sure that they are in line with each other and at right angles as shown on the side view and the view on *a*.
4 Glue part K into the hole in the platform and orientate the assembly as shown on the side view.
5 Glue the supports M into the holes in the platform, making sure that the holes line up with each other by passing a wire through them. *Check that the wire so positioned is parallel to the platform.*
6 Glue the handle P into the hole provided in the platform.
7 Glue the treadle elements together as indicated in the plan view on treadle and side view.
8 Form the kink in the wire axle as shown on the projected view of the platform and pass it through supports M, wheel hub and arm R. *To prevent the axle coming adrift, I glued a small piece of timber to each end, with a hole drilled to fit over the axle.*
9 Connect arm R to the treadle, by means of a pin made from a cocktail stick rubbed down and glued in place.
10 Pass some thin cord around the wheels, as shown in the photograph, and using superglue, join its ends together.
11 Finally, prepare a base for the model to stand on. I used a thick piece of card covered in velvet and glued the legs of the spinning wheel to the card.

FINISHING

I left the timber in its original state but there is no reason why you shouldn't apply a coat of clear polyurethane varnish just to protect the timber. You could, of course, stain the timber if you would prefer the model darker, but you must allow plenty of time for the stain to dry before applying a wood sealant, followed by a suitably coloured varnish.

TAPESTRY FIRE SCREEN

This model would fit into most period style dolls' houses and would add to the overall ambience of such a setting. The timber used was beech, except for parts E, F, and H which were made from lime.

FRONT AND REAR VIEWS AND CROSS SECTION

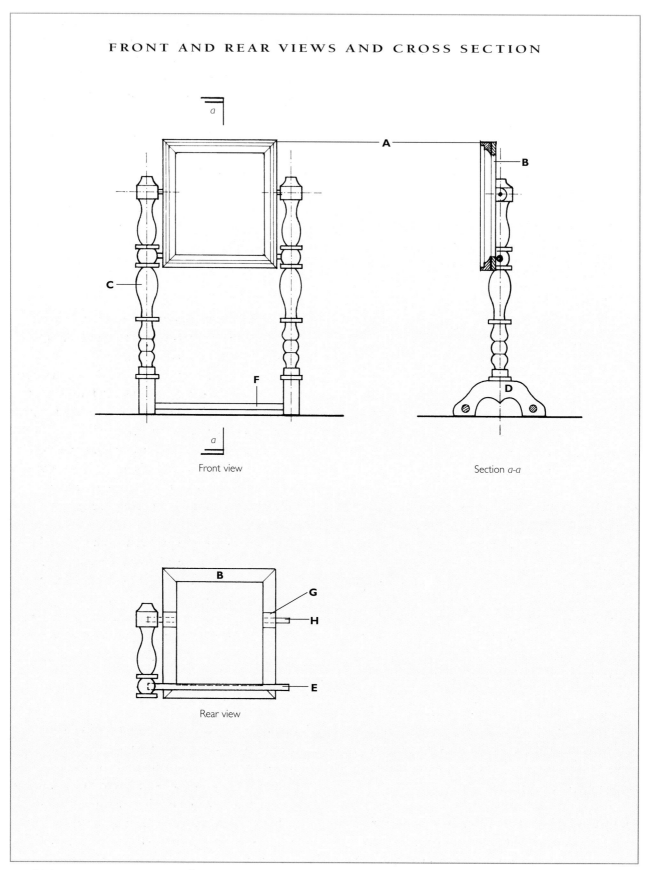

a

A

B

C

F

a

Front view

Section *a-a*

B

G

H

E

Rear view

Fig 29.1 Tapestry Fire Screen: Plan

CUTTING LIST

Beech; lime.

A Frame (1), from picture frame moulding, 150mm (6in)

B Frame (1) 150 × 4 × 1mm (6 × ³⁄₁₆ × ¹⁄₃₂in)

C Legs (2), dowel, 200 × 10mm diameter (8 × ³⁄₈in)

D Stands (2) 50 × 10 × 5mm (2 × ³⁄₈ × ³⁄₁₆in)

E and **F** Stop and stays (3), dowel, 120 × 1.5mm diameter (4³⁄₄ × ¹⁄₁₆in)

G Pivot parts (2), can be made from pieces of scrap timber

Miniature picture frame moulding is obtainable from mail order suppliers if there is no supplier near you. Sizes given allow for cutting, shaping and fitting.

PREPARATION AND CONSTRUCTION

LEGS C Cut out sufficient length of dowel to fit into the chuck of your lathe and turn to the details shown on the front view. A suggestion for marking out the principal points is shown in Fig 10.4. Drill a 1mm ($^1/_{32}$ in) diameter hole part way in to receive the peg H (made from a short length of brass wire, 1mm ($^1/_{32}$ in) in diameter) and a 1.5mm ($^1/_{16}$ in) diameter hole to receive stop E. The lengths of these can be fixed at the assembly stage. Check that they lie on the centreline and are in line with those in the other leg.

FRAME A Cut out the lengths obtainable from the front view and mitre each corner, as you would do with a picture frame. Place the parts on a flat surface and glue them together, making sure that the sides are at right angles to each other.

FRAME B Follow the same procedure as for frame A, above. Frames A and B should receive their finish before they are glued together, to avoid getting varnish on the tapestry.

STANDS D Trace the shape of these from section *a-a* onto the timber surface, using carbon paper, and cut out with a knife. Drill 1.5mm ($^1/_{16}$ in) diameter holes where shown to receive the stays F. Again, the length of these can be fixed at the assembly stage.

SCREEN Tapestry screens are readily available commercially through dolls' house suppliers and outlets, or you could make up a screen yourself.

PIVOT PARTS G These are made from scrap pieces of timber with a 1mm ($^1/_{32}$ in) diameter hole drilled to receive the peg H.

ASSEMBLY

1 Place the tapestry between the frames A and B, making sure it is drawn taut in all directions, and then glue the frames to each other.

2 Carefully position the pivot parts G onto the frame B and glue them in place. *Pass a stiff wire through their holes and check that the wire is parallel to the edge of the frame whilst the glue is still wet.*

3 Glue the 1mm ($^1/_{32}$ in) diameter brass wire pegs H into the hole provided as shown on the rear view.

4 Glue stands D to the feet of the legs. *Check that their faces are parallel to the centreline of the legs.*

5 Fix the length of the pegs H, the stop E and the stays F, by fitting them into the legs and stands. Adjust where necessary, cutting a piece from the ends if they are too long. When you are happy with the fit, glue the parts together. *Check that the stands and the legs are parallel to each other and that the stays F are at right angles to the stands D.*

FINISHING

I used a darkish varnish for this model, but if I was to repeat the project, I would prefer to stain the timber first. To prevent the stain from leeching out, it is advisable to apply a wood sealant before the varnish is added, and to wait until this is perfectly dry before you do so. Should you want to apply more than one coat, you should allow up to eight hours between coats and rub down with wire wool before the next coat is added.

AGA COOKER

This is one of the older type of farm house cookers which
has become fashionable again. Therefore, it would not look out of place
in any old or new setting.
The model can be made from any kind of timber and so gives you the
opportunity to use up any scraps you have lying about. I used some
birch-faced plywood amongst other types.

FRONT AND PLAN VIEWS

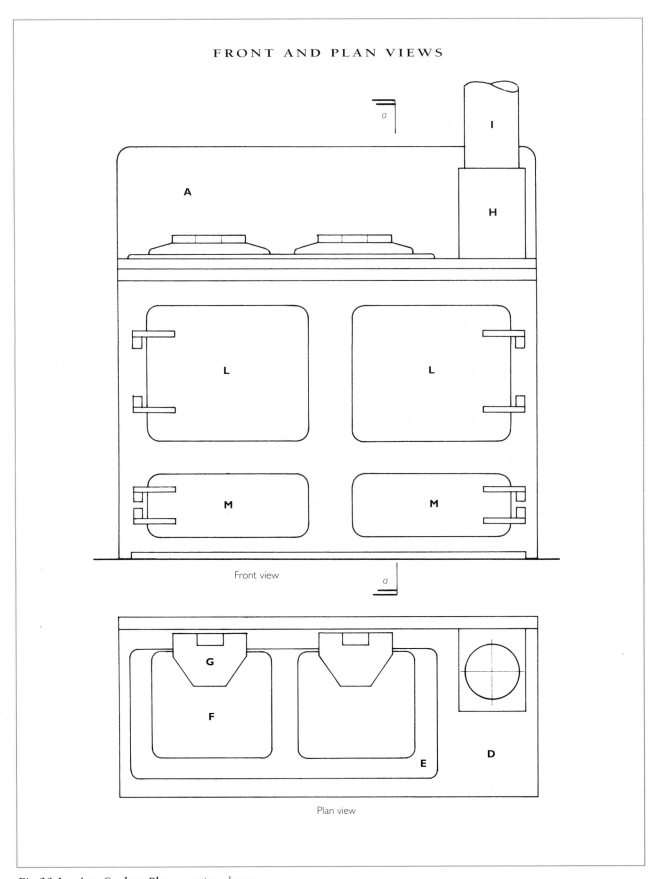

Front view

Plan view

Fig 30.1a Aga Cooker: Plan - *continued over*

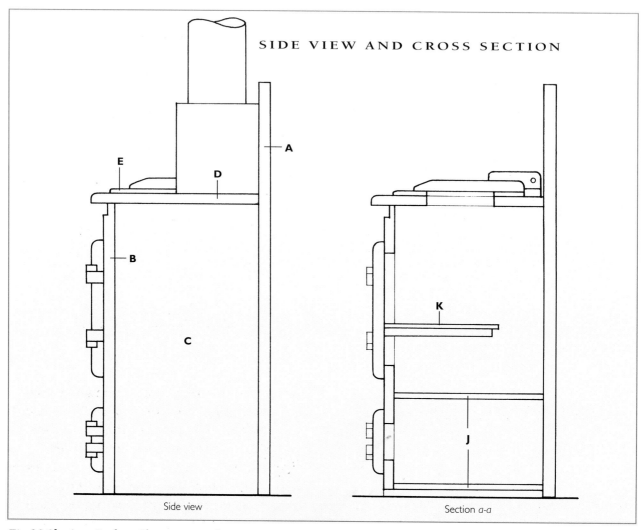

Fig 30.1b Aga Cooker: Plan - *continued*

CUTTING LIST

Any timber.

A Rear panel (1) 113 × 110 × 3mm ($4^7/_{16}$ × $4^{11}/_{32}$ × $^1/_8$in)

B Front panel (1) 113 × 77 × 3mm ($4^7/_{16}$ × $3^1/_{32}$ × $^1/_8$in)

C Side panels (2) from 2: 78 × 39 × 3mm ($3^1/_{16}$ × $1^{17}/_{32}$ × $^1/_8$in)

D Top panel (1) 113 × 45 × 3mm ($4^7/_{16}$ × $1^{25}/_{32}$ × $^1/_8$in)

E Panel (1) 83 × 35 × 1mm ($3^9/_{32}$ × $1^3/_8$ × $^1/_{32}$in)

F Lids (2) from 2: 32 × 28 × 3mm ($1^1/_4$ × $1^3/_{32}$ × $^1/_8$in)

G Hinges (2) from 2: 20 × 15 × 4mm ($^{25}/_{32}$ × $^{19}/_{32}$ × $^5/_{32}$in)

H Stack base (1) 24 × 22.5 × 18mm ($^{15}/_{16}$ × $^7/_8$ × $^{23}/_{32}$in)

I Stack (1), dowel, 15mm diameter ($^{19}/_{32}$in)

J Shelves (2) from 2: 117 × 40 × 1mm ($4^{19}/_{32}$ × $1^9/_{16}$ × $^1/_{32}$in)

K Grid (1) 34 × 30 × 1mm ($1^{11}/_{32}$ × $1^3/_{16}$ × $^1/_{32}$in) + 80 × 2 × 2mm ($3^1/_8$ × $^3/_{32}$ × $^3/_{32}$in)

L Doors (2) from 2: 43 × 36 × 3mm ($1^{11}/_{16}$ × $1^{13}/_{32}$ × $^1/_8$in)

M Doors (2) from 2: 43 × 17 × 3mm ($1^{11}/_{16}$ × $^{21}/_{32}$ × $^1/_8$in)

N and **O** Partitions (2) 75 × 40 × 1mm ($2^{15}/_{16}$ × $1^9/_{16}$ × $^1/_{32}$in)

P Hinges (8), scrap timber

The sizes given are actual sizes except for the partitions and the strips supporting the grid K.

Chain-dotted lines indicate the relative positions of panels J, N and O

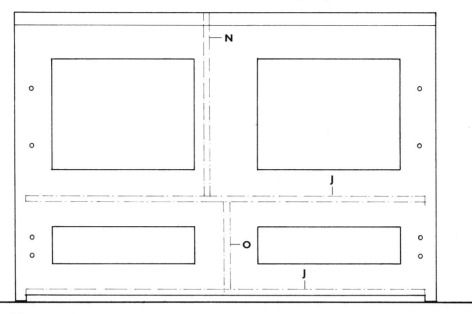

Fig 30.2 Detail of front panel B

PREPARATION
AND CONSTRUCTION

REAR PANEL A All you need to do with this is round off the top corners as shown on the front view.

SIDE PANELS C Make sure that the corners are at right angles and that the edges are square. (*See* Fig 30.1b).

FRONT PANEL B Ensure that the edges and corners are square and then cut out the rectangular openings with a fret saw after first drilling a small hole near the inside edges to receive the saw blade. Clean up the holes with a sanding block or a flat file.

You will notice on the side view, a recess along the top front-edge. This is purely for effect. If you want to include it, you will have to cut along the face and edge with a knife and straightedge, and clean up with a sanding block. There is a recess along the bottom edges which can be cut out with a bead saw and knife.

The eight small holes shown on Fig 30.2 are to receive the hinge spigots indicated on the exploded view in Fig 30.3 and should be left until the doors L and M have been fitted with their hinges.

PANELS D AND E Trace the holes shown on Fig 30.4 onto the timber surface of panel E, using carbon paper. Ensure that the edges and corners are square and that the edges and corners of panel E are rounded off as shown on the front and side views, and then glue panel E to the top surface of panel D in the position shown on the plan view. Use clamps to ensure that there is complete contact between the panels.

When they are fixed together, drill a small hole near the inside edge of the larger hole, through which to thread the fret saw blade, and then cut out their profiles, finishing off with abrasive paper.

LIDS F Round the corners and chamfer the edges as shown on Fig 30.5, using a sanding block.

HINGES G These are to be cut out to the details shown on Fig 30.6, using a bead saw and chisel for the knuckle recesses and a bead saw to thin down the top surface. The underside surface must then be rounded where indicated so that it will fit snugly onto the curved edge at the top rear-edge of lid F. The hinge knuckle can now be cut from a scrap piece of timber to fit into the recess of the hinge, and rounded along the top edge as shown.

Now comes the tricky bit. With the knuckle held in place, you have to drill a 1mm ($^1/_{32}$ in) diameter hole, very carefully, through the edge of the hinge and knuckle to receive the hinge pivot.

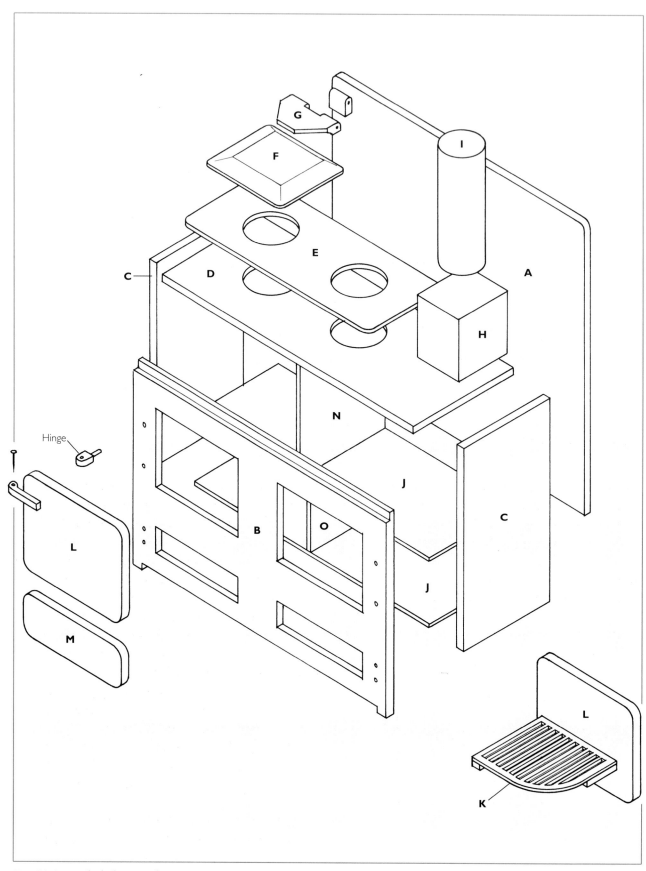

Fig 30.3 Exploded view of Aga

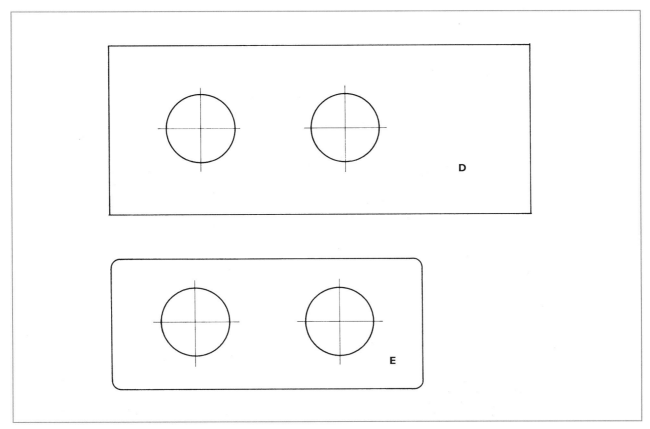

Fig 30.4 Detail of panels D and E

DOORS L AND M Ensure that the sides are at right angles to each other and then round off the edges and corners as shown on the front and side views, Figs 30.1a and 1b, and on Fig 30.7.

HINGES P The hinges can be made up from odd scraps of timber and shaped as shown on Fig 30.8.

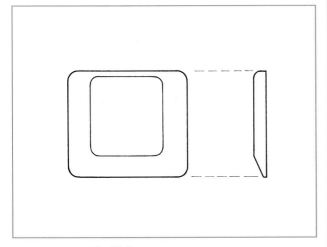

Fig 30.5 Detail of lid F

Try to get all eight looking the same and then drill a 1mm ($^1/_{32}$ in) diameter hole through each piece, as indicated, in order to receive the pin. See the exploded view for clarity.

Glue the hinge leaves to the doors, as shown on the front view, making sure that the pivot holes line up by passing a wire through them whilst the glue is still wet.

Having satisfied yourself that they are positioned correctly, the next thing to do is to place the front panel B onto a flat surface and then lay the doors in place with the hinge knuckles in position. Now determine the location of each of the eight holes needed to receive the spigots on the knuckles and drill them, using a drill bit to match the size of the spigots, so that a tight fit is assured. When the holes have been located, make sure that they line up with the other holes, in both directions, before you drill them.

GRID K A steady hand is required here, when you come to cut out the slots. If you trace the shape from Fig 30.9, including the slots, onto the timber surface, you can then cut out the slots in one of two ways. You

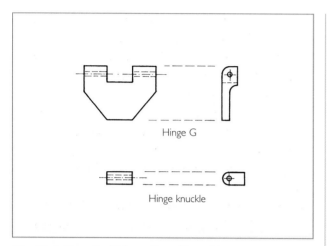

Fig 30.6 Detail of hinge G and knuckle

can first carefully cut out the ends of each slot with a miniature chisel, and then use a straightedge and knife to cut along their length, or you can drill a series of holes around the two sides through which you can cut out the slots with the straightedge and knife. The danger with material this thin is that it does tend to split very easily. If, after the umpteenth attempt you have managed to cut out the slots, you can then shape the curved portion as shown on Fig 30.9 and glue the two short lengths of timber strip and the crosspiece to its underside (*see* section *b-b,* Fig 30.9).

SHELVES J All you need to do with these is to make sure the sides are parallel to each other and that all corners are at right angles.

PARTITIONS N AND O Cut these out to the sizes obtained from Fig 30.2 where they are shown as chain-dotted lines on panel B. Again, make sure that the sides are parallel to each other and that the corners are at right angles.

STACK BASE H Make this as square as you can from the details shown on the front and side views. It is necessary for the top and bottom faces to be parallel to each other and at right angles to both vertical faces so that when the stack is glued on, it won't appear to lean like the tower of Pisa.

STACK I This has to be cut to length so that it reaches the underside of the ceiling in your dolls' house kitchen.

ASSEMBLY

1 Place the one side panel onto a flat surface and butt and glue rear panel A up to its edge and in the position shown on the side view, making sure that the panels are at right angles to each other.

2 Glue the lower shelf panel J to the rear and side panels by first placing a 3mm (¹/₈ in) panel of timber underneath it to act as a spacer. *Remove the spacer before the glue sets.*

3 Glue partition O in the position shown on Fig 30.2, once again making sure that it is at right angles to its adjacent panels.

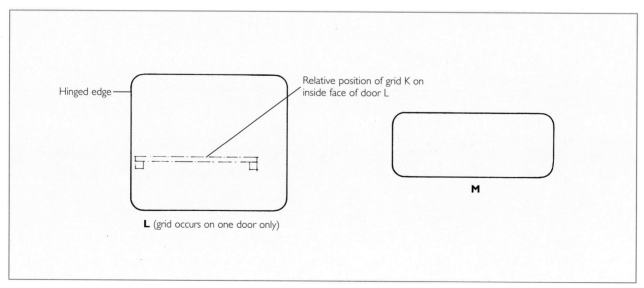

Fig 30.7   Detail of doors L and M

4 Glue the upper shelf J to partition O, rear panel A and side panel C. Make sure that it is parallel to the lower shelf.

5 Glue the other side panel C to rear panel A and to the ends of shelves J. *Check that the front panel B will fit, such that its sides are flush with the faces of the side panels C. If it won't, rub down the side panels with abrasive paper wrapped around a block of timber until it does.*

6 Glue front panel B to the edges of panels C, N and O and to the shelves J. *Check that all exposed edges of panels C, N and B are flush.*

7 Glue top panel D to the edges of panels C, N and B.

8 Fix the pivots through hinges G and their knuckles and then position them as shown on the plan view, Fig 30.1a. Mark off the position of each knuckle and glue the base of the knuckles in place on top of panel D. *Check that the lids operate properly whilst the glue is still wet.*

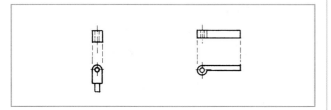

Fig 30.8 Detail of hinges P

9 Fix the pivots to doors L and M as indicated on the exploded view and then glue the spigots into their respective holes. *Check that the doors operate properly, before the glue sets, in case last minute adjustments are required.*

10 Glue grid K to the inside face of the right hand door L, in the position shown on Fig 30.7. *Check that the grid does not foul the edge of the opening when the door is operated, before the glue sets.*

11 Glue stack I to stack base H and stack base H to panel D in the position shown on the front and side views. It should be noted that no handles are to be seen on the lids or doors. If you would like to add them, you can easily do so using either small timber blocks with a finger grip carved in them, or brass pulls, which can be obtained by mail order. You could even make your own from bits of brass wire.

FINISHING

Go over the surfaces on display with a wood sealant and when it is completely dry, apply a coat of black enamel. If, on the other hand, you want it to be a bit more modern you can apply a coat of more brightly coloured enamel instead.

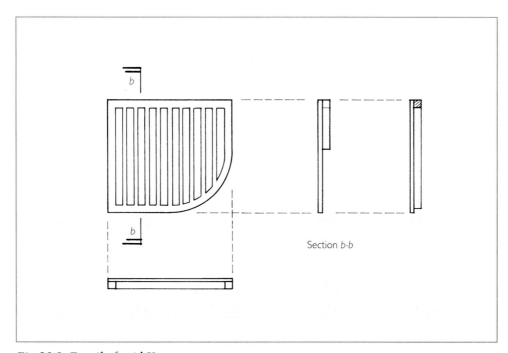

Section *b-b*

Fig 30.9 Detail of grid K

METRIC CONVERSION TABLE

INCHES TO MILLIMETRES AND CENTIMETRES						
mm = millimetres cm = centimetres						
inches	mm	cm	inches	cm	inches	cm
1/8	3	0.3	9	22.9	30	76.2
1/4	6	0.6	10	25.4	31	78.7
3/8	10	1.0	11	27.9	32	81.3
1/2	13	1.3	12	30.5	33	83.8
5/8	16	1.6	13	33.0	34	86.4
3/4	19	1.9	14	35.6	35	88.9
7/8	22	2.2	15	38.1	36	91.4
1	25	2.5	16	40.6	37	94.0
1 1/4	32	3.2	17	43.2	38	96.5
1 1/2	38	3.8	18	45.7	39	99.1
1 3/4	44	4.4	19	48.3	40	101.6
2	51	5.1	20	50.8	41	104.1
2 1/2	64	6.4	21	53.3	42	106.7
3	76	7.6	22	55.9	43	109.2
3 1/2	89	8.9	23	58.4	44	111.8
4	102	10.2	24	61.0	45	114.3
4 1/2	114	11.4	25	63.5	46	116.8
5	127	12.7	26	66.0	47	119.4
6	152	15.2	27	68.6	48	121.9
7	178	17.8	28	71.1	49	124.5
8	203	20.3	29	73.7	50	127.0

ABOUT THE AUTHOR

Maurice Harper's interest in dolls' house furniture began with the birth of his daughter, in 1978. Making her a 1/12 scale dolls' house led him to making furniture to go with it and to an interest which has continued since.

A chartered structural engineer by profession, Maurice has over 40 years' experience in the building trade, half of this time spent in the industry and half in education.

Having now retired from his position as Head of the Department of Building Technology at Sandwell College of Further and Higher Education, he is able to devote more of his time to envisaging and making wonderfully varied items of furniture to 1/12 scale.